VIRGINIA HAMILTON

Speeches, Essays,
and
Conversations

❧

Good quotes: p119 (bottom)
    on entertainment
p. 139- Top ⫪
p. 303- bottom- used for review

VIRGINIA HAMILTON

Speeches, Essays, and Conversations

EDITED BY
ARNOLD ADOFF & KACY COOK

THE BLUE SKY PRESS
An Imprint of Scholastic Inc. • New York

THE BLUE SKY PRESS

Our deep thanks to all of those sources
where some of these speeches and pieces first appeared.
"Everything of Value" © 1993 by the American Library Association
With great thanks.
"Slow Dance Heart Break Blues" © 1986 by Arnold Adoff

Library of Congress catalog card number: 2009031676
ISBN 978-0-439-27193-6
10 9 8 7 6 5 4 3 2 1   10 11 12 13 14
Printed in the U.S.A.   23
First printing, February 2010
Designed by Kathleen Westray

For our children,
Leigh and Jaime
—A.A.

For my mother,
Marny Cook
—K.C.

CONTENTS

Contents

9

INTRODUCTION

*I*N THE THIRTY-FIVE years between the publication of her first book, *Zeely*, in 1967 and her death — too soon — in 2002, Virginia Hamilton earned a place of honor in the pantheon of children's literature. *Zeely*, with its focus on an ordinary black girl and her family, its implicit celebration of "black is beautiful," and its evocation of black history, opened the modern era in African American children's fiction. *Zeely* and all of Hamilton's subsequent books were about illuminating black experience in America, the journey of black people across what she called the American hopescape. She stated, more than once, that she saw her work as helping to portray "the essence of a people who are a parallel culture community of America," while at the same time revealing the universality among peoples.

That Hamilton was enormously successful in this endeavor is evident from the honors and awards she received throughout her distinguished career, during which she published more than forty books. She was given, for example, four honorary doctoral degrees and was the first children's book author to receive a MacArthur Fellowship, popularly known as a "genius award." In the field of children's literature, she garnered every major national and international honor for which her work was eligible — the John Newbery Medal, the Coretta Scott King Award, the Boston Globe–Horn Book Award, the National Book Award, the NAACP Image Award, and the Hans Christian Andersen Award, to name just a few. By the close of the twentieth century she had become the most highly honored American author of children's books.

This collection of Hamilton's essays, speeches, and conversations is significant, then, in part because it sheds light on the genius behind her profoundly important body of work. These pieces show Hamilton as a serious scholar of history and folktales and make clear the importance of place, time, family, and history to her and to her work. At the same time, they present a portrait of the writer as literary artist—her creative use of language, her far-reaching imagination, her innovative mixing of the everyday with the unusual or near-bizarre, her sure sense of who she was and what she was about. They illuminate the process—the blending of "the known, the remembered, and the imagined"—through which she created her unique and critically acclaimed canon.

These pieces also show how and why Hamilton's work is central to the canon of African American children's literature. Through various genres—including biography, fiction, and folktales—her books explore some of the major themes of those genres, themes relating to family, history, and heritage. In her first published essay she wrote, "Perhaps someday when I've written my last book, there will stand the whole of the black experience in white America as I see it." She had other interests, too, such as the environment, but she never wavered from her determination to relate her version of black people's journey across the American hopescape. She also never wavered from her determination to have it understood that the story of that journey was a vital part of the American story and her work a vital part of the canon of American literature for young people.

This collection, then, helps to clarify why Virginia Hamilton was one of the premier writers of African American/American children's literature. It is a gift to anyone with an interest in American literature, but especially to the many scholars, teachers, librarians—and readers of Hamilton's books—who understand the importance of her work. For those of us who knew and admired her, this collection offers the chance to "hear" her voice again and be reminded once more of the enormity of her talent and the richness of her legacy.

—Rudine Sims Bishop

VIRGINIA HAMILTON

Speeches, Essays,
and
Conversations

ಞ

PORTRAIT OF THE AUTHOR AS A WORKING WRITER

*This is believed to be the earliest nationally published essay
by Virginia Hamilton. It appeared in* Elementary English,
*an official publication of the National Council
of Teachers of English, April 1971.*

Now the portrait of an author has always been awesome, although the gilt fleur-de-lis motif which framed past portraits is replaced these days by the institutional sleekness of polished chrome. Picture, if you wish, the author posed with profile prominent, with eyes seeming to look inward and backward at the same time, and seated in her Mies chair in the manner of a modern-day Whistler's mother. She appears superbly matter-of-fact. Still young, the calm expression of her face bespeaks the functional competence of the suburban matron.

A portrait is only as good as the artist who created it. For an accurate portrait, the artist must have experienced something of life and must translate his own experience into the interpretation of the author.

A close look at the portrait reveals what we were unable to see from a distance; from afar, the chrome frame had bewitched and beguiled us. Up close, we see that the author has lines of stress and strain on the forehead, around the mouth, and under the eyes. Her hands, which had seemed to rest delicately in her lap, actually claw at the fabric of her culottes.

The author is tired. The author drinks too much coffee, gets too little sleep, and is overweight. No longer a delicate mystery shrouded in possibilities, students open doors for her and old gentlemen tip their hats. Such is the coming of Over Thirty for a born lady writer. The portrait is disappointing to the author when she stands in front of it, but it is undeniably true. Still, she wishes that somehow the portrait might show all the years of living and partly living that went into it—that the portrait could say more than its simplistic statement of time's passage. There is more to it, she feels—oh, much more—and so she decides to write it out. That's always her way, to write it down. Thus she holds on to time and makes it solid. She gives time quality and thereby denies its quantity.

Time is of quality: I do not have the time, I tell you. A grand time was had by all. Remember that time?

I remember the time I stood uncertain on the backward edge of the Beat Generation wondering what forward motion I should attempt. The generations of Pepsi people, of hippies, of peace and freedom, and of black and beautiful were out of range, beyond me and others like me who, although a bit lost, anticipated what was to come by our urge to be on the move.

Maybe that's why I felt compelled to strike out on my own for the Big Apple of Manhattan, that institution for reformed wastrels. I knew a few things even then. I knew that I would be a writer. I knew that I had to learn my craft away from all the kind people who wanted to help and did help but maybe hadn't realized there came a time when help was not what was needed. I knew a poem by Langston Hughes: "My soul has grown deep like the rivers," the poem sings (Hughes, "The Negro Speaks of Rivers," 1921). Deep. Yes, that's what I was looking for.

When I lived in the East Village of New York City, it was known as the Lower East Side. There were no lifestyles such as Puerto Rican, hippy, and head. There were the teachers from the newly defunct Black Mountain College; resident Poles, Yugoslavs, and Czechs;

a Shakespearean theater group; and eastern European Jews in black greatcoats and wide-brimmed hats. There existed little communication between the groups or between the groups and myself. No police cars cruised through the streets at ten-minute intervals. No plainclothesmen searched for runaway teenyboppers and no troubled fathers exhausted the known crash pads hunting for lost sons.

We of the Lower East Side isolated ourselves from one another and insulated ourselves for that which we thought was worth the loneliness: independence, self-knowledge and self-expression, and safety from the intrusion of a chaotic world. If there was a time at all when we came closer together, it was on the day of the week when we publicly acknowledged our debt to the rivers. On Sunday, we all made it over to the river, either the East, which was never my favorite, or the Hudson, the kind of river I especially took to heart.

People in cities always go down to their rivers. They pay tribute in a way that at first was inexplicable to me. But as time passed, I began to comprehend the tribute and the need. I moved across town to Greenwich Village and closer to my favorite river. I could spend days writing and get nowhere. But if I went down to the river to sit awhile, I could come back home feeling as though I had partaken of a healing potion.

Eventually, my writing grew better as the experience of myself alone and cut off from all things familiar deepened inside me. Soon I could spend a day writing and, by evening, rather than incoherency I had created a kind of unity of thought. I hadn't learned to write a whole story yet, but there were themes that continued throughout. I knew enough to take hold of those themes and separate them from the rest by cutting the rest away. Then, rewriting those themes, I concentrated on sentences. And if a sentence did not follow what had gone before, it, too, was cut away.

Eventually, also, I knew the writing of Carson McCullers pretty well. I learned from her what a good sentence was. "In the town there were two mutes and they were always together," she had written

(McCullers, *The Heart Is a Lonely Hunter*, 1940). For a working writer, such a sentence is profoundly exciting. It stays in the mind for years.

Having learned in the Village that my writing had progressed thematically, I no longer needed to stop the process of time and my own experience. I had lived a rather solitary existence. I often went for days without talking to anyone. Working half days as a cost accountant in order to eat occasionally, I hid myself within columns of figures and made no friends.

However, it was time now to step into the flow of the city and to wet my feet in the stream of city people. I moved out of the Village and uptown, closer to my people and still near the Hudson River. My river changes uptown. It has Riverside Park along its steep banks, and the park is beautiful, full of children and dogs. All sorts of people rest, lounge, read their papers, sunbathe, and sing. They all needed the river in some way as I did.

My writing grew better as I grew older inside. I came to understand that the river's flow was the flow of freedom inside us all. We wonder about it in this way: What do you suppose is beyond the bridge there—a town, another park? What sort of place is Bear Mountain—are there really brown bears? I think I'll walk awhile and see what's beyond that bend in the river.

So it is that the river is the mind of people, ever flowing to some other where. Whenever any of us grow deep like the rivers, it is because we have learned to allow our minds to flow free as rivers flow. And so the reason rivers figure so largely in my writing and ever will. But it was years before I realized that the Hudson River was not the river which had nourished me. From the time I discovered my need to move, it must have been another river that had caused the need. I am talking about the Ohio River, sixty miles from the place I was born, and the river so necessary, so symbolic for my people.

The Ohio River needs no orchestration to explain it. It needs no fury of words nor purple narrative for an image of it. It is simply grand the way an Ohio sky is grand for those of us who are related to it through the quality of time and memory. Wherever we go, we carry the quality—that piece of sky, that particular reach of land, and that river—with us.

Having lived ten and more years in New York, I discovered that my mind had never left Ohio. And so I returned to the river and the country. I could write. I had done it. I had pulled past and present, memory and experience together and grown deep like the river. Time now for the author to become a working writer and, indeed, I have. Whatever else I do—buy groceries, raise my children, take care of my husband, plant crocuses—I write each morning and every night. I think, I dream writing, and writing is who I am. How much time I spend at it, who I write for, why I write, and what next I will write, fall in the realm of propaganda. The fact is that I must write, and writing is work, hard and exacting. The best job I've ever had.

The portrait of the author is complete. Know that I don't mind if it reveals the lines of stress and time. It is my own picture as I created it. I am the artist, the author, and the working writer, and we are doing what we set out to do.

I write of the black experience. You've heard the phrase often enough, perhaps understood it, wondered about it, or even dismissed it as a kind of subversive nationalism. You may not have thought of children's books using that term or of my books in particular. But the black experience is the fact of my writing from my first book, *Zeely*, through the third, *The Time-Ago Tales of Jahdu*.

I attempt in each book to take hold of one single theme of the black experience and present it as clearly as I can. I don't mean to make the writing of fiction sound cold or calculating—it isn't at all. In the beginning, an idea takes hold of the writer in a special way which demands the getting it down on paper. From there, using whatever skill or craft he has learned, the writer develops the idea into a theme which becomes the basis of the plot.

A professor at Antioch College once gave me some advice. He told me I would go far if I would concentrate on using conventional forms of structure and simple language in my writing. "Your stories are wild enough without your inventing a new novel form." I took his advice. More and more I reach for the unconventional theme while depending on the solid base of tried-and-true structure and easy language.

The black experience in America is deep like the rivers of this country. At times through our history it became submerged only to emerge again and again. Each time it emerges, it seems strong, more explicit and insistent.

There are themes in my writing that are strains through the whole of black history. The strain of the wanderer, like the theme of Jahdu; the strain of the fleeing slave or the persecuted moving and searching for a better place becomes the theme of the Night Traveller in *Zeely*. And the black man hiding his true self, ever acting so that those who betray him will never touch him. Thus we have such a man in the actor son of Mr. Pluto in *The House of Dies Drear*:

"We wear the mask that grins and lies," he says, speaking from the [Paul Laurence] Dunbar poem (Dunbar, "We Wear the Mask," 1896).

The books I have written can be seen as a reflection of my past experience. I have brought myself up to the present and into the eye of the future. What will be the themes of my future writings? There are two books which I am working on, and they are as different from one another as the three already written. They do not attempt to cover the whole of black experience; rather, they each take a theme out of it, as did my other three books. Perhaps someday when I've written my last book, there will stand the whole of the black experience in white America as I see it. Actually, I never write thinking in these terms. It's only when working out a book that I realize how hugely logical is the writer's unconscious life.

Examining the first of the two themes I'm working on, we have the failure of a black, quite obese junior high school youth to develop any area of successful contact with the white world that determines the limitations of his life. By the time we first meet the boy, who is called

Junior Brown, his unique intelligence and his mental isolation are already apparent. He spends his anguished days trying to cope with the monstrous fantasy that has come to live in the home of his deranged piano teacher, Miss Peebs. The youth, Junior Brown, tries desperately to save the sanity of Miss Peebs by entering her fantasy and dealing with the apparition who lives there. Junior Brown and Miss Peebs both live in the same isolation caused by the same conditions, and Junior instinctively knows that by saving her he may save himself.

The second book concerns the boy M.C. Higgins, whose country of hills and mountains along the Ohio River is being destroyed by strip mining. As the earth is poisoned by the mindless force invisible behind the invading mining machines, so, too, are the hill people annihilated. I am speaking mainly of a spiritual annihilation. These people do not prevail over the condition of their lives, which causes an atrophy of the spirit. They endure — the emptiness, the oppression, the dull sameness. They endure it. That is, all save M.C., who lives by means of his courage, and his strength and daring. There are boys like M.C. who when they become men are legends, and there are legends — pure fictional men — who have become real to us. We know Wild Bill Hickok and Billy the Kid, Nat Turner and Crispus Attucks, all who once lived. We have C.C. Rider, High John, and "Staggalee," whose lives are far more fiction than fact. Finally, we have the extraordinary legend of John Henry, not the song, but the legend, which states that when John Henry was born he spat in the fire and asked his mother why everyone including the dog had been fed and not he. Not waiting for a reply, he ordered his mother to prepare him an enormous, sumptuous meal. His mother prepared the food but John Henry did not eat it. He rose from his pallet. He turned his back on his mother and stalked out of the house never to return.

Nothing erases the legend of the man-made man, the natural man from our memory. Such men hold an essential lifestyle in common. They do not need to prevail as we do. I suppose that is why I created my own M.C. Higgins. He, the same as the others of his kind, will not

21

prevail or endure, either. He is content to survive when he understands that the aim of his life is to live it in terms that only he can define. And so he lives it up and, if he is like Nat Turner, may destroy himself in the process. If he is a John Henry, he will burst his heart proving he is a man. In any event, he will live not just some life he was born into but his own life, never loving it and never hating it, either.

What sort of world is it I create, where the people seem imbued with an isolation of the spirit? Old Mr. Pluto, alone for years in his cave; Zeely, separated by her very height; and little Jahdu, a lone traveler born of no woman but in an oven. You might well ask: What is it I'm getting at? Not actually knowing, I sense that finding out is the reason I persist. I sense also that finding out is far less important than the quest and the pleasure of writing along the way.

I've attempted here to make the writer and writing more understandable. Those of us who write have a deep love of language and a need to make reading an extraordinary experience for children. In my own young days, I knew the excitement of coming across a book which touched and changed me. Now I experience while writing the shock of finding out that I might have a good story working. It hits me as though I had been asleep and awoke with a start. Always when that happens, I am reminded of my childhood when, skimming a book with only mild interest, I would start suddenly alert and begin reading in earnest.

For children, reading is the discovery of new worlds of color and texture. For me, writing for children is the creation of worlds of darkness and light. There is an essential line between us, a line of thought and ultimately of communication. Each book must speak "This is what I have to say," in the hope that each reader will answer "That is what I wanted to know."

Thank you.

22

THOUGHTS ON CHILDREN'S BOOKS, READING, AND ETHNIC AMERICA

Essay from Perspectives in Reading No. 16: Reading, Children's Books, and Our Pluralistic Society, *compiled and edited by Harold Tanyzer and Jean Karl, prepared for a Joint Committee of the International Reading Association and Children's Book Council, 1972*

I VIEW FICTION, the writing of novels, as an experience that should reveal emotional truths rather than arguments. Moreover, I see the principal fact of my life and all life as the mind at liberty. I see mankind as a free, creative spirit evolving a world in constant creation. The human race is yet to come, and its *becoming* makes for the chaotic world in which we struggle, a world of change and attempts to change.

We range wildly between being and becoming and find ourselves in conflict between the new idea and the old. A writer has to recognize and understand the new idea whether it is called the Black Revolution, Ecology, Consciousness III, or the Third World. And a writer must know that the new idea may not be new at all; for instance:

It is the race-conscious black man cooperating together in his own institutions and movements who will eventually emancipate the colored race, and the great step ahead today is for the American Negro to accomplish his economic emancipation through voluntary, determined cooperative effort.

The quote is from an editorial in the *Crisis* magazine on planned black economic segregation, written by W. E. B. Du Bois in January 1934.

In a conflict world such as ours, we have but two choices — one for life and one for death. In order to live, we must persuade one another through language communication that every life is equally valuable and that all life is worth living. But if we should decide that persuasion is too time-consuming and that, indeed, individual life is not worth the effort, then we might as well get on with the business of killing one another on a grand scale — man-to-man and one-to-one the world over and have the annihilation done with.

Surely, most of us prefer life and living, and sporadically we try seriously to communicate with one another. We don't do very well, but it's obvious that those of us who have learned to use language persuasively and who have a particular linguistic style have a certain advantage over the less-verbal majority. This edge is true especially in democracies where, at once, politicians come to mind. But it has been noted many times that revolutions are led by poets, writers, and those who have great style in persuasive public speaking. And today, in black communities across this country, poets, not politicians, are filling the lecture halls and the street corners.

The linguistic stylist may be a demagogue, a crook, a saint, a hero; whoever he is, he possesses the power to persuade; and no matter what he says, whether I think it is for the good or not, I know it is better that he say it than that I pummel him into silence or he pull his weapon on me and shoot me down.

In the world today, we have countless millions of people and we still haven't discovered how two people communicate; although we do know that once communication between two people is no longer possible, one will attempt a series of complicated maneuvers to escape the other.

For example, one day two individuals exist quietly with each other, although for one of them that life has been vaguely discomforting for quite some time. The next day the life he is living becomes totally unacceptable to that one individual, so he leaves it and goes to nothing. From nothing, he begins again, sometimes in a radically different style. He may move himself away only mentally or mentally and physically; but by whatever method he chooses, he will escape in order to renew, to become himself.

In my past books, I wrote of characters who, among other things, were reaching for their black American history or their African heritage; or, as in the Jahdu stories, I wrote of discovering what power there can be in black pride. But in a new book I am moving toward an entirely different feeling. The new novel is *The Planet of Junior Brown*, in which two black youths have a friendship of long-standing at the time the book begins. Pretending to go to class every day, they actually are hiding out in the basement of their school. They are protected by the janitor of the school, an extraordinary fellow who has constructed a ten-planet solar system for their amusement, the tenth planet being the planet of Junior Brown.

But unknown to either of the youths, to engage in the friendship each has had to carry on an outlandish secret life. The friendship is a hollow shell, for their secret lives have run away with the limb and mind of reality. In this instance, you have two individuals, both of whom escape because life as they lived it had become unacceptable.

Why should a friendship that had always been fine suddenly become unapproachable? Perhaps because evolution of minds at liberty does not take place over millennia, as it will with species, but over every day and hour. Individuals grow together, or they will grow apart. But individuals always change, evolve, and grow.

I believe modern life to be extremely difficult for most people, and yet, through often miserable lives, most people make a fair effort at living with spirit. The opportunities for pride in ourselves are awfully slim in our modern world of waste and of man against man. Still, many of us are taking pride in having found ourselves less frightened, silent-suffering, or self-pitying than we were at other times. The black revolution beginning in the fifties and continuing now is more pervasive and ambitious for itself than the similar though more limited New Negro movement and Harlem Renaissance of the twenties. Although both reaffirmed this uniqueness of a people, the new revolution — or revelation — refuses to accept an entrenched American way of life that is exclusive of thirty millions of a race. That way of life has seemingly substituted a pattern of behavior and morality for mental evolution and spiritual growth. The new black revelation attempts to purge from its spirit a Calvinist conscience and substitutes self-awareness and self-criticism for entrenched patterns of behavior. It has, with justification, viewed America's lack of commitment to its own people as having the baseness of a war crime.

For a writer such as myself, the new black revelation gives rise to fictional characters who become heroic by simply surviving their own mental and spiritual evolution. When you find yourself up against the wall long enough, you begin to calculate your endurance against the wall. You begin to know how strong you are. You are beautiful, and you think in terms of going through the wall.

I'm interested in that. I'm interested in human beings who have changed emotionally, who have evolved so fundamentally and extremely that they see no difficulty in going through walls. Walls are the sides of buildings, and enough buildings make cities. As the black poet Raymond Patterson has written:

> There is the sorrow of blackmen
> Lost in cities. But who can conceive
> Of cities lost in a blackman?
> (Patterson, *26 Ways of Looking at a Black Man
> and Other Poems*, 1969)

That's what I'm talking about, turning poetry around, literature around, bringing characters and action beyond what is already conceived about them.

It should become possible, then, to write in fiction what was written in poetry ["The Song of the Smoke"] by Dr. Du Bois in 1899:

> I am the Smoke King,
> I am black!
> I am swinging in the sky,
> I am wringing worlds awry;
> I am the thought of the throbbing mills,
> I am the soul of the soul-toil kills,
> Wraith of the ripple of trading rills;
> Up I'm curling from the sod,
> I am whirling home to God;
> I am the Smoke King,
> I am black.

The Smoke King and the blackman with cities lost within himself survive only in terms that they themselves define. And they will prevail, having evolved beyond all known means of survival.

In *The Planet of Junior Brown*, the lead character, Buddy Clark, lives by his wits on the street. Homeless, he has learned how to cope with the city, with hunger and suffering. He has learned all that the street has to teach him and has become as finely tuned a human sensation as one could imagine. He no longer needs the street; after all, what are streets but walls flattened out. Literally, he goes through it or beyond it.

He finds others like himself. They teach one another in a joyful school. They go beyond survival, beyond institutions, families, lack of families, and deprivation to that joyful sense of cooperation and communication, of learning together.

Only by going through walls, by going beyond streets can a youth like Buddy Clark escape to become one with himself and others. But this is fiction, as the Smoke King and the blackman with cities lost within himself are poetry. What do they have to do with reality? I'm sure I don't know, and that may not even be the question. The only thing I am certain of is that a writer must deal in possibilities, not with what is but what might become. And I believe, so must institutions of learning and practitioners like yourselves of arts and sciences, of education, and reading. Our institutions are not equipped to solve four-hundred-year-old grievances, but there is the distinct possibility that they may well have to become so. As practitioners, you and I must be aware of evolution. Our children can and do progress beyond us, and the progression isn't fatal. If we become finely attuned, we might even discover how it is they can go through walls. That knowledge won't kill us, either.

I deal with their growing by writing of the possibilities these forms of growth may take. I know you must deal with it by knowing that education must be a joyful sound. It must evolve as they evolve: The books from which they learn must reflect movement and change and all of the infinite possibilities of minds at liberty.

LITERATURE, CREATIVITY, AND IMAGINATION

Speech given November 11, 1972, at George Peabody College for Teachers, in Nashville, Tennessee (since 1979 a part of Vanderbilt University and renamed Peabody College of Education and Human Development); the third in a series of regional workshops sponsored by a Joint Liaison Committee of the Association for Childhood Education International and the Children's Book Council. Reprinted by ACEI, 1973, with an afterword by Professor Emeritus Roma Gans, Teachers College, Columbia University, which follows Virginia Hamilton's speech.

I CAN ADMIT with certainty that as a writer, I was a late developer. To be more precise, I wasn't convinced that I would be a writer until about the age of twenty-five. First, having fled academe, I became a singer in obscure nightclubs; then, an esoteric folk singer; and, after that, a guitarist for a modern dance ensemble. But all along—since the age of nine or ten—I *had* been writing. At age nine, I started "The Notebook," which was an accumulation of mysteries my parents and other adults talked about—whispered gossip couched in symbolic language so that my young ears would not comprehend. As I recall, I filled "The Notebook" with all manner of secrets, knowing that one day I would be old enough to understand what I had written down.

What a wealth of grown-up talk graced its pages. What monstrous, wonderful, snide, and vindictive secrets!

I lost the thing. I mislaid it or merely forgot it in my enthusiasm in growing to ten. I have never found it. And I know not what lay stark and open within its pages.

By age eleven, I had turned grim with the loss and had started my first "Novel." I called it that. I must have read some novels, although I have no idea what they were about or what were their titles. Nevertheless, I filled page after page with vehement prose under the hot summer sun while lying on a slant atop the burning tin roof of the hog barn.

I was a country child. Writing must come easily and early to country girls when they discover pencil and paper before they learn about horses. Since horses of my childhood were fitted to the plow and not the saddle, I never had much love for them. But I did discover boys at age twelve and found them sickening. By age fourteen, I found boys marvelously intriguing and ever more so; yet, by then, paper and pencil had established themselves as my most constant friends. Boys might come along, tease me, and go away, while *p* and *p* remained ever present.

I cannot remember when I gave up the pencil for my first Olivetti, and it would be boring to catalog the number of Olivettis I've conquered. The foregoing is merely an introduction to the subject of "Literature, Creativity, and Imagination." I am a creative person with a vivid imagination who, some say, occasionally writes literature. Moreover, I am a grown woman who never quite recovered from the loss of a notebook and who now writes books in order to rediscover a mislaid mystery.

That reason for writing is as good as any. But, of course, it isn't the whole truth. I also write because as a child, a youngster in my mother's enormous Perry clan, I was considered strange, even stranger than my father who was an outlander from Iowa and by definition eccentric.

For I was the one who wandered away from home for hours on end at age six and wandered home again a few seconds before the arrival of the local gendarme. I was the one who had nightmares and walked the house, the night road, and the fields in her sleep. I was the worry, the trouble, the one with the unusual voice who would never perform for Sunday aunts and cousins.

In short, I was born to live within my mind, to have thoughts and dreams more vivid to me than any daylight. The wisest thing my family ever did was to realize early on that there was no changing me and to leave me alone. They left me to discover what I wanted and to learn what I could. In my whole life, I have been left alone to be what I wanted to be. No one ever objected to my writing things down. Teachers from grade school on through college only encouraged me. I can't recall anyone saying that being a writer was a stupid idea for a girl. Growing up in rural Ohio, with all sorts of possibilities for neglect, rejection, this encouragement was indeed very odd. I can only assume that I was lucky. I told people I was a writer. They would look at me quizzically for a long moment, then nod and believe.

So it is that if you say something long enough, you will be what you say you are. Now, I am a writer and by no manner of logic that I can discover.

Twenty years ago, François Mauriac wrote these words in a French literary magazine:

> Every novelist ought to invent his own technique . . . Every novel worthy of the name is like another planet, whether large or small, which has its own laws just as it has its own flora and fauna. Thus, Faulkner's technique is certainly the best one with which to paint Faulkner's world, and Kafka's nightmare has produced its own myths that make it communicable.
> (Mauriac, *La table ronde*, August 1949)

Mauriac's premise holds true as well for children's books. I hesitate to use the term *children's literature*, for not only have we in the past narrowed our view of children but of literature, also, so that either view has become limited to individuals and their moment in time.

Today, happily, all manner of children's books are being written, reflecting on that which is provocative in our society. It is a grand time to be a novelist, rather scary, but a time full of challenge. Our real world has become so bizarre that a novelist must go very far to get beyond it. More and more, she must turn inward upon herself, searching for what she suspects is true: Society may change, books and writers may change, but the essence of that which we call *literature* might possibly remain the same. A good novel may have its own laws; it may well be another planet, as Mauriac wrote.

When I write a book, I don't often ask myself about the kind of technique I am using or who or what motivates the characters. For a time, I simply write it out, carried along by a strong sense of story unfolding with no limits on what the story can or cannot be. I never worry about why the story occurred to me at a particular time or why such a character came into existence. It is enough to know something of the plot in order to continue. Therefore, I don't often think about literature, creativity, and imagination while I am working. I am content to let things develop, using all of the craft learned so painfully long ago — that myriad of technique and style which my instinct suggests is right. This is the way I began writing and it is still the way I write.

Not meaning to suggest that I write in any unconscious way, I believe there is an odd ability most writers have of dividing themselves into two entities. The first entity writes down the story as it occurs in a particular form; the second analyzes the worth of the story and form. It adds dimension and cuts away all that is unnecessary. Neither entity has anything to do with the initial act of creation. Of the books I have written, I am unable to tell how the initial act occurred. I never remember the first idea, the first thought, of any of them. That knowledge, like the long-lost "Notebook," is mislaid and forgotten forever. No need to try to rediscover it, for I believe the loss is the way in which the mind protects its primordial dream.

The mind doesn't separate creativity from imagination. And both combined form the act of making sense and logic out of images stored in memory. Memory can be as new as the last minute and as old as childhood, past generations, all of the experience and history of experience one has ever learned. It is the Freudian archaic heritage and the Jungian collective unconscious; it is at times primordial and inexplicable. I rediscover what I can of memory and heighten it to new understanding through story, character, mood, technique, and style.

Memory is what I have stored away, what did happen, what I think happened, what never happened but might have been great if it had, what I fear could have happened—on and on. It is the essence of my mental and physical exploration brought to bear on a specific idea I wish to write. Smell, sound, sight are all part of memory during this act of writing. And creative imagination plays an enormous role in how one uses them and how much of them one uses.

The system of creating characters which either do or do not make a book come to life involves the energy of life that I, the writer, possess. That energy is like an unending stream. I dip into it for as much of it as I need for a given character. I may draw out of the stream an energy entirely unexpected, such as sadness, the abject loneliness and mental isolation of Junior Brown. For the energy of life is not only a capacity for living, but also its opposite, the rejection of life.

Now, it occurs to me that *The Planet of Junior Brown* is a war between the capacity for living and the rejection of life. Both Miss Peebs and Junior Brown establish their fears as apparition, with no chance for communication for life in the real world. Mr. Pool and Buddy Clark allow the energy of life to flow into them from reality and from them into reality.

In all of my fiction, the characters win out for life. And life is a benevolence which permits the characters to move and experience with utmost freedom.

33

Can you imagine what would have happened if life had not been good to Geeder Perry in *Zeely*—or if she hadn't had an uncle there with a nice farm where they could visit?

Can you see what might have happened to Thomas Small in *The*

House of Dies Drear if his father had not a chance for education, a job waiting for him in Ohio, and a car to get the family there?

Benevolent life is the one concession I make to wish fulfillment. It is the single romance, the unreality, that I consciously allow myself. For in reality, life isn't so "good" for black families. It is never so sweet and so free.

Poet Nikki Giovanni wrote that, after having read *Zeely*, she sat in a closet and cried—"We never had an Uncle Ross who lived on a farm in the country. We never knew a big, old house with the smell of generations of my people in it. . . . We remembered our childhood—long gone—never having been" (Giovanni, *Negro Digest*, August 1967). Thus, she cried for a childhood she wished she had had and for something lost she had never known.

That is the point of most of my writing, of course. I concede benevolent life to open the world to readers who never experienced the rare freedom I knew as a child. I concede it so that they will know that if my mind can conceive of freedom, so can theirs. I want them to wish for fulfillment while knowing that fulfillment is never easy.

Only in *The Planet of Junior Brown* do I depart from the concept of benevolent life as a certainty. The backdrop of the city with its hard-edged institutions is not friendly to Junior Brown or Buddy Clark. It is not unfriendly, either, but indifferent, which is the closest I have come to writing about real life. Thus, *Planet* is not a pretty book in the sense that *Zeely* might be called so. But it is an honest book and one that I am extremely proud of. I shall not soon forget the uneasiness with which it was written, the anxiety of never knowing whether all the time and energy I spent writing it was worth the trouble, or whether it was truly a good book. For I had done something I had not tried before. I had not used benevolent life to allow my characters freedom. And without it they not only survived, but they prevailed. That was an extraordinary breakthrough for me as a writer. It meant that I had complete faith in my own power to create fictional life; I no longer needed benevolent life to help me.

Ah, but when I grow weary of the hard work of novels, I turn to my little friend, Jahdu, a fictional character of mine who has absolute power in his world and who has magic. Jahdu is free to play tricks, to roam, to do good or be bad. He can turn grass green; he created the tide. He puts things to sleep and wakes them up. He is that stuff from which our folk myths are made and for me a relief, a rest for my mind in his world of mischief and magic. So I have written new Jahdu tales, which will be out in the spring. Then, another hard novel and on and on with more books.

I hope someday something I write will match the perfect pictures I hold in my head. I judge myself and other writers and books on how unique is their failure to do the impossible, to match the perfect pictures from which all writers write and all books are made. This is what literature and writing mean to me: the book, not always a perfect success but, with luck, a worthy failure; the writer, not trying to be better than past authors or her contemporaries particularly, but always attempting to be better than herself.

That for me is happiness.

AFTERWORD:
THE AUTHOR SPEAKS

BY ROMA GANS, PROFESSOR EMERITUS
Teachers College, Columbia University

THANKS TO the Joint Liaison Committee of the Association for Childhood Education International and The Children's Book Council, three groups of teachers, librarians, administrators, authors, editors, and publishers have recently had the privilege of meeting and hearing authors speak.

Many writers, well-known for their books, are seldom presented live to listening audiences. To many young readers, authors are old, queer, unreal, and, in today's juvenile language, "not with it"—even if these youngsters have read and enjoyed any number of books. Getting acquainted with an author not only as a reader does, but as a seeing, listening member of his or her audience, can make that writer's works come truly alive.

This was my privilege at the joint meeting of these two organizations in November 1972, in Nashville, Tennessee. As I listened to Virginia Hamilton speak I became increasingly grateful to those who dreamed up this wonderful idea. But I kept wishing that thousands of young readers, too, had been in this audience to see Ms. Hamilton, relaxed and at ease as if in a living room, and to hear her tell the story of her life. I was already acquainted with Virginia Hamilton as an author when I met her as a speaker at this joint session. Her ease, warmth, and great personal charm are qualities one hopes for in professional speakers and lecturers, but does not necessarily expect of writers. She is fortunately gifted in both arts.

In a direct simple style she told of her early years, family incidents, first efforts at making a living, and then the steps in becoming a writer. Every now and then she sprinkled in a touch of humor. There were no harsh words or flashy phrases, no frayed tones. All, like her writing, was underplayed and in a low key. She said of herself that she was not given to rousing people and stirring their anxieties. This was evident. Yet everyone in the large audience welcomed every word.

Today's youngsters need to be exposed to more personalities with charm, warmth, honesty, and knowledge, and the ability to convey these qualities in an audience situation. The three joint sessions that the Association for Childhood Education International and The Children's Book Council have sponsored have proved to be professional highlights for all privileged to attend.

NONWHITE LITERATURE AS AMERICAN LITERATURE: A PROPOSAL FOR CULTURE DEMOCRACY

Speech for unknown audience, 1973

I T'S MY PLEASURE to be here today and bring to you a discussion of literature from this writer's point of view. I was tempted to say just then "from a nonwhite point of view." But it occurred to me that the truth is that I don't always run around thinking of myself or defining myself in terms of my race. And you shouldn't, either. Race, like nationality or background, is only one type of definition of a human being, as nonwhite is one definition of literature of a particular kind.

Literature can be thought of broadly as any type of writing on any subject produced by citizens of any country. Or less broadly, as a written expression of form and ideas that, over a period of time, might be of permanent interest.

Recently, the British journal *Growing Point* ran a review in which the reviewer writes that "literature is a matter of privilege — not of class or money but of intelligence and sensitivity." Moreover, the reviewer went on to say that it was also a matter of choice, that a book such as *The Planet of Junior Brown* "cannot appropriately be offered to any and every child," but that young readers might learn to respond to it in the manner in which they learn to listen to music. I believe the reviewer was speaking from another concept of literature and approaching one of my books as an art form. And needless to say, I appreciated her thoughtful and penetrating statements, particularly since my books have had difficulty crossing the sea and in the whole process of translation for non-English speakers.

What I had in mind while writing *Junior Brown* was to tell a whopping good tale, to entertain while blurring the lines between sets of values.

Here in America, the tendency is to view children's literature as books for all children. Historically, Americans have thought of themselves as deeply egalitarian, some more so than others; but all of us are aware at least of a constant assertion of the equality of all. That assertion has caused many a teacher to worry about teaching their children to be sensitive to every book. They will search out those books that reflect heterogenous groupings — those too-few *nonwhite* books which, when thought of in terms of world populations, would represent the literature of the majority peoples of the earth. Teachers are naturally upset when they do not find enough of these books and often disturbed when they may not understand every line and nuance of such books they do find.

All of this has its basis in the proposition that American children have the right to books that reflect their cultural and racial heritage. This is a stunning, absolutely unique concept for which numbers of nonwhite and white Americans have worked hard to make a reality. Certainly, it is not a concept that has yet found practical application in foreign countries with or without nonwhite populations. I have been consistently told that English schoolchildren (Danish, French, Italian, as well) would have no frame of reference for my books. That's interesting, for I know American children of all races who diligently read English novels in which not only points of culture but often the very language is foreign. Naturally, I was pleased by the review of *Junior Brown* in the British publication, although the book has yet to be published abroad. However, there will soon be a German language translation, and needless to say, I don't worry about these barriers to translatable culture. For I think it is only a matter of time, as it has been in this country, until more of us realize the richness of cultural diversity.

Cultural democracy in American literature, like many a fledgling idea, has in some ways already been exploited beyond recognition. I am often confronted with questions and statements such as these: "Why aren't you writing books about biracial children? We *need* them." "My children are inner city and recently from the South, we need books about them." Or, "Half of us don't live in the inner city. What about the suburbs, the middle class?" And "My kids can't relate to your *Zeely*. Write about the poor, the ghetto." And finally, "My kids love *Zeely*, write another *Zeely*!"

Pressure is great on all writers and particularly nonwhite writers today to be relevant to an extreme and beyond, serving the cultural needs of our heterogenous society. Generally, children's books fall into two broad categories: those that are written to fill a need and those that are written and may or may not fill a need. In either category, we have good and lousy books. There are also a plethora of groups below these categories, so that it is possible for a book like *Zeely* to fall, or rather stand, in Column A: Black Books. Column B: Books About Women. C: Books for Free Children. D: Interracial Books. And E (a New York Board of Education group): *Zeely* — Rural. Farming.

Books such as my Jahdu tales, unlike Coyote tales of The People, are frequently categorized as fantasy when actually they represent my belief that folktales and myths are not only of past origin but evolve legitimately in the present.

There is nothing at all wrong with categories and groupings as long as they serve as informative guides. But what has happened is that categories of books have become institutionalized as a kind of multiple segregation, and woe to the books that can't fit a category.

A long time ago, I first noticed that in the month of February I am in much greater demand than at any other time of the year. February

39

is, of course, the month when Americans justly pay tribute to the historical accomplishments of American blacks. For Black History Week, schoolchildren in all-white, all-black, and racially mixed schools diligently read my books. I dutifully make appearances in classrooms to explain how I write, why, and with what singleness of purpose. Once, upon asking students by what means they came to read my books, they informed me that in February they had to read books by black authors, that the rest of the year they could read anything they wanted!

Now that gives me a chill. And however much I value Black History Month, and I do, I'm made uncomfortable by the fact that books written by blacks are made to serve as a substitute for true evaluation of nonwhite literature. Many black studies programs in schools and colleges have failed to attract even black students time and again because they represent a subtle kind of "final solution." Rather than surveying nonwhite literature as part of course offerings in American literature, such courses were segregated in black studies areas and ignored by so-called American literature department chairmen. With the present financial crunch, many black studies programs have disappeared throughout the country. This is tragic — to eliminate programs before we have achieved cultural democracy; however, we may now have an opportunity for curriculum integration.

So it has been with keen interest that I've observed the growth of new language arts programs in our public schools. Numbers of writers have found that their books or parts of their work have become subjects for serious study as teaching material for writing, reading, and literature programs. I, too, have lent myself to the cause of childhood education, sometimes with the spirit of cooperation and other times with a distinct feeling of apprehension.

I have bared my life in two hundred words or less; I have told how I write — not from inspirational moods but because writing is a necessity for me, more so than sleep. My writing has been and is being anthologized, analyzed, dissected, explicated, and distilled in tens of not-so-provocative end-chapter questions. Even my first drafts have been utilized; I suppose to demonstrate to students that even a poor speller can learn to write. However, I hope my books haven't become the token representation of nonwhite literature in the United States.

While soliciting some of my material, one reading specialist wrote me that my stories have "more of the reality about today's world and its less-than-happy endings that children will be needing to grow up whole." Something about that opinion still bothers me, and I think it's the part concerning "reality about today's world."

Good Lord, children don't need my books, or any books for that matter, to know the reality of today's world. In fact, if I had to write that reality, I'd give it up in a day. No, I find my concerns begin at some point on the far side of reality. You'll find no true documentation of early 1970s nonwhite America in my books. No true rural language, no true street language or documentary history that you could say is precisely the way people speak and behave at the moment. If I were writing a sociological tract, I might attempt to do that. What I do write is best described as some essence of the dreams, lies, myths, and disasters of a bunch of my blood relatives whose troubled footprints we are first able to discern on this North American continent some hundred and fifty years ago. Some essence of language and feeling which I project as the unquenchable spirit of a whole people through imagery, space, and time.

The fact that you come to believe it and see it as real simply reveals how similar is the spiritual struggle of one group to that of another. It's that essence, that soul which concerns me, not the ofttimes grim reality.

I wonder seriously how one is to approach teaching an animating principle of a race or races. And I wonder if the very abundance of pro-grammatic learning material—metal teaching machines, kits, boxes, and answer cards—does not signal a certain perplexity and an inabil-ity to trust ourselves to teach and guide, to interpret, while bringing our own experiences to the reading of books and to children.

In my own life, it has been the teacher and not the program that influenced me profoundly. Teachers brought to me knowledge of literature made more significant through the crucible of their maturity and understanding. Teachers taught me to cherish reading by their very love of the sport and their ability to pass that love on to me. It's no mystery that through these literary offerings I came in contact with no nonwhite literature. This can be ascribed to the times and the state of American life in which I grew up. An all too familiar period when individuals such as Mary Bethune, Richard Wright, and Paul Robeson were internationally renowned, while, at the same time, they and the rest of their race remained significantly segregated at home.

It does not amaze me that the segregated experience continues to revive in one form or another throughout our history. Or that again and again we must reassert the assumption of nonwhite literature, not only as minority group literature but as American literature; that in a world in which the majority of peoples is nonwhite, the term *minority*, with its connotations of less and of less importance, is detrimental to the education and self-image of nonwhite children.

I am bored by proponents of the "Black of the Month Club" or "Black of the Year Club," who conceive only one kind of nonwhite book or nonwhite writer existing at a given time. They will condemn books that do not conform to the image of an experience popular at the moment, and they narrow the myriad of marvelously diverse possibilities of nonwhite literary contribution. Too often, we worry whether this book is written in black English and whether the other one is authentically black. I would agree with Dr. R. L. Williams, one of the founders of the Association of Black Psychologists, that the concept of black English has become a "common hustle," created out of a glamorization of and fascination with ghetto life.

What we all should be interested in is good writing, no matter what the source, the idiom, argot, or social dialect. We need more good books, fiction, that will bring characters, past and present, to life through uncontrived situations.

In order to discover good writing and good books, one must have the broadest base possible for comparison. One needs to have access to and knowledge of what is being written and be empathetic to cultural diversity as expressed through literature. I don't say that one must have an abundant knowledge of diverse backgrounds in order to present various kinds of books to school-age children. I would be happy if more teachers would subscribe to the periodical *Interracial Books for Children*, which over a period of time gives a comprehensive view of nonwhite literature and varying nonwhite attitudes.

Always, the attempt should be made to startle and surprise children with the allure of totally different books in order to generate awareness of the enormous possibility of their American heritage. But the attempt will be a failure if the presenter has little or no real respect for the generations of living built up by groups of individuals. If the presenter suggests by negative attitude that one group is less equal than another, or that one group's contribution is better than another's, then I can see no improvement in the instruction of literature or anything else.

I would think teachers would want to make use of stories having to do with black culture, specific tribes of The People, Spanish culture—not as supplements to the body of offerings in American literature, but as tributaries feeding into and increasing and strengthening the body. And not only presented one month of the year, either, or only in conjunction with a social science section on Spanish Americans or Indians—our term, not theirs—but at any time, with no elaborate, self-conscious explanation of why these books have to be read. Rather, in the manner in which you would present Pippi Longstocking, or tales from Narnia or from the Little House series. Simply as good books to be enjoyed and not necessarily as educational tools.

43

NEWBERY ACCEPTANCE SPEECH:
M.C. Higgins, the Great

Given at the meeting of the American Library Association,
San Francisco, 1975

*I*T IS MY GREAT pleasure to accept the Newbery Medal. I am so very grateful to the American Library Association, whose Newbery-Caldecott Committee selected *M.C. Higgins, the Great* as the most distinguished contribution to American literature for children in 1974.

In my hometown, which is a small, relatively obscure Midwestern community, my family has been, if not well-known and well-heeled, at least talked about from one generation to the next. My mother's large, extended, and complex Perry clan literally plummets individual Perrys into the spotlight. For example, it was an uncle of mine who single-handedly cornered the culprits who robbed a nearby bank. Rather than be taken in by a madman—wearing nothing more than a flannel nightshirt and with Jack Daniels on his breath—who shot at them with two gold-plated pocket pistols, they jumped down an empty well, breaking first arms and ankles and then legs and wrists when Uncle staggered too near the edge and plummeted down the well on top of them.

It was another uncle of mine who in 1937 had the finest, sleekest black touring car in the county. And in the same year, on the clearest, sunniest summer day on record, he met his maker when he spotted an elk in the trees at the side of the road; grabbing his shotgun at the ready, he took careful aim and with deadly accuracy shot it whilst he and the touring car sailed serenely over a cliff at twenty miles per hour. If that isn't plummeting, I don't know what is.

It was my favorite, immensely superstitious aunt who was the first among the Perrys to come in at the middle of Orson Welles's alarmingly realistic radio version of H. G. Wells's *The War of the Worlds*. On that scary night of mists back in 1938, Aunt Leah terrified and aroused Perrys in three counties to limited action against invading Martians. Apparently my own immediate family of Hamiltons knew enough about Perrys to spend the next six hours sensibly in Grandpa Perry's root cellar, while all of the male relatives and Aunt Leah searched the skies and shotgunned anything that moved.

Don't blame me if tomorrow you discover that the three tales I've related are exaggerations. For they were told to me by other Perrys, and none of us is known to tell a story the same way twice. What I meant to imply by the above confessional is that folks in my community have been primed for three-quarters of a century to expect some action from my end of town. I'm sure little or nothing is known of the exploits of Perrys in the last quarter of the last century because they were too busy, I suspect, acquiring land and seed and wives and generally keeping their hands on the plow so that subsequent Perrys might raise hell and tell tales on one another in the relative security of mounds of millet and manure.

So that when it was announced in the local papers that one of the Perry clan was the recipient of this medal, older members in particular of my community were more or less conditioned to respond.

"I wasn't a bit surprised," an octogenarian of my acquaintance told me at the reception given me by the Greene County Library, Yellow Springs Branch. Although my elderly friend did seem a bit disappointed that the medal had not been given to me for something slightly more outrageous than writing the best children's book of the year, still she soon seemed happy enough, and pumped and patted my hand long and hard.

I'll never forget the gentleman who, after regarding me from a distance for a time, quietly came forward, his face still wet and glasses foggy from the rain. It rained a total of thirty-eight hours before, during, and after my reception; the land flooded, but still hundreds from my county and from miles around came out to visit with me. This gentleman, red-necked and suspendered, solemnly spoke: "You may not recollect me," he said, "though I do recall you from a child. I am the elder Standhill, and I knew your dad, and I must say, Kenny Hamilton would have been good and proud of you upon this day."

Something inside me went dead quiet at the sound of the man's stark Midwestern voice, sweet to my ears and so like my own late father's stirring accent. I caught the essence of it and filed it away in that place where writers keep extraordinary human sounds, while struggling with my memory and the gentleman's not unfamiliar face.

"I think I remember you," I said.

"Surely," he answered. "Your brother, Buster, went to school with my boy, Don." When I looked on blankly, he was quick to say never mind. "What I wanted to tell you," he said, "was that we are all so proud of you. And I want you to know—we are aware of the significance of this award in the *lit'ry world.*"

I was speechless and near to tears when the gentleman, whom I still couldn't place, grinned and patted my hand.

"I wasn't going to tell you this," he said, "but I was the one, against my wife's will, who let you charge your potato chips and those of a slew of your friends on your dad's account each lunch-noon. You remember me now? When you were in fifth grade? And I had the grocery?"

I nodded, a flood of memories of wooden shelves reaching to the ceiling and glass counters of candy coming to me, clear as water.

"I knew you'd remember," he said, "and I'd like to think that through that small indulgence, I was one who helped you get your way in life."

I am certain he was one, as were many others; and I told him as much.

Experiences such as that are some of the small wonders of receiving this award. And through all of the kindness shown me in relation to it, nothing has so moved me as that reception in my hometown. All of my mother's Perrys turned out, looking, as usual, absolutely different from other people, black or white. For Perrys you can single out of any crowd by that mysterious combination of furious intelligence and shrewd humor seen in their eyes. I hope I resemble them, if only slightly. But they *are* standoffish from all others at the best and worst of times. So they were at my party, never quite overcoming their Midwestern shyness. I like them a lot. That look they have says to me that Perrys are here today because through thick and thin we knew how to survive — that there would always be at least one of us to remember those who had gone before. And when my own mother, Etta Belle Perry Hamilton, told me after having read *M.C. Higgins, the Great* that young M.C. atop his outlandish pole was no less than a Perry in disguise, I knew she had to be right. For M.C., too, knew well how to survive.

No book of mine was ever in more danger of being a failed labor of love than was *M.C. Higgins, the Great*. None was to bring me more pleasure and pain in the writing. I had worked through one chapter of *M.C.*, another, and another — when abruptly nothing more of it would come. So I put the manuscript aside, trusting my instinct, which warned me I wasn't yet ready to write this one. What is instinct but a natural, primordial aptitude for foreknowledge and forewarning? Call it *muse* or *in the mood* if you like, but I trust it equally with reason and understanding. I know that the one will not work without the other. Instinct, then, is that sudden capacity for limited precognition, that half-conscious idea that inexplicably causes a writer to be absolutely certain there is a perfect story waiting just up ahead.

So it was that over the years *M.C.* was never far back in my mind, although other books intervened. Then imagine the day in New York in early 1972 when I burst in on my editor and shouted the news that I had this wild, barefoot youth atop a forty-foot steel pole on the side

47

of a mountain called Sarah's. And if this weren't enough of a really swell story idea, at the summit of Sarah's Mountain was a spoil heap left from strip-mining the land, and this heap was moving relentlessly an inch at a time toward the kid atop the pole. Moreover, to cap the whole thing off, I had this incredible redheaded family of six-fingered vegetarians who were capable of healing mountains.

Picture if you will Susan Hirschman: My editor's capable smile seemed to thin on hearing the news. Her cautious-kind reply was, "I can't *wait* to read it, Virginia."

However, Hirschman has nerves of steel. Wait she did over the next few months until the second of our consultations in her office in New York. I anguished and protested to her that this time the book defied solution or completion. *How do I write*, I worried, *when all of my subjects upon creation immediately suggest intangible objects?* And I said to Susan, "How do I keep mountains, rivers, and, yes, black people from turning into myths or emblems of themselves? They are somehow born on the page too large," I said, "and no sooner do I put them there all together than the river becomes The-One-That-Has-To-Be-Crossed; the mountain is The-One-That's-Got-To-Be-Climbed; and my people? A mere symbol of human STRUGGLE, in capital letters, *Against Adversity*, in italics. And that would be playing them cheap," I said.

Having said that, I slumped back, glumly eyeing Hirschman, the smell of defeat as unsavory as wild onion in my nostrils.

She stared back rather unsympathetically, I thought at the time, and totally uninterested in my fading confidence.

"What about the pole?" she asked.

"What about it?"

"What's *it* a symbol of?"

"It's . . . just what the kid sits on?" I asked, tentatively.

"But why doesn't he 'just' sit on the mountain or on the porch; why a forty-foot pole on the side of a mountain?"

"Well, it's not his mountain," I said, feeling unaccountably annoyed. "It's Sarah's . . . but the pole belongs to him and that's why he sits on it."

"But where did he get it," she persisted, "and what for, and—"

I cut her off. "It's his!" I said, nearly shouting. "He won it. . . ." I was getting this really fantastic scene in my head.

"What did he win it for?" Hirschman asked, carefully removing sharp objects from her desktop.

"Swimming!" I shouted with glee. "For swimming!"

"Remarkable," she said. "I hadn't known he was a swimmer."

"Not just any swimmer," I said, "but a great swimmer. And once he swam the Ohio River . . . and there's a lake in the mountains . . . and there's a tunnel!"

"A train tunnel?" she said.

"No, no . . ." By then I was out of my chair, grabbing my suitcase and, in my mind, already on the plane home.

"Don't forget to write," Hirschman called softly as I reached the door.

"Yeah, sure," I said, by way of farewell.

That was it. There would be no more of those talks between us for quite a spell.

Actually, I've oversimplified an interesting method between editor and writer of defining story area and limits. It is never as simple as I've described it, nor does it happen so quickly. However, when symbols begin to build at the outset, they must be made to yield at once to the things they stand for. In other words, before one can see the mountain, one must know its heat, its flies, its wind, and its place against a total breadth of sky. Writing such fascinating detail keeps me going—over long months of plotting; but it is with character that I must always begin.

I began with M.C. atop a forty-foot pole, lofty, serene. Too serene, perhaps, too above it all, and so I conceived of Ben Killburn, created out of darkness at the foot of the pole. Earthbound, Ben is dependable in a way M.C. is not. Ben, in turn, is constricted by Jones Higgins,

M.C.'s father, a man of strength and integrity, yet superstitious and unyielding. So, too, is Jones illuminated by the Dude from out of nowhere, who clarifies for M.C. his father's inability to face the reality of the endangered mountain.

As though in a spiral from the top of the pole, each character bears light to the next until they all form a circle revolving at the base of the pole. The Dude in his turn is made less imposing in the presence of M.C.'s mother, Banina, and the simple magnificence of her voice. Finally, how easily random chance in the slim shape of a whimsical teenage girl might have brought tragedy to Banina's beloved family.

Thus, the circle of characters moves about the pole, their lives as intertwined and fragile as the thin, flashing ribbons of a May dance. There they reel precariously on the side of Sarah's Mountain under a black cloud — the spoil hovering above. The Higgins's mountain has within it the element of its own destruction in the form of coal; yet it also contains the building materials of rock and dirt which become the means for M.C.'s affirmative action. At the last, M.C. builds a wall in order to stop a spoil heap. Correction: he begins to build a wall. Whether it would really stop the force of tons of falling debris is open to question. But in terms of story and fiction, it is necessary that we see him move to save himself.

We do know the truth, however. In truth, Appalachian hills are flattened; the Harrison and Belmont counties of Ohio are decimated by the GEMs (Giant Earth Movers) of Hanna Coal. Acids released by mining destroy wells, crops, livestock, and land. Because of them, people starve and people die.

But no one dies in *M.C. Higgins, the Great* or in any of my books. I never have written demonstrable and classifiable truths; nor have my fictional black people become human sacrifices in the name of social accuracy. For young people reading *M.C.*, particularly the poor and the blacks, have got to realize that his effort with his bare hands to stay alive and save his way of life must be their effort as well. For too long, too many have suffered and died without cause. I prefer to write about those who survive—such as old Sarah McHiggon of the mountain, Banina Higgins, and the Killburns, who have good cause for living.

A letter I received from a young female student in Toronto is typical of letters I receive from young people of various racial groups. She said, "Miss Hamilton, I am white, but I just as well could be black. Either kind, I'd be okay. Your books taught me to say that."

Most young people who write me tell that my books teach them things—ways to live, how to survive. Having set out to be nothing more than a teller of tales, I have come to feel more responsible—that what I have to say is more worthwhile than I had first thought.

I would like to thank everyone who helped make *M.C. Higgins, the Great* the book it is. To my family—Arnold, Leigh, and Jaime—thank you for bearing with me. To Phyllis Larkin and Elizabeth Shub, I appreciate all you have done. To Janet Schulman, who unstintingly saw *M.C.* through—you are here with us in spirit and we thank you. And last and most, to Susan Hirschman. The past is prelude, and you are the best there is.

One final note: This event here this evening is, in part, an historic occasion. I am the first black woman and black writer to have received this award. May the American Library Association ever proceed.

ILLUSIONS AND REALITY

*Library of Congress Lecture presented at the Library of Congress,
November 17, 1975, in observance of National Children's Book Week,
under the auspices of the Gertrude Clarke Whittall Poetry and Literature
Fund. The speech was reprinted in* The Openhearted Audience:
Ten Authors Talk about Writing for Children, *edited and
with an introduction by Virginia Haviland, published by
the Library of Congress, Washington, D.C., in 1980.*

WHAT I DO for a living and what I do daily as, generally, a most pleasurable pastime are one and the same. I make up people and places. I write fiction. Occasionally, I write a work of nonfiction, which is no less important to me. But I am predominantly a fiction writer.

The best definition of fiction I've come across is a dictionary definition which states that fiction is "an assumption of a possibility as a fact irrespective of the question of its truth." Put another way, the fiction writer works within the realm of illusion. Without the benefit of visual aids or even background music, the writer uses a single system of language to create the illusion of reality.

The most frequent question asked of writers of fiction is "Where do you get your ideas?" I've yet to find a satisfactory answer to that question, but usually I reply rather lamely, if not desperately, "Well, they just come into my head." It's obvious from the ensuing silence that the questioner might well be thinking, "Why do they come into your head? Such ideas certainly don't come into mine."

I think it can safely be said that there is no one answer and no one place where a writer gets ideas. Rather, there are many answers and many places, perhaps as many as there are writers. What I'd like to suggest is the particular direction I take in uncovering the scope of an idea as it relates to reality and illusion in fiction, and also in biography. For ideas do just come into my head and I create fictions out of them, often long before I uncover their source.

Anyone who has been asked by a child whether what he or she views on television is real or unreal is familiar with the confusing elements of reality and illusion. Before the most recent restrictions on the depiction of violence on family-hour television, my own son was mightily confused when the bad guys fell mortally wounded. "Are they actors?" he asked. "Are they acting dead? Will they get up after the show? How can they be shot and get up after the show? How do you *know* they will get up after the show?" I never convinced him that the actors did indeed get up. But unknown to me, my young son had gathered evidence for the proof himself. For in all those dramas in which bad guys fell down dead, there had been one element of truth missing.

A few years ago, when suddenly the horrid scene flashed on the air of a prominent individual being shot and falling seemingly mortally wounded, my son happened to see it. He covered his eyes. "It's real!" he whispered and ran from the room. Later I asked him how he had known it was real, for he had come in the midst of the scene and not at the announcement of a special bulletin. "Because," he said, "there was blood on him. There was blood on the ground." My son had noticed what I had missed when the bad guys fell on Saturday-night television. Earlier restrictions had cleaned up some of the violence. Blood was never shown.

This example is, of course, a much too vivid and tragic way for a child to learn the difference between the real and the unreal. My own children now often watch the evening news and documentary programs because I think it's important that they understand the

53

difference between reality and illusion in life, in entertainment, and in books as well.

A work of fiction is an illusion of life in which characters attempt to transfer a basic reality by casting their desires and their subjective view upon it. In essence, the attempt creates internal conflict between elements of the real and the unreal. Characters must sort out the conflict through experiences that enable them to discover what truths finally exist.

In *M.C. Higgins, the Great*, an environment of plot and characters is based upon the supplanting of reality by the wishes and dreams of one main character. M.C. Higgins desperately seeks escape for his family through a single misconception which becomes for him the only reality: His mother will become a great singer, acquiring enough money for them all to leave their ancestral home on a threatened mountain. Within the misconception, M.C. is able to sort out certain truths by means of experience. Finally, he sees there is no way for him to rid the mountain of its spoil through illusion. At the end, the scarred land, the spoil heap, and the immense mining machines remain to be dealt with by means of whatever reality is left to him.

The two books of Jahdu stories I've written fall outside the realm of the reality-illusion principle of the novels and delve, instead, into the rich vein of American black folklife, both past and present. These tales are based less on a fantasy tradition and more on African prototypal folk myths of animal heroes. The African jackal, hare, tortoise, and hyena were translated on the American continent into the fox, rabbit, terrapin, and wolf. The shaman-hero of Africa is here transformed into the trickster-hero, who personifies the wit and cunning of individuals once condemned within a slavocracy. The amorphous Jahdu of the Jahdu tales, born of no woman but in an old oven, suggests the transcendental nature of present-day black experience in America.

Aware as I am, and was, of the limitations imposed upon purveyors of black literature in this country, perhaps I sought through the Jahdu tales to expand and elevate concerns beyond real and imagined limits of nonwhite American experiences. From this, some few critics have deduced an eccentricity of character delineation and definition within my fiction.

Virginia Hamilton's characters are said to deviate from the recognized or usual. They are variously described as peculiar, odd, and queer — strange, columnar figures fixed somewhat off center of known human orbits. They are detached, as was Zeely, separated by her very height; or like Mr. Pool in *The Planet of Junior Brown*, barred from his professional group by a self-imposed disengagement; or Mr. Pluto in *The House of Dies Drear*, isolated because of the locals' superstitious belief in his supernatural activity; or Junior Brown, rejected because of his ugly fat; or M.C. Higgins, literally risen above mere mortals by means of a forty-foot pole. These are some of my eccentrics. But why the need for them? Why are they created with this quality of spiritual isolation, of other-worldliness, when I, their originator, feel so normal within, having no mental aberrations that obsess me?

We find a clue in my past. Back in college, I tested "normal" as part of the control group in a series of psychological experiments. Translating normal to mean that I was average, I came to detest the term. In vain, I searched within me for a secret hate, a trauma. But it seemed that all of my conscious and unconscious fears and "bumps in the night" were boringly within the limits of normalcy, if we are to believe the results of the tests. Even my childhood anemia and bed-wetting were blandly attributed to the zealous but normal strivings of an overly protective father ambitious for his children.

Later on, I was amused and ultimately relieved to discover in the writings of Gertrude Stein that, while at Harvard Annex (now Radcliffe) and a student of William James, she was a subject of a student project in experimental psychology. Another student complained to Professor James that Gertrude Stein had no subconscious reactions; therefore, she invalidated the results of his experiments. "Ah," said Professor James, "if Miss Stein gave no response, I should say that it was as normal not to give a response as to give one. . . ."

Gertrude Stein always disliked the abnormal, which she felt was so obvious. And she believed that "normal" was "so much more simply complicated and interesting," a statement which gives us an insight into her writing of objective subjectivity (Stein, *The Autobiography of Alice B. Toklas*, 1933). For Stein is the focus and center of all her own work. Writing only of what she was hearing, feeling, and seeing at the moment, she nevertheless always viewed herself with complete detachment.

As a student then, fortified by my reading of Gertrude Stein and her mentor William James, I came to accept my condition of being normal less as a terminal disease and more as something solid, like bedrock, upon which some sort of individual mark might be made. Coming to the present, I wonder whether eccentric creations in fiction are not as normal for me as the totally conscious but seemingly automatic writings were for someone like Gertrude Stein.

Few writers are as un-*self*-conscious as was Stein, with the ability to write alone, as it were, with no involvement with the past. Most writers work within and through a framework of myths, delusions, dreams, and realities of the group to which they bear allegiance. This may hold true for black writers more than for other American groups, for the survival pattern of their group pervades the generations, as though it were an inherent collective trait. Black people, who in recent history were born into bondage as property, had to be different from other people. Even for those born free within the bonded group, slavery must have become a stigma that bled their hearts and marked their minds.

My own grandfather had to be different. Born a slave, as an infant he was sold away with his mother, never to know his father. The years he lived as part of my child life, I knew him as this old friend, chewing tobacco, barely five feet tall, who at eighty, could jump from a standing-still position into the air to click his heels together three times and land still standing. Never ever could I do that.

One of Grandpa's hands was forever maimed to an inch of being closed tight. He had been employed in a gunpowder mill near Xenia, Ohio. One day, the explosive mixture caught fire; the mill burned to the ground. There were great flames and, for some reason, Grandpa reached out for the fire. In a moment of confusion, perhaps he thought the flame would melt away the stigma. His hand was burned hideously. It was bandaged shut and it healed that way, a closed fist from which the generation of his grandchildren, from which I, would hold tight and swing.

How eccentric an image is that fiery hand and the closed fist! How easily it becomes symbolic, even for me. How eccentric is the total history of blacks in America, imbued as it is with the spiritual isolation of the fugitive alone and running, with weird tales which are true tales handed down from one generation to the next. The characters I create are descendants of slaves and freemen. All carry with them the knowledge of former generations who were born as livestock, as property. That sort of knowledge must corner reality for them and hold it at bay. It must become in part eccentric and in part symbolic for succeeding generations. So it is natural that I try through fiction to break down the symbols and free the reality.

As an example, simple curiosity caused me some time ago to attempt to discover the depths of the term *the Street*. Trusting my instinct, I felt there was more to the inordinate use of the term in the lexicon of subculture language than mere ambience.

I had made use of the term in *The Planet of Junior Brown*, where both Junior Brown and Buddy Clark are involved in some way in the Street. Buddy is a street youth, having no home and no normal family as we know family. He lives by his wits in the Street, and he takes from the Street, as he learns from it, only as much as he needs for survival. However, Junior Brown is the opposite of a street youth. He has a home, he has family, but these do not nourish him as the Street nourishes Buddy Clark. Thus, to fill his emptiness, Junior creates the illustration of the Red Man, in which he paints the Street—all of the people he sees are free and together, sharing all, even misery. It is interesting that Red Man is the name of a well-known tobacco and that my grandfather was the only one of my relatives who chewed tobacco. *The Street* also refers back to my grandfather, although I was not conscious of this when I wrote the book.

Many times my mother had told me of the song her father sang to her while she swung from his closed fist, as I did in my youth. "Dad would tell about the Rag Man," she said. "Coming down the street, the Rag Man would sing his song: 'Any rags, any bones, any bottles today,' he'd sing. 'The big, black rag man's coming your way. Any rags, any rags,' he'd sing, all along the street."

I loved that street cry and often sing it to my own children. It's only recently I've wondered at the phrase *the street*, as referred to by my mother in relation to the Rag Man. For there were no *streets* as such in our rural country a hundred years ago when my grandfather was a boy or eighty years ago when my mother was a small child. Was the term *the street* a simple accident, the result of an unconscious shift to a more modern expression? I asked my mother about it. Now that she thought about it, she said, the Rag Man came down the road or the lane, but they always said he came down the street. She insisted on that. "Even Grandpa said 'the street'?" I asked. "Yes," she said, "always."

Occasionally, I wondered about the expression, not actually aware that I had begun to search for something. I knew that in the forties Ann Petry's novel *The Street* had been published. And I made a note when Mordecai Richler's book entitled *The Street* was published in 1975 here in Washington by New Republic Book Company. I remarked to myself how many different cultures view the Street as a particular reality. So it was with Richler's Street and Petry's Street in Harlem. Was it the same with my grandpa's street, and if so, what particular place or reality did it represent, and in what period of time?

Things do fall into my hands rather unexpectedly. I have a habit of seeking the old — old curios and old people whose long memories I admire. I even follow old roads in the country which twist and turn, change names suddenly, and end just anywhere. One of my favorite old roads leads to a stupendous shopping mall, acres and acres of it out in the middle of nowhere. Surprisingly, the mall has turned into a gold mine for old things.

Perhaps all over, but certainly in my part of the Midwest, the great shopping malls built in the sixties and still being built have fallen on hard times. With lines of sleek stores opening on to one gigantic enclosure of fountains, potted palms, and rest areas, these monstrous malls are hit hard by a depressed economy. Consumers, suffering through long periods of unemployment, have given up making the long drive out when they can save gasoline by shopping in town or not at all. Mall lights are dimmed, stores are uncomfortably chilly, and sales personnel have disappeared. Viewed from a distance, surrounded by huge, empty parking lots, my favorite mall is eerily quiet, like the giant launchpad for a dream ship that has come and gone.

I find it all very sad, for shopping malls have always seemed to me particularly American — our adventuresome, garish ode to good times — what with their massive promenades and thirty-foot display windows. We show off, like to think big. But I can envision a day when the whole extravaganza will fall into the hands of the populace. Displaced farmers will come forth on giant tractors to plow up acres of cement. Workers will plant boutiques of corn and wheat. Hired hands will lay out endless holding pens for Black Angus under massive skylights.

Yet, suddenly, something has happened out there in nowhere that is far more interesting than any future sight of fountains irrigating fields. These days, one expects to see camels drinking at marble watering holes. For every inch of the spacious promenade has been taken over by incredible bazaars. Hawkers of every stripe and character are out selling Americana to America. They drift in on Harley-Davidsons, or in minibuses and campers like gypsies, and then melt away again. While they're out there, you can buy old coins, handwoven blankets, old oak furniture, handblown bottles, rolling pins, quilts, Kewpie dolls and carnival canes, and books. Area communes produce afghans and pure honey. One dude wearing chaps and a leather vest came strolling in leading a matching team of Leopard Appaloosas, but they threw him out. On weekends, we go out to the mall to be astonished and to pick over and fondle the past.

The first item my hand fell upon one Saturday was an album of old postcards. I can't say why I paused there, since I collect little of the past beyond that which I store in memory. But as I leafed idly through the album, I came to a section labeled "Negro Postcards." These were a ghastly commentary on an uncertain black history—painted portraits of toothy "pickaninnies" slurping watermelon or photos of ragged black children grinning and dancing. At once repulsed and fascinated, I flipped over one card depicting a melon eater, to discover this message: "Dear Mildred. I am here where I was going. I was going no farther and, Mildred, I hope to die here. I thought you would want to know. Alice."

Such a stunning, sad message. I stood there for a half-hour reading other messages, but the whole time wondering what kind of journey Alice had embarked upon. Were these cards with their stereotyped portraits used solely by white wanderers? Would even white users of the cards believe that these crude portraits truly represented blacks? I thought of buying up all of the "Negro" cards to study them at my leisure. But in the end, I left them there, every one of them. At the last, one intrusion into the privacy of the dead and gone was enough. I had learned all I needed to know.

I did find something at the bazaar that day which I had to have, and which is the point of this long exposition. A slim paper volume entitled *Homes of the Freed*, published in the twenties and written by Rossa B. Cooley. Its cover illustration is a woodcut of a crude cabin with a figure seated before it, a clouded sky, and a road winding by the cabin. Below the title is the notation, "The oncoming of three generations of women from the plantation street. . . ." Here was the Street again, but used in a wholly unexpected way.

Homes of the Freed hoped to demonstrate how "the purely

academic character of the early Negro schools" started by Northern teachers during Reconstruction could be thoroughly eradicated by means of domestic training and service programs and supplanted by "the self-dependent households of freedom and . . . what this has meant to the women of the race." It was a terribly biased approach to the education of black women, but interesting to me personally for the story it tells of the great transition from the black Street of slave days.

Homes of the Freed gives testimony of old black people remembering what their parents and grandparents told them. An elderly man relates the history of a row of slave cabins, always calling it the Street.

Women worked from *dayclean*, as the dawn was called, until tasks in the fields were done. The fields were isolated, lonely places where, apparently, women often worked separately from men and were cut off from the comparative security of the cabins, from newborn babes, and from their very young children. A whole system of day care had to be arranged for these children in the Street. Black women too old to work the fields became the maumas, or nurses, and the newborns were carried out into the fields to be suckled by their mothers and then returned to the Street.

In the Street in front of the cabins, the old maumas built a huge fire and, in one great cooking pot, cooked the meals for children, for themselves, and for the field hands. The food for the pot was supplied by the whole of the Street. The maumas and babies all ate from it. When the workers had completed their tasks in the fields, they returned to the Street, and they too ate from the pot.

They ate and talked quietly. They were tired to the bone now, but they gained strength again from one another and the communal life of the Street (Cooley, *Homes of the Freed*, 1926).

So it is that "the Street" down which came the Rag Man of my grandfather's song and the Street in *The Planet of Junior Brown* may both hark back to the old time in the plantation Street. The Street may well be that which the slaves gave up in order to be free. To flee from the only security they had ever known must have terrified many, but break away they did, from an old order, to discover a new reality. Still, the Street exists, not only in racial memory but in the daily lives of those who escape from mean rooms to the camaraderie, sometimes even the danger, of Petry's ghetto Street, or the stupefying drudgery of Richler's Street; in the lives of Street people, the voice of Street poets, the drama of Street theater and the prose of Street literature; also, in the lazy times on the Street corners of boring small towns. The meaning of the Street in all ways and at all times is the need for sharing life with others and the search for community.

Knowing that the Street is so connected to past life in a special way which is personal to me makes the language of it richer and makes the past always present for me.

Every fiction has its own basic reality, as does the Street, through which the life of characters and their illusions are revealed, and from which past meaning often creeps into the setting. The task for any writer is to discover the "reality tone" of each work—the basis of truth upon which all variations on the whole language system is set. For reality may be the greatest of all illusions. We each know our own reality through which we seek a common ground of communication with others. The fiction writer seeks the common ground by relinquishing her own reality for the creation of a new one. No number of past successes helps this writer in the creative process of a new writing. For the very process must be created for each new reality. The way to do is never mastered and never really learned.

It would be interesting to create a fiction in which reality and illusion are completely personified. The thought of attempting such a fiction came to me from observing my own children and their contemporaries. All seemed to be trying to find out who they really were through testing and by changing roles. I have watched them for days playing at being one another, using one another's language, walks, and hairstyles. When one Elodie D. Dangerfield from Little Rock, Arkansas, entered the seventh grade at the beginning of this year, a number of her twelve-year-old classmates began affecting syrupy

Southern accents. For a time, they discarded their blue jeans and talk of sisterhood for pink dresses and evening prayer meetings. I have nothing against Elodie D. Dangerfield—not her real name, of course. In fact, I find her fascinating as I attempt to discover just who it is *she* is playing at being, or whether she is really being herself.

My observation of these young girls started me thinking. To write about a family unit in which some members are in the process of learning who they are and in which others are living a fiction they admire seemed to be the perfect sort of risk for me. Which of them would live a true portrayal and which would live an illusion? On what basis of truth can be measured the reality and the illusion personified? Moreover, it occurred to me that we all carry with us the somewhat tattered baggage of our pasts, so why not personify the past in the present as well? How does one accomplish this without reducing characters to symbols or creedal types? Add to this questions of racial identity, and it becomes clear how diverse an environment of illusion and reality might be created.

The whole idea might sound rather complicated for children. Actually, it's the approach to the process of creation that gets complicated, not the idea or the manner in which it's to be written. Moreover, we've all observed children struggling daily with an incredible array of identity forms. One nine-year-old youth of my acquaintance who is white was asked what he wanted to be when he grew up and replied, "I want to be black." His father, telling me this, was pleased by his son's answer. I was not so pleased and I told the father so, for I believe it is poor mental health for a white youth to want to grow up to be black, as it would be for a black youth to want to grow up to be white.

Said the father, "David admires black athletes. He also sees black people living around him just the way he lives. He sees no difference."

"If he sees no difference," I said, "why wouldn't he want the group to be white, to admire white athletes as well? And suppose he weren't living in this middle-class community where most of what he sees includes only one class of black people? Suppose he were to see the hungry and out of work. What then?"

"But the truth is," said the father, "David's living here where black people are living in the same way he lives."

"You must never let him believe it is the whole truth," I said finally.

We ended our discussion there, with the question of truth unanswered. But David nags my mind. My instinct tells me that he must be made to understand that being white is quite all right, as is being black. Perhaps he should be told that he can wish to be black if he so desires, but that the wish will not be fulfilled. Even as I say these words, they seem to melt in illusion. For me all are at least aware of the fact that there are whites among us who live as blacks, and blacks among us who live as whites. There are biracials and multiracials among us, such as my own children, who might more realistically be termed Other Kinds, or Composites, or Betweens. Can you hear children of the future saying, "I'm a 'posite. She's an o'kind. The others are 'tweens." I don't doubt anything.

Transracial peoples are nothing new in this country. The Shawnee Nation Remnant Band of the Tecumseh Confederacy has set up a nation house in my hometown, and although they appear to be white and do not seek recognition from the Bureau of Indian Affairs, they nevertheless live as Shawnee Native Americans. The Wesorts — a people who are probably Native American, but this is uncertain — live in large groups in the swamplands of southern Maryland. In the Piedmont and Blue Ridge areas of Virginia there are groups known as the "Amherst County issues," brown people who may or may not be Native American and who for years have intermarried. Many of us have long been familiar with those mysterious people, the "Jackson Whites," living in New York and New Jersey, who number more than five hundred and whose origins are unknown.

We have yet to deal successfully with American transraciality in real terms, as we have failed to redefine race in light of the modern, twenty-first-century progress of humankind. Certainly, here is an arena for serious study by anthropologists, sociologists, philosophers, and, of course, writers of fiction.

Delineating such areas of a writer's thoughts as these may give an inkling of the difficulty in answering the question "Where do you get your ideas?" For ideas come from without as well as from deep sources within. They may just as easily come from my son's original knock-knock jokes as from quiet moments of contemplation in my study. They come from memory, from sight and sound. They come from living.

I've only made mention of a type of writing besides fiction and folktales which has given me a good deal of satisfaction. Although I've written just two biographies for young people, one concerning the life of W. E. B. Du Bois and the other the life of Paul Robeson, they are no less involved with the subject of reality and illusion.

I had hoped, by writing the personal history of a real individual through a disciplined presentation of facts, to create the illusion of total reality; to give readers the feeling that they walked along with the subject in his life; and through the creative use of source material, to allow the subject to speak as closely as possible in his own voice.

In this respect, of the two biographies, the Robeson biography is the more successful. The research and study of the Robeson material took a number of years. When that phase of the work was completed, I discovered it was possible during the day to evoke the Robeson spirit in my mind and to live with it as though the man were a guest in my house. I began to know Paul Robeson quite well, and slowly two aspects of him emerged to trouble me and to pose definite problems in the actual writing of the book.

The first problem, and the one easiest to deal with, was the problem of Robeson emerging not as a man but as a symbol. The same difficulty occurred in the writing of *M.C. Higgins, the Great*. In that fiction, I had to come to terms not only with the symbolic nature of mountains and rivers but with all the preconceived notions about

65

blacks being in a state of nature or nearly so. In my Robeson research, it was almost impossible to find a single newspaper account that did not depict the man as somehow supernatural and larger than life. Take this one by a sportswriter when Robeson was barely eighteen and playing football for Rutgers: "He rode on the wings of the frigid breezes; a grim, silent and compelling figure. . . . It was Robeson, a veritable Othello of battle" (Arms, *New York Sunday Tribune*, November 25, 1917). Or this one: "A dark cloud . . . Robeson, the giant Negro" (Taylor, *New York Tribune*, October 28, 1917).

Hardly ever was Robeson described as a man. Rather, he was "this giant," "that great, noble prince," or "the original stuff of the earth." Individuals who knew him and whom I interviewed often seemed at a loss for words or struck dumb with awe, and when they *could* put their experiences into words, the superlatives would roll forth in god-like descriptions.

Eventually, I learned to use these overwrought passages to an advantage. But it became necessary for me to write in a very tight, simple style: to write close up to the individual in the hope that a concise and straightforward revelation of his life would finally produce a composite of the man.

The second problem was more difficult and became clear to me only after I had written a first draft of the book. Then Robeson still seemed elusive. I could not get a handle on him. He stood alone, but he did not stand out in a way I knew he must. Something about him remained out of focus and out of time. It took months for me to realize that no simple factual presentation of Paul Robeson's life was likely ever to reveal the man in his true stature. For the basic difficulty of writing about blacks in America was intensely a problem here: The origin of black American history is fundamentally different from that of traditional American history. I have said that that history is eccentric because it departs considerably from the usual or traditional. Because of slavery, because of continuing discrimination, segregation, and exploitation throughout the history, it was and is necessary for blacks to make extreme changes in their view of themselves in American life, in their evaluation of themselves, and in their institutions.

In order to understand Paul Robeson or W. E. B. Du Bois, it is necessary that we understand that what the majority viewed as radical in their time was quite a normal point of view for these men whose lives were profoundly restricted by a whole system of established mores. Thus, it was not possible to write about Paul Robeson without a thorough understanding of the political and social times in which he lived. Furthermore, it became necessary to go beyond the usual thorough and traditional histories having to do with political America, Europe, and the rest of the world, such as those written by Commager and Leuchtenburg, and to search for and find those revisionist historians, like Gabriel Kolko, whose historical truths emerge as radically different from what we have taken for granted as the truth.

In revisionist historiography, the alliance of Great Britain, the United States, and the Soviet Union at the time of World War II becomes not a matter of high ideals, deliberation, and choice, but one of ruthless necessity to defeat an enemy. The European aid program instituted by the United States after the war becomes less a program of recovery for Europe from pain and suffering and more the deliberate attempt to take from Britain control of foreign markets and Middle East oil and to advance American investments and economic and military power by means of the extension of a capitalistic system throughout the world.

Paul Robeson's drift toward radicalism and the appeal radicalism had for him become understandable from the viewpoint of a colonized people. Robeson saw himself as a citizen of the world and identified himself, as did Du Bois, with the world's workers and colonized people, whom he deemed criminally exploited under capitalism.

Whether the view is wholly correct or partly inaccurate, it is not possible to write about either man without recognizing that they were in a position to make contact with the world, to travel it and study it, in a way few Americans other than statesmen ever had.

Writing these two biographies from a more radical perspective was quite a challenge, and the perspective is as justified as any other, if not more so, with regard to blacks. Curiously, my studies in radical history and research into black life and history have tended to radicalize me not so much in terms of world political views as in fictional terms. I would be a rather useless individual in any revolutionary situation. I hate violence and tend to view it as a human aberration — certainly not a very radical point of view. I also tend to view capitalism as an aberration which provokes extremism, which I suppose *is* radical. In any case, we must remember that radicalism is as American as apple pie. The men who wrote the Declaration of Independence were radicals who were not above trickery, rabble-rousing, rioting, and murder to aid fugitive slaves.

For myself, I deliberately attempt a kind of literary radicalism in the hope of removing traditional prose restrictions and creating new ways to approach literary forms from a perspective other than that of the majority. It is a way of continuing to legitimize nonwhite literature, bringing it into full view to provoke curiosity and discussion. Many in this country are attempting to bring not only good literature but representative literature to the country's children. I don't believe that anywhere else in the world has such an attempt been made. Here it is not always successful; it meets with varying degrees and kinds of resistance. Still, few of us would deny the right of nonwhites to a literature reflecting their concerns. I am not talking about a literature that merely satisfies a need, though that's important; I'm speaking about a literature whose themes and philosophy may begin now, and in the future continue to be, entirely different from what is traditional. Indeed, it would be radical.

Tracking down the source of an idea and discovering the true components of a fiction are intriguing work. But they are work that is, in a sense, a sideline and after the fact. It is not necessary to know the source of an idea in order to expand upon it. For to get an idea and from it create a system of illusion we accept as reality is the most exciting prospect of all. Through the use of words alone, the writer creates sight and sound and emotional response. By reading words alone, the reader sees, hears, and feels. Both are demonstrating an act of mentality, the connection of minds through which belief is suspended in the interest of illusion. One would be at a loss without the other. I for one would find it impossible to write indefinitely with only myself to read what I had written.

That is why, when eager young writers seek me out for help when they know their work isn't ready and I know it isn't, I understand so completely their impatience. It is not just the need to see their work and their names in print, although that is part of it always. It is the overwhelming desire to make that connection of mind with mind, to have demonstrated the act of mentality and to have communicated. For the writer, there is nothing quite like having someone say that he or she understands, that you have reached them and affected them with what you have written. It is the feeling early humans must have experienced when the firelight first overcame the darkness of the cave. It is the communal cooking pot, the Street, all over again. It is our need to know we are not alone.

MISSION TO MOSCOW

Essay from School Library Journal, *February 1980; a report on her trip
to Moscow in October 1979 for the Second International Conference
of Writers for Children and Youth, discussing the conference
and conveying her impressions of the city and its people*

"UNFORTUNATELY," said Ismail Uyaroglu of Turkey, "most of the children of earth live today in cold and hunger; they have no necessary clothes and can neither read nor write."

Vasil Vitka of the Soviet Union commented, "The Nazis killed more than two million two hundred thousand people in the land of Byelorussia (a Soviet republic) . . . and not even the children were spared. The children's literature of Byelorussia and of the whole Soviet Union has faced the challenge of talking to the youthful reader about concepts and phenomena very difficult for the child's understanding."

Shigeo Watanabe of Japan added, "I am obliged to touch upon a subject which might seem unexpected. I am asking whether we grown-ups are able to save children from death. In Japan, many adults and parents find themselves in an extremely complicated situation when it is necessary to save a child from death but not because the child is doomed to die of an incurable disease or heavy wounds. It is the physically sound children who die. In my opinion, the main cause of children's deaths is the suppression of children's psyches by adults: the latter's selfishness. Parents spare no effort so that their child may study in a privileged school in order to guarantee material well-being in the future. Such upbringing arises in children an abnormal feeling of rivalry and makes them ready to take a step for the sake of superiority. The children who are unable to withstand competition commit suicide. This threat of children's deaths is apparently incorporated in the very system of school education."

Miriam Morton of the United States spoke about the fifty-two million children who have to work to eke out an existence. "If present trends continue," she said, "the number of children six to eleven years of age not attending schools will reach one hundred and thirty-four million by 1985. Children and adolescents must not remain voiceless in the struggle for their survival and welfare. We writers can, through our books, help them become advocates of their own human rights."

Again and again, authors from around the world spoke somberly of the suffering of the world's children at the Second International Conference of Writers for Children and Youth held in Moscow on October 15–24, 1979. One hundred twenty-nine writers from thirty-nine countries, including fifty-nine foreign writers, took part in the conference sponsored by the Writers' Union of the USSR.

There were five participants from the United States: James Fraser, president of the International Research Society for Children's Literature and editor in chief of *Phaedrus* magazine; Sybille Jagusch, member of the executive committee of the International Board of Books for Young People (IBBY) and member of the Hans Christian Andersen Award jury; Miriam Morton, chairman of the international committee for the Jane Addams Children's Book Award; and authors Eloise Greenfield and me.

Despite the litany of grim statistics on the children of earth, the conclave of children's authors from around the world — all holding diverse political views — was enthusiastic and committed to good literature for children.

My first thought was to simply report on the conference — what the speakers had to say, how their concepts of children's literature

7 1

differed according to their ideology, and so on. But after a few days, I realized that I (and so many others) hadn't been invited to the Soviet Union merely to take part in a series of sessions on writing books for children, however unique such a conference might prove to be. It was clear that a significant intention of the Writers' Union was to show us a pretty swell time while revealing the best side of one of the most successful socialist systems in the world. I was eager to see whatever my hosts wanted me to see while judging for myself, of course, the truth—the value and completeness—of the picture.

MOSCOW — FIRST IMPRESSIONS

WE LEFT Kennedy Airport on Aeroflot, the official Soviet carrier, and arrived in Moscow after a nine-and-a-half-hour nonstop flight. Flying on a Soviet jet was unlike anything I'd experienced before—I have yet to hear the voice of the Russian pilot, let alone see him. The plane was crowded, noisy, and a cold draft ran along the floor. The stewardesses were usually unavailable until mealtime, but the service was good—although a couple of hours late the evening of the first flight—and the food was fine. Otherwise, the flight was uneventful. I stayed awake all night, watching the sun go down and the stars come out, the stars go down and the sun come up—a pleasant and satisfying feeling of oneness with the heavens.

We landed unexpectedly at an airport which was not the Sheremetyevo International Airport, at which most tourists arrive. Fortunately, the interpreter from the Writers' Union located us within an hour, loaded us and our baggage into two cars, and we set out for the long, fascinating drive to Moscow.

With a population of over eight million, Moscow, located on the Russian Plateau, sprawls immensely over three hundred and fifty square miles. It is the capital of the Soviet Union as well as the capital of the Russian Soviet Federative Socialist Republic (RSFSR), which is the largest Soviet republic. As the cultural, industrial, and political center of the Soviet Union, Moscow is a workers' city having more than one hundred nationalities.

We drove (actually, we barreled) along the eight-lane, divided highway—there was no speed limit! My terror at traveling 110 kilometers per hour in a strange new world was overwhelmed by stunning vistas: uniform strands of lovely birch trees, a huge apartment city with new rose-tinted buildings fading into the softest blush on the blue of the horizon. Everywhere workers with hoes and shovels crisscrossed the highway. I felt we had landed literally in one of the many oversized billboard murals which exalt the greatness of communism. Before us lay the workers' paradise, or so it seemed.

As a guest of the Writers' Union of the USSR, I had been given a ten-day, expenses-paid visit to the country of which I have long been a student. I had written biographies of W. E. B. Du Bois and Paul Robeson; both had been friends of the Soviet Union—a friendship which had caused them grave consequences. I felt that, at last, I was seeing for myself that which I had heretofore researched and only imagined. And I remembered the Du Bois creed I'd memorized years ago:

> I believe in Socialism as well as Democracy. I believe in Communism wherever and whenever men are wise and good enough to achieve it . . . I despise men and nations which judge human beings by their color . . . I believe in free enterprise among free men and individual initiative under physical, biological and social law. I hate war.
> (Du Bois, *In Battle for Peace: The Story of My 83rd Birthday*, 1952)

It was a creed that set a proper frame for openmindedness. I settled back, then, as we flew down the highway and the immense city rose from the tableland. It's tiresome using words such as *immense, awesome, massive, gigantic*, again and again; yet there is little about the

Soviet Union that can be characterized in other terms. The first impression one has seeing Moscow is that it has heroic immensity. The buildings are not unusually tall, but they are often awesomely wide and long. A massive architectural style pervades, and the huge Hotel Ukraina where we stayed was no exception. Situated at a wide loop in the Moscow River, it was a monolithic edifice and reminded me of a gigantic crown.

After we had registered, we were taken to our rooms, which were quite pleasant. I headed downstairs to explore the lobby and the shops. (I spent rather madly the first few days, never forgetting that I was beyond Europe, and I experienced a perverse delight at throwing away my hard-earned bucks in a communist country.)

The conference participants were given a reception the first evening sponsored by the Writers' Union. The food was a smorgasbord set out on banquet tables in the center of a large room. We moved down the line of tables, sampling dishes. Simply by asking everyone to pose for my camera and to talk into my microphone, I managed to photograph a number of writers and tape their views on literature for the young. There is some difficulty to juggling a camera, tape-machine, and glass and plate with grace. Eventually, jet lag got the better of me — I suddenly realized I'd been awake for thirty-six hours. When voices began to fade so did I — to my room and welcomed sleep.

THE CONFERENCE

THE NEXT MORNING, October 16, the Second International Conference of Writers for Children and Youth officially began at nine o'clock with breakfast at the Writers' Union at 52 Verovsky Street. Interpreters informed us about some of the history of the Writers' Union and patiently answered all our questions. By ten o'clock we were seated at tables in the Oak Hall of the Union building. There were table signs designating our countries — the United States was situated across from West Germany and Finland. Syria was on one side and Thailand on the other. A microphone was located conveniently within reach of each delegation, and every participant was equipped with earphones for one of seven simultaneous translations. Translators were to be seen on a balcony above the hall and also on a platform outside the hall. (All the writers stayed at the Ukraina. An interpreter would meet every two writers at the hotel each morning.)

The inaugural address for the opening session was given by Georgy Markov, first secretary of the board, the USSR Writers' Union, who welcomed us to the Soviet Union.

The first paper was delivered by Sergei Vladimirovich Mikhalkov, secretary of the board, USSR Writers' Union. Mikhalkov is one of the most popular writers for children in the country, with millions of his books in print. I asked for an interview with him at his convenience and he contacted me the next day. Mikhalkov is a formidable-looking man, quite tall, with white hair and mustache. In his address, he said the aim of the International Year of the Child was to "attract the world's public attention to the conditions of children in various regions and to identify ways of bringing speedy help to the young wherever it is necessary. We all agree," he said, "that a reading child is far better than a child who does not read. . . . The challenge before us is also to see to it that progressive children's and youth literature should become an even more effective helpmate in the noble cause of international détente, and in promoting cooperation, peace, and friendship among the peoples."

Much of Milhalkov's paper praised the socialist system and railed against the capitalist system. He spoke of what he called "cheap literature" from some Western countries as the "cultural poison . . . exported to the Third World countries."

"Nothing of the kind exists or can exist in the Soviet Union and the other socialist countries," he said, "where *commercial and corruptive trash is banned and where there are no, and cannot be, social forces or groups interested in producing and purveying it*" (italics mine).

When the ideological differences came crashing down during the sessions, I was heartened when, on the second day, Fraser (United States) spoke up:

"As writers and researchers we feel even more frustrated about the print and film violence which we see confronting children in most Western countries and in the Third World countries *which continue to import the worst American television programs or international comics* (italics mine). I regret as an American that the picture of the United States is held by many children from watching such programs and not from reading our many fine and socially engaged writers, two of whom you have met here. . . ."

CHILDREN'S PUBLISHING

EACH DAY of the three-day conference, fifteen writers read papers in two sessions that ended at 4:30 PM. Participants concentrated on the extent of children's publishing in their countries, what types of books authors were engaged in writing, the trends in youth literature, and so on. Ena Noël from Australia mentioned that the world produced a book every minute. But publishing in her country was not extensive enough to service Australia's children. Thus, Australia imported many books from various countries in English and also in languages relevant to Australia's ethnic communities.

Jens Sigsgaard of Denmark said that 60 percent of books in public libraries in Denmark were lent to children although children are only 20 percent of the population. "A writer is paid for every book of his kept in the library," he said. "Annual counts give writers a considerable addition to their earnings. A sixteen-page illustrated book for children gets equal pay with a four-hundred-page novel for grown-ups."

Speaking about major trends in children's literature in socialist countries, Christian Emmerich of East Germany said, "Our authors seek to acquaint their youthful readers in a way that they can readily understand with the heroism of the fighting and suffering peoples and with international solidarity. Children come to understand the worldwide class battles and to compare these events with our socialist world and its historic achievements."

Lena Friedell of Sweden spoke about a plan her country has for a new mass-market edition of quality books supported by the state. "Many people doubt the effectiveness of publishing five or six cheap quality books a year," she said, "while the real mass-market production of many hundreds of books is still here. We should perhaps restrain the import of commercialized literature, but it is quite a problem in the conditions of a free market prevailing in Sweden. . . . Hardly any publisher dares to publish a new Swedish picture book if he is not guaranteed international coproduction or a support from the state. This is a serious threat for the original Swedish picture books."

Over and over again was heard the lament from poorer nations similar to what Ismail Uyaroglu had to say about Turkey (which has a long-standing tradition of children's literature). He felt obliged, he said, to mention some unfortunate facts. "Turkey's population is about forty-five million people," he said, "while the circulations of children's books do not exceed five or six thousand copies because our people, as a result of the domination of capitalist economy in the country, lack sufficient means for subsistence. People have no money to buy children's books," he went on, "and the level of literacy is very low, so the picture is rather sad."

One sensed from these speeches, a solidarity and certainty of purpose among the socialist countries as well as strong state control over what can and cannot be written and published. Said Sergei Mikhalkov in his opening address, "I think it would be fair to say that the life of children on earth would have been very happy if all the governments treated them with the same cordial concern as the socialist countries treat their young citizens. Our country stands like a loving mother at the cradle of every baby. . . ."

Entertainment was provided for us on each evening of the conference. We saw children's films, comfortably traveling to and from our destination by bus, and attended a performance at the Central

77

Children's Theatre. The musical play, entitled *Maximka*, was about a Russian seaman who had lost his son in some tragedy but gains another—a slave youth who escaped from a pirate ship. Before the play's end, the youth is recaptured and sold to a flamboyantly wealthy couple who speak English. But he is rescued, finally, by Russian sailors and adopted by Maxim, the one who had lost his son. The costumes and the fine stage settings depicted a time a century earlier, which was the period of the play. All the adult actors, including the woman who played the boy Maximka, had exceptional voices.

But I was having some difficulty with the play, or rather with the questions I had which arose from it. What was I, the granddaughter of fugitives from slavery, doing in Moscow watching a somewhat obvious lesson in class struggle and white saviors-to-the-rescue? The young woman who played the slave youth had been painted dark-skinned and wore a short, black, kinky Afro wig. And the character, so helpless and alone, brought out the maternal and paternal instincts of all who watched. What I was seeing staged was an old, familiar colonialism, which made me rather sad. So I got rid of the contents of the satchel of black contemporary literature (my own and other authors') I'd brought with me. This was accomplished with no trouble since the Soviet authors wanted whatever books we could give them. This didn't change the play I had seen; it simply made me feel better.

In our free time, we were bused to schools and to "pioneer palaces," those remarkable after-school centers where Soviet boys and girls concentrate their efforts in fields of their choice under the guidance of experts. Some of us visited the Publishing House of the Central Committee of the Young Communist League, "Young Guard" (Molodaya Gvardiya).

We had a frank discussion with Inessa Feodrovna Avramenko, the deputy editor in chief, about the publishing of contemporary American youth literature in the Soviet Union. After a presentation of the books Young Guard published, Avramenko said we might differ in our opinions, but she was confident we could find levels of mutual understanding and respect through which the exchange of good literature could be made.

On October 18, the conference officially closed with *An Appeal* "Of the Participants in the Second International Meeting of Writers for Children and Youth to the World's Workers in the Field of Literature for Young People":

> We were inspired by a common desire to see our planet at peace and all of the children on earth happy. We therefore resolved to reaffirm and protect the principles advanced in the *Declaration of the Rights of the Child* proclaimed by the United Nations two decades ago.

The *Appeal*, read to the participants by Miriam Morton and unanimously approved, ended: "May each year on this earth become the Year of the Child. Humanity's future depends on the destiny of today's children."

SIGHTSEEING IN LENINGRAD

THE PARTICIPANTS of the conference stayed on until October 24. They had a choice of travel—an overnight stay in Leningrad, Tallinn, or far-off Baku. Baku was tempting, but I had studied the Siege of Leningrad and the heroism of its people. I was eager to see the city I knew only through war memoirs and through fiction.

The Leningrad Writers' Union had planned a dinner reception for those participants who spent the final night there. I, with about twenty-five other authors, took the Red Arrow express train to Leningrad, which left promptly at midnight. We were served steaming hot tea in tall glasses in silver holders and then went to bed.

At eight AM, we disembarked in the pastel city of Leningrad, which is constructed on one hundred islands in the Neva River and is linked by bridges and canals. The "white nights" of Leningrad, when the sun does not set, are legendary—it seemed a more European city than Moscow. The Hotel Mockba was a mammoth, modern circular structure with small contemporary rooms and bunklike beds with suede bedspreads. Mockba is the perfect hotel for the tourist on the run: its modern, fast-service cafeteria had a variety of food.

We spent Saturday sightseeing at the town of Pushkin and the Catherine [the Great] Palace where Alexander Pushkin was educated, the Cruiser *Aurora* museum, and the grand Hermitage Museum (the former Winter Palace). Those of us who still had energy by evening sampled the nightclub life at the hotel. The floor show had varied acts including a traveling circus, and the band played Western-style dinner music. My beef stroganoff was tender and tasty. Later I had vodka with a Pepsi chaser—a rather curious new custom the Russians have adopted.

On the last evening, we visited the Leningrad Writers' Union. The writers were pleased that we had enjoyed their city and that we had come to spend this time with them. They were very cordial. We were greeted with toasts that were witty and full of good humor. We answered toast for toast but, I must say, were not as quick with the wit. As if shedding heavy cloaks, we all relaxed and had fun, ate fine food, danced, and talked.

We sang American songs—anything at all. Remembering Robeson, I sang "Meadowlands." The Russians grabbed my hand and cried, in English, "Thank you!" Poet Raul David from Angola sang beautifully the ballads of his homeland. The literary scholar from Japan played the piano. The night wore on. Someone thought to toast the writers who had fought at the Siege of Leningrad. Glasses were lifted again and again. Then, it was remembered we had a train to catch. The evening had come all too quickly to an end.

The authors from the Leningrad Writers' Union saw us to our hotel again, helped us with our luggage, and accompanied us by bus to our train for our return to Moscow. The night had turned bitter cold, yet none of us wanted to say good-bye. But Soviet trains run on time.

Whatever books by American authors that I had left I gave to those around me. We left (again on the midnight express) after promising to return someday.

LAST DAYS IN MOSCOW

I LEARNED THAT we would be returning to America on October 23, rather than 24, which meant that the day we arrived back in Moscow would be our last day in the Soviet Union. There was time, however, to visit Red Square and walk within the Kremlin walls.

Hundreds of people were in the square—tourists as well as Soviet citizens from all over the country. All carried red carnations symbolizing freedom, to be placed on the Lenin Mausoleum. As we watched, in silence, the spectacle of the changing of the guard, two young women, still in wedding gowns and with their attendants, laid wreaths on the mausoleum in a gesture of love and respect.

The enormous square with the gigantic GUM department store along the length of one side was still in contrast to the large numbers of people there. Snow began to fall. A cold wind came up. The mild October weather we'd left behind had changed to winter as we streaked back from Leningrad. The skies now grew leaden, and the ton-and-a-half red stars revolving slowly above the Kremlin heights were rose-hued and misty. Our group had grown large now as we shuffled out, blowing our breaths before us, and joined those who had returned from their trips to Tallinn and Baku.

I decided not to spend my last afternoon packing—I could do that after midnight. I wanted to spend whatever time was left seeing more sights and continuing those delightful conversations I'd been having with my interpreter, Helen Kotkin of the Foreign Language Institute. She and I visited the marvelous Pushkin Museum, and we found time to take a long, last look at the Kremlin and Red Square. Later, at the Writers' Union, we saw a fine film about the disintegration of a Soviet nuclear family, which pertinent subject matter took me by surprise.

All that day I had tried, unsuccessfully, to put my thoughts in order. I hadn't been transformed in a surge of revolutionary zeal into a Soviet-style socialist, yet, the order, the dedication, and the lack of chaos made a deep impression. I wondered if the Soviet writers whom I had come to know, who seemed quite satisfied with the system, were *good* writers in the Western terms that I understood. Had I come with the assumption, perhaps naïve, that if these writers were happy with communism, they could not be good writers?

Serghei Mikhalkov told me in the interview I had with him that only one of his books had been published in the United States, although he'd been publishing for forty years, with one hundred and forty million copies of his books in print throughout the world. He said that works such as he wrote were seldom translated to foreign languages in capitalist countries. He gave me three of his volumes in the Russian language, all colorfully illustrated. I don't know the language so I cannot read the books, and I find it disturbing that I will never know what they say, that I can't make a judgment about them.

When at last I found myself able to summarize my thoughts and feelings about the Soviet Union, I admired it for acting upon the belief that children are the world's treasure and for holding the literature of children in the highest esteem. It was a privilege to have been invited to Moscow to partake of a unique mission in the interest of earth's children. It took enormous effort on the part of the Soviet Writers' Union to bring together children and youth writers from around the globe. Ours was a truly international conference, and those of us who participated better understand the conditions under which our colleagues live and work. We have been given a broader view and, it is hoped, a greater scope through which to create honestly for the young.

Soviet citizens were gracious and kind to us. Staff people, such as Frieda Lurie of the Foreign Language Commission of the USSR Writers' Union, were unstinting on behalf of all of us. Throughout the Russian film I had seen, it was she who translated every word for me and, it seemed, even the pauses! My young interpreter, Helen Kotkin, of whom I had grown fond, stayed with me throughout the evening. We had become pals of sorts—her cautious questions, my guarded answers. Finally, we were able to express a frank curiosity about each other's lives. We had a pleasant meal together at the Writers' Union. Late in the night, we shivered in the cold waiting for a bus. (As in New York, buses are few and far between on a winter's night in Moscow.) We gave up and gaily flagged down a passing motorist who dropped me off at the hotel entrance. Helen dashed for the subway; she would see us off to the airport the next morning, after shyly asking me if I would like to have her come.

I stayed up most of the night packing and listening to Radio Moscow World Service, an English language station of news and American jazz and country music. Often, I stared out of the window at the night and windblown snow. The really awesome thing about Moscow was that it comes to a compete standstill, with not a car or a truck moving, from midnight until morning—eight million people in a vast, mysterious silence.

Then, when it was dawn, we left Moscow for home.

FACE-TO-FACE WITH SERGEI VLADIMIROVICH MIKHALKOV

Essay from School Library Journal, *May 1980; an interview Virginia conducted with the noted Russian writer during her trip to Moscow in October 1979 for the Second International Conference of Writers for Children and Youth*

SERGEI VLADIMIROVICH Mikhalkov is a poet, prose writer, and dramatist who has won the Lenin Prize and is a nominee for this year's Hans Christian Andersen Award. He is secretary of the board of the Writers' Union, USSR, and chairman of the board of the Writers' Union of the Russian Soviet Federative Socialist Republic (RSFSR). He is also a deputy of the Supreme Soviet of the USSR and a member of the parliamentary board dealing with the problems of youth.

Mikhalkov is said to be one of the most popular writers for children in the Soviet Union with millions of copies of his books in print. He is apparently in his sixties, tall, and powerfully built. His commanding appearance often seems so forbidding until he smiles, and his eyes are enlarged behind thick lenses. There is an easy camaraderie between him and members of the Moscow Writers' Union, with no sense that he is in a position which is separate or superior to theirs.

We are seated in Oak Hall, the meeting room for the Conference of Writers for Children and Youth in the Moscow Writers' Union building. The conference tables are empty now, save for myself, Mikhalkov, and the interpreter provided by the Writers' Union. It is lunchtime. At the other end of the hall from where we sit can be seen the spiral stairs leading to the balcony where some of the translators work.

At our end of the hall, the wall behind us soars for two stories. There is subdued light filtering down from long and narrow stained-glass windows. The atmosphere is utilitarian and simple. Voices can be heard outside in the spacious anteroom. Occasionally, individuals enter the hall at the far end, pass through and on out another exit.

I prepare my tape recorder for the interview and open my note-book to a page of questions. From the beginning, my idea was to ask questions concerning the writing and publishing of children's books in the Soviet Union. Later, if there was time, I planned to get into more controversial aspects of the Writers' Union and its criteria for member-ship.

Mikhalkov and I sit on the same side of the table facing each other. The young woman interpreter is seated between us. I wait, interested in seeing whether he will impose limits for the interview. He does not. Yet, once we begin, it becomes obvious that he intends to control the flow of the conversation.

VH: *So that we in the United States are clear on the subject of the Writers' Union of the USSR, could you give an explanation of its function and its organization?*

SVM: The union of Soviet writers of the USSR represents fifteen Soviet republics, and each republic has its own writers' union and its own board of writers' union. The biggest body of the Writers' Union is the Russian Federation, and I'm the chairman of the Russian Federation Writers' Union. The Russian Federation is subdivided into areas of regional organizations and all in all they come to seventy-five. The biggest one is the board of all Moscow. And coming after it is Lenin-grad. So our Moscow organization numbers two thousand writers.

Every five years, the writers of the RSFSR congress gather here in Moscow, and they elect the leadership of our Russian Federation organization. They elect the board; the board elects secretarial staff—about thirty-five members; the staff chooses the chairman. So

85

this is the second time that I have been elected chairman. This is a great tribute to children's literature because I write for children, although I write for adults, too, which proves that popular writers for children are well respected here.

VH: *Yes, that was something I wanted to ask about. You make little distinction . . . [Here, Mikhalkov says something to the interpreter in Russian. At once, she ceases translating what I am saying to allow him to speak.]*

SVM: There is one small thing I would like to mention. Uzbekistan, the Uzbek Republic, exists here, and they have their own Uzbek Writers' Union. Everybody there writes in Uzbek, but in Russia where I am the chairman, they write in fifty languages of the Russian Federation and books are published in fifty languages, too. Within the Russian Federation, there are fifty autonomous regions—Tartars and others. So the Russian Federation is the biggest as far as the languages are concerned and as far as the number of writers' organizations, too.

VH: *How does the organization help the Soviet writers make a living at what they do?*

SVM: Naturally, the organizations do take care of the writers. Well, I will start with one thing. The main mission of the writers' organization is to help young, emerging writers. Very often, you know, we gather or have meetings of young writers who have just written their first book or those who have not published their books yet. And if the book or the manuscript is talented enough, then our authorities help to publish the book. Well, our recommendation means a lot.

VH: *Is that how you got started as a writer for children?*

SVM: No, my way was a little bit different. Well, it was long ago. I worked. I was a geologist. I was nine when I wrote my first poem. And when I was fifteen, my first work was published. When I was a schoolboy, I worked and continued to write and was published. But I could not make my living by literature. When finally I got the chance to make my living by writing, I got completely involved only in literary work and did not do anything else to make a living. You know, the relation between the writer and society is a little bit different in our country than in yours. For example, the editorial offices pay the writers for the complete future circulation. They are not waiting for the book to be sold. The writer is paid immediately.

VH: *[laughing] It's a good system!*

SVM: Yes. Yes. And then, the rents are very low. It doesn't matter how much a writer makes, the rent is only 13 percent.

VH: *Of what he makes?*

SVM: Taxes. Yes, they are very low, just 13 percent. It doesn't matter how much he has made.

VH: *I see . . . interesting.*

SVM: And the circulation of works by children's writers is really big.

VH: *What do you mean by big?*

SVM: Well, for example, one hundred and forty million of my books have been published in all of the languages of the Soviet Union. Not only the languages of the Soviet Union, but both in languages of the Union and foreign languages.

VH: *Your books alone?*

SVM: Yes.

VH: *In America, you would be a very wealthy man with sales like that.*

SVM: I'm not poor here, either!

[Later, I was told that Mikhalkov probably was a millionaire. I asked if, therefore, Mikhalkov was a capitalist and was informed that, no, since he gave so much to those less well off. I said that so did Rockefeller give much away. There was laughter, and I was assured that Mikhalkov couldn't be a capitalist since he did not exploit anyone.]

VH: *I see! That's an enormous number of books. We have nothing comparable to that in the United States. But I would like to go on here—* [*Again, Mikhalkov cuts off the interpreter who then begins interpreting him as he speaks.*]

SVM: But it doesn't mean that a writer will get royalties from any book that's published.

VH: *Why not?*

SVM: The agreement that is signed between the author and the publishing house is different from what is going on in your country (as far as I know), especially if you write for the youngest, the little ones. Then, the publishing house can publish one hundred thousand copies. They pay the author; the royalties sometimes are not bad, but not each book is taken into consideration.

VH: *Oh, you have a flat fee, yes?*

SVM: If two hundred thousand copies have been published, and the agreement was for one hundred thousand copies, double price is paid. And if a very popular book has been published many times, the royalties are going down a bit.

VH: *I see, but I'm having trouble, difficulty understanding this, because we think that in your socialist republics that the state owns the publishing houses. Therefore, the state publishes the books, and nobody gets paid, or at least, not very much for it.*

SVM: No, that's wrong. Every publishing house is paying royalties, of course. That's their duty, and they do pay them.

VH: *All right. Okay.*

SVM: Example. The complete editions of my works are being published—six volumes. For the first volume, I should get 30,000 rubles, about 30,000 dollars.

VH: *That's one payment only—is that the final payment?*

SVM: For one volume, final payment. For one volume of the complete edition. It would be the circulation of one hundred thousand copies, the final payment.

VH: *But forever, that's what you get on that one book?*

SVM: Yes, but if in five years or in ten years they would like to republish it; I would get it again.

VH: *I see, I see, that* is *very interesting.*

SVM: But the next payment would not be 100 percent of the first payment, but 60 percent.

VH: *I see, I understand now.*

SVM: And if we publish it for the third time, it would be 50 percent; then 40, and then 30. They don't pay less than 30 percent. They can go on publishing me for the rest of my life, but I won't get more than 30 percent of the first sum.

VH: *Is this true for all writers or only for ones that are long established like yourself?*

SVM: Well, the other side of the problem may be like this: The author who is not very famous and long established will never have the complete collection of his works published.

VH: *Tell me, do you have an American publisher?*

SVM: One book. One book, and it was not printed very well because I'm writing satire, fables, and the book of my fables in the United States—the things that were written by me in poetical form have been published there in prose.

VH: *I see. You believe it's not good.*

SVM: So, it doesn't make much sense.

VH: *I understand.*

SVM: And then, I think poems that are written here for children are not often, very seldom, actually, translated to foreign languages in capitalist countries. The book that I gave you as a gift, Miss Hamilton, the collection of poems has been published here for forty years. It has been published one hundred times.

VH: *I understand that your poems are very popular. You answered some of the questions I had in your opening address and now, too. I am interested in the minorities here.*

SVM: National minorities, yes. That's a very interesting question. They are writing in their national languages. They are publishing in their national languages, and their people are reading them in their languages, in their republics. But the best books of national writers are translated into Russian and into the other languages of the Soviet Union. So they overcome their national isolation, if we can call it that, and they get to the market of the whole USSR. And some people sometimes translate into English, into French, and into German. But first, they are translated into Russian.

VH: *And you say how many copies are printed at one time in one edition?*

SVM: One hundred thousand. Well, it's a very low circulation. It's impossible. To get a book like that is not difficult, it's impossible.

VH: *What do you mean?*

SVM: Because it's immediately sold.

VH: *Oh, I see.*

SVM: From the moment it gets on the counter — five minutes at the bookshop — it's sold out.

VH: *I should think that they would print more then. They do print more?*

SVM: If it were a publisher who is a capitalist, he would publish it until it sold. Until there is demand. He would not think about one more thing. Other writers would like to be published, too. And our state should think about it. So, our state thinks that if I want any books to be published, well . . . the state takes care of all others who were sitting here; who were sharing that table with you today. They think that their books should be published, too. They do think about it. And still talented writers are published more than less talented.

VH: *It sounds like a very attractive program.*

SVM: Well, I should criticize ourselves. I should mention that we run a shortage of paper in our country. That's why we can't satisfy all the demands of children's books, which are very cheap here, which are necessary for every village and every country place.

VH: *Yes, is that so?*

SVM: And in every family. So we satisfy the demand by only 30 percent.

VH: *I understand better now. You take children's literature very seriously here.*

SVM: Well, we do have the state prize for children's literature. And every year, one prize, the State Prize of the Soviet Union, is given. This is a gold medal and 5,000 rubles. Every republic has its own prize for all types of art — especially for children's literature. There is also the

Lenin Prize, the biggest, most honorable prize. Once every two years they give this prize. One can get it only once in your life. I have got it. This is 10,000 rubles and a gold medal. Five categories of prizes are given every two years for all kinds of art. There is a special Lenin Prize for children's literature. It is not given if there is no proper candidate.

This Lenin Prize, it was I who managed to promote this and do everything possible to persuade the government to adopt the prize for children. It was not an easy thing. I visited Brezhnev and told him that writers for children—artists and composers—can't compete with the adult artists; that the symphony written will seem much more important to the jury than a little song written for children. My idea was that the things should be treated separately with a particular attitude to them. They understood me; they realized how important it was. And the prizes have been confirmed.

VH: *One question about the makeup of the conference and the people: I notice there seems to be no black Caribbean writers here.*

Interpreter: From Cuba, you mean?

VH: *I'm not talking about Cuba but other Caribbean countries. There are some fine writers. I was curious if they were invited.*

SVM: We invited people from eighty-one countries, from the Caribbean, too. Some had things to do. Some will still come, but I'm afraid there are not many people writing for children there.

VH: *I read recently that a Chinese delegation had come to the Soviet Union* [to Moscow]. *Were there any Chinese writers invited here?*

SVM: No.

VH: *Do you care to comment further on that? Do you care to elaborate?*

SVM: Well, it's so hard to explain what is going on in China and to give some reasons for the politics. Crazy people!

VH: *May I write that? Can I quote you? I would like to know.*

SVM: Welcome! It is so difficult to understand, to realize, to comprehend their politics. First they [the Chinese] tried to state one thing, then they state an absolutely different, opposite thing. For so many years, they kept saying that we were their best friends. And now, they are saying that we are their worst enemies. Very often, they ignore all the invitations that are sent to them.

VH: *But they were just here.*

SVM: There were no writers in that group. Well, there is a group of Chinese people here who are discussing our border problems. While no information concerning this meeting is published, and while the only thing that is mentioned in the press is that the conference, the meeting took place—because it is very difficult to come to some mutual agreement with them. They are Chinese!

[There are a few more interruptions with people coming in to speak Russian to Mikhalkov. I decided to end the interview.]

VH: *Well, you've been very gracious. I thank you very much. If I have more questions, I'll come back.*

SVM: Any time you like.

VH: *Thank you.*

The interview seemed to end abruptly, yet it was quite lengthy with every word having to be translated from English to Russian back to English. Obviously, Sergei Mikhalkov hoped that the American reading public might better understand him, his country, and his work. I regret there was never another opportunity to continue the interview; however, I did talk to him again for a moment or two at a Moscow restaurant where I was one of his guests. He presented me with several of his books and drank a toast in my honor. Perhaps the publication of this interview will serve as a toast in return.

AH, SWEET REMEMORY!

Essay from the Horn Book Magazine,
December 1981

R EMEMORY IS A *reword* out of my past. It is not poetic license but a volunteer, like a self-sown seed come forth unbidden. A given. I was fourteen, and I met a dashing fellow who told me he wasn't much on names, but he had a perfect rememory of my smile (i.e., "Haven't I seen you somewhere before?"). *Rememory* stayed with me through the years; I don't know what happened to the dude-with-a-line. Fortunately, I was able to use rememory as a device for indicating a change in the time frame in *Arilla Sun Down*.

There were a number of words back then that I got wrong quite on my own — words I'd seen in print but never heard spoken. I used what I considered long, sophisticated words principally on my mother to impress her with my maturity. A favorite one was de-ter-min-ED, hard accent on the last syllable, as in, "Mom, I'm de-ter-min-ED to stay out until twelve; all of the other girls are allowed to." Whereupon, Mother informed me that as long as I was de-ter-min-ED, *she* was de*ter*mined I would be home by eleven.

Thereafter, I was careful to look up the pronunciations of peculiar-looking words. How I cringed that I might have fractured *amiable* or *amicable*, had I not made use of the dictionary. Looking things up, I discovered *rememory* wasn't a word. Of course, it should be. If one recalls or remembers something remarkable, such as a high compliment

93

from a jiving dude, then one must need use one's rememory in order to do so. Therefore, I take it upon myself to define the reword for the sake of réchauffé: *Rememory*: An exquisitely textured recollection, real or imagined, which is otherwise indescribable.

Which brings me around again to Mother. The local PBS radio station and its zealous young reporter discovered my going-on-eighty-nine feisty mother. The station was preparing programming devoted to Underground Railroad history in Ohio, which — I suppose — it intended to use for a decade of Black History Months. Mother was to give a commentary of whatever length she desired on the escape of her father and his mother from slavery.

I was present for the interview. Mother looked like the canary who had had the cat for lunch. The reporter suddenly reminded me of that sincere folk-collector fellow, called the Dude, who visited the Higgins family in *M.C. Higgins, the Great*; each generation, in or out of fiction, has its faithful compilers. Mother kept her eyes on the tape machine as she began; it was clear to me she didn't trust a small black box with about six keys to take down her every word. And at last, she asked the reporter to play it back so she could hear how she sounded. When he did, sure enough, there she was.

"That's not *me*," Mother announced.

"Of course, it's you; who else would it be?" I said. But I understood what she was getting at. She meant it didn't sound like her in every which way, the same as I don't sound quite like me when I stand before an audience. Mother was not used to hearing herself as chronicler, utilizing unlikely tones and rhythms in order to reveal the action. There were cadences and inflections that had to have been similar to her father's speech peculiarities when first he told about the incredible journey that took him north across the Ohio River to freedom. She definitely didn't sound like Mother. And what she had to say wasn't what I'd heard before. We had spent lots of time, over the years, going into family history.

The reporter fellow must have been thanking his lucky stars. It was clear he considered Mother a great *find*. Anyone could see his excite-ment—eyes shining, gasps escaping him. Mother always knew she was a find. She gave a glance at me with a look of reproach, I thought. The fact that I hadn't laid bare the spectacular information she was freely giving away to a perfect stranger served me right, the look seemed to say, and there was a lesson in that.

Well, I am for the most part a fiction writer. I use from the source, but I *create* my characters. Mother *is* a character. And all these years she'd been waiting to reveal herself. All that rememory! Real and imag-ined places and times—thank goodness the young man came along and got it all!

Place and time are at the heart of the fiction I write. The place being a minuscule, unlikely piece of southern Ohio, where I was born. The time is the period of my early life that is transformed and heightened to uniqueness through the creative process. Or it is the memory of my life or my mother's memory of her life as told to me, revised by me toward rememory; or it is that of her mother's and her grandmother's and of old friends'. Time and place are bound together, a solid sensa-tion in the present and past of that which has been accomplished.

Subject matter is for me derived from intimate and shared places of the hometown and the hometown's parade of life and all that is known, remembered, and imagined throughout time therefrom. Home is where I find the emotional landscape for my own spiritual growth and the geographical location for the fictions. Time and place become almost mythical. I suffer through them as I imagine, historically, oth-ers have suffered through them. The progress of a people across the hopescape of America gives to my writing a sense of continuity and a narrative source.

Which brings me to a kind of source that is narrative and a way of talking. Going down an open field from where I live to Mother's house. At a certain hour in late day, the ancient hedgerow marking the west property line is backlighted by the slanting sun, and great old Osage hedge trees are a mystery of growing depths and sparkles. I slip quietly inside the house from the back door. I find Mother in the "front room" talking with my aunt Sarah Perry. They greet me kindly enough, but I am young; I can wait. They must get back to their talking in the quiet, semidark that holds past and present like loops of an invisible bow. I settle back in an easy chair redone in deep plush velvet.

Aunt Sarah Perry is in her late sixties and troubled by arthritis. Mother likes to pretend she's ninety and is troubled by nothing. They are discussing Mother's sister, Aunt Leah, who is seventy-two. These ages are not relevant, for they see one another as they were in their prime. Aunt Leah, being the "Auntie Mame" of Mother's Perry clan, carries on as if she were as free as a bird. This ruffles Mother's feathers; probably because at her advanced age, she considers any sudden movement a personal affront. Aunt Leah continually flies off to distant places, buying one-way tickets only.

"Why only one-way?" I asked, captured in the overwrought chair.

"Leah never knows how long she will stay somewhere," said Aunt Sarah Perry.

"Because she never knows when to come home, you mean," said Mother. "Sarah, you are too polite. Leah won't leave until she's told."

"Where is she going?" I thought to ask.

"To Kansas City to spend the summer," answered Aunt Sarah. "You know, Early Lee is out there." Early Lee is my second cousin.

"And if Early asks her to leave early," said Mother, aware of the play with words, "she will go on to Germany."

I was startled by the lack of transition and dared ask, "Who's in Germany?"

"Some people she once knew," said Aunt Sarah, smiling her sweet, shy smile.

"Who won't know she's coming," said Mother, "until she arrives."

"She'll stay in Germany or Kansas City until summer's over," explained Aunt Sarah.

"Leah never could take the summers in this town." Mother sniffed. "Sarah, you remember the first time she got married, it was summer?" Aunt Leah is somewhat overextended when it comes to marriage.

"It does get hot here," I thought to say, "but surely it won't be as hot as it gets in Kansas City."

"Virginia, it's not the heat," said Aunt Sarah Perry. "It's the spiders. Leah says they come in the house where it's cool and wait until nightfall to get on her pillow and in her slippers. She can't stand the thought of them crawling in her ears and her hair."

I shuddered in sympathy.

"And in her slippers," Mother added, sounding disgusted.

I had to smile, knowing Aunt Leah well enough to have figured out how carefully she must have combed her vivid imagination to come up with an explanation that had *style*—as a reason for escaping a stifling village in its steamiest season.

Suddenly, I wondered what sort of children they had been—Aunt Sarah Perry, Mother, and Aunt Leah. Yet I felt moved to leave this question unanswered as shadows deepened around my mother and my aunt. Both were comfortable on the Autumn Gold couch. Their heads were thrown back as they created light and time, past and people, with just their talking.

I am a teller of tales, in part, because of the informal way I learned from Mother and her relatives of passing the time, which they also utilize for transmitting information, for entertainment, and for putting their own flesh and blood in the proper perspective. The Perrys are interesting talkers. They began as farmers who had been fugitives from injustice. Acquiring land and homes, place and time, was to them the final payment in the cause of freedom. After long days, a long history in the fields, they talked their way into new states of mind. They could appreciate a good story in the companionship of one another, not only as entertainment, but as a way to mark their progress. Stories, talking, grew and changed into a kind of folk history of timely incidents. And these developed in lines of force that had beginnings, middles, and endings—a certain style. True memory might lapse, and creativity come into play. It was the same creativity and versatility that had helped the first African survive on the American continent. An uncle of mine told the most astonishing lies. An aunt whispered in perfect rememory the incident of Blind Martha and how she found her way down the dusty road to the spot where the log cabin had stood in which she had been born. The day Uncle Saunders was killed, all of the ivy fell from the Pasony house. Pasonys were neighbors, quiet and shrewd. But they could not save the ivy.

There's the story I remember always knowing about my Grandpa Levi Perry and how his hand burned shut from a fire in the gunpowder mill where he worked. And from the time that his life and mine coincided, his hand was a fist with burn scars hidden in the tightly shut palm. I would lace my fingers over his closed fist when I was a child, and he would lift me up and up, swing me around and around—to my enormous delight. Ever after, the raised black fist became for me both myth and history, and they were mine. Grandpa Perry was John Henry and High John de Conquer. He was power—the fugitive, the self-made, the closed fist in which I knew there was kept magic. Oh, but the rememory!

What is transformed from myth, history, and family narrative in my own fictions is not a play-pretty to be held in the hands of children. My fictions for young people derive from the progress of black adults and their children across the American hopescape. Occasionally, they are lighthearted; often they are speculative, symbolic, and dark and brooding. The people are always uneasy because the ideological difference they feel from the majority is directly derived from heritage. In the background of much of my writing is the dream of freedom tantalizingly out of reach. Echoes of long past times serve to feed my imagination. They may sound of African dreams, family truths, and even speculations on the future. All of it grows from my own experience in some way. The writer will uncover ways of expressing the source and essence of living which belong to her, alone.

In my daily professional life, I see myself as a woman working at a complicated job. The way I approach the job changes, consistent with the changes going on inside me, as a woman moving through time. I keep the vision of the writer which I started with, that of the humble crusader locked in the garret room. The writer up there suffers for life, creating all-purpose prose with bruised, delicate hands. The works of crusading sociologists, such as Lincoln Steffens, Jacob Riis, Shirley Graham, and W. E. B. Du Bois, made an indelible impression on me. No wonder then that there is something of the social reformer in the back of my mind while I work.

The job—laboring through a fiction from the beginning to the end—takes from eight to fifteen months. I never lack for beginnings of fictions. But what I find I need is the process for uncovering the art form that will transform ideas into coherent fictions. The challenge is to deal with the revelation that there is no way of knowing beforehand how a fiction is to be written. I discover how it's done only by writing it; and when it's finished, I am able to say, "Ah, so that's the way!"

The fictionist occupation is the only one I know in which acquired knowledge cannot be applied. What is learned concerning the writing of a single novel is hopelessly inadequate in writing the next—or any others, for that matter. Each book is like a new system that must be uncovered. It is not precisely created, as we sometimes like to believe. All of it is inside but hidden. In order to begin one must find the system of it each time. I find the system and the way through. If a concept occurs to me, so must its creative development follow. Therein lie instinct and intuition. Solving must be the natural tendency of writers. And yet, to paraphrase T. S. Eliot, between the idea and the reality falls the shadow. In the shadow, then, the woman working lives. In the shadow, life is very long and worth the time it takes. In the shadow I recall, reconstruct. I create. I am the shadow.

I begin with a fairly clear concept of story, only to have the characters who must live it take it over. They become individuals who change and shape plot according to their needs. Created characters express their power of intent on the page. I may not alter the intentions to suit myself. In the early books I tended to exaggerate the physical traits and quirks of the characters in order to control what they might do. Zeely Tayber was six-and-a-half-feet tall and thin as a beanpole. Mr.

99

Pluto from *Dies Drear* was lame and looked like the devil with green eyes. Junior Brown from *Planet* was in danger of drowning in his own fat. Grotesqueries were my props, my crutches, which I didn't need. The characters did whatever they wanted, anyway. The fact that Pluto looked like the devil did not stop him from sitting in the first pew at church, and Junior Brown climbed over the rocks of the Hudson River, despite his weight.

In later books, emotions and the way characters act upon them tend to reveal who they are from the beginning. Jack Sun Run from *Arilla*, bare chested and golden, riding his horse, is a still shot—an old sepia print—and a revelation of his commitment of being Amerind. I concentrate on the emotions all of us share, and I use the most comfortable milieu or vantage from which to reveal them. These fictions may involve folk wisdom and superstition, since I am interested in archetypes and archaic heritage. Black-being may be significant to a story, and it may not be. I enjoy the freedom to make that decision.

In the fantasy books of the Justice Cycle, race has nothing whatever to do with plot and the outcome for the characters. The powers of extrasensory perception, telepathy, and telekinesis the children have are not meant to be peculiarities. They represent a majestic change in the human race. We find that Justice and her identical twin brothers, in *Justice and Her Brothers*, *Dustland*, and *The Gathering*, have unleashed new gene information, which provides them with psychic powers allowing them to extend themselves into an extraordinary future where things are not as they seem. With their friend Dorian Jefferson, they travel through time as a unit, and only as a unit are they able to return to the present. The fictions depend for effect on the weirdness of location or setting and on the increasing strangeness of the characters. A golden animal, Miacis, roams, talks, and telepaths; a band of wild children communicate through song; winged Slaker begins search for an end to Dustland and their despair; a cyborg, Celester, and a stupendous computer, Colossus, go about saving civilization.

There is not a formal way such speculative fiction should be written. But it does assume the individual will pit himself or herself against a world or worlds that have grown cold and impersonal. I write all fantasy, from Jahdu to Justice, to bring the power of magic into a world that seems increasingly lacking in the marvelous. There enters into my work a sense of melancholy, however, which has its origin in black history and life in America. It is often an inherent quality of the writing and inseparable from the lives of the characters. It pervades the fictional hopescape with the reality that black life is at once better and worse than it has ever been. Better for some, worse for most. This is not bitterness; it is truth.

The challenge for the fictionist is to deal with the truth through youth literature with an evolvement of a fiction of compassion, hope, and humor. There is no question that the young should appreciate and share the truth. For it is not merely subject matter that occasionally turns grim. It is the history of a people and their life at present. What can be shared of it is its depiction as serious entertainment through the art of writing.

Within the heritage and history are boundless possibilities for creative writing. There begins a literature that indicates a people's range and unique capacity for living. But it is not accomplished as simply as other kinds of writing with less historical grounding. On the surface the stories are straightforward. And young people are capable of varied reading levels and of several degrees of difficulty when given the opportunity. My own books don't have to be understood in a hard and fast sense. Certainly, they don't need to be *taught* in elementary and junior high school. The best way to read fiction is to open the mind and enjoy.

CHANGING WOMAN, WORKING

Essay from Celebrating Children's Books: Essays on Children's Literature in Honor of Zena Sutherland, *edited by Betsy Hearne and Marilyn Kaye, published by Lothrop, Lee & Shepard Books, New York, 1981, honoring the late Zena Sutherland, who edited the University of Chicago's Bulletin of the Center for Children's Books *for nearly 30 years and wrote the textbook* Children and Books

IT IS PLACE and time that are close to the heart of so many of my fictions. The *place* is a minuscule, unlikely piece of Midwestern America where I was born, which made a profound impression. I was all of nine when I realized I could not be for long without a hot, wet, whelming scent of fresh-mown green grass on the oppression of August. The *time* would be that period of my early life transformed and heightened to uniqueness through the creative process; or it is the memory of my life, or my mother's memory of her life as told to me, revised by me; or that of her mother's and her grandmother's and her old friends'. Time and place are bound together, no longer real; yet, they remain a solid sensation in the present of that which has been accomplished. The longer I remain in this small village, my time and place in Ohio, the more deeply I comprehend it as the source for all of the fiction I create.

There is no glamour for me in the sight of distant places, although I enjoy exploring them. My subject matter is derived from the intimate and shared place of the hometown and the hometown's people, and all that is known and remembered and imagined through time over time therefrom.

Here, I find my emotional landscape as well as the geographical location for the stories. Time and place are so very important to my spiritual self. For I have suffered through them in the same sense that the black people have suffered through them toward freedom. The progress of the people across the hopescape of America gives to my writing a sense of continuity and a narrative drama—the spiritual impact called *style*—so important to any writer.

In my daily life, I see myself not at all as a writer but as a woman working, a day laborer. Hidden behind the picture, I suppose, is still the unfocused vision of the writer that compelled me in the beginning, that of the humble crusader locked in the garret room, suffering for life, "creating" all-purpose prose for the bruised, delicate hands. So important to that vision were those below on the ground, who, looking to the garret window, whispered in awe, "There lives the *author*!"

The truth is, the work I do is a long haul day after day from the beginning of a fiction to its end. I never lack for beginnings of fictions. What I do lack at first is the knowledge of the process for discovering the art form that will transform ideas into coherent fictions. It is a challenge for me to come to terms with the stunning revelation that there is no way of knowing beforehand how a fiction is to be written. One discovers how it is done only by writing it. And when it's finished, one can say to one's self, "Ah, so that's the way!"

The work I do is the only occupation I know in which acquired knowledge cannot be applied. What is learned about writing a single fiction is hopelessly inadequate in writing the next, or any others, for that matter. Each book is like a new system that must be uncovered. And realizing that I will have to find the system of it each time I begin is what keeps me startled, awake, through bleary-eyed mornings.

Each day, I labor through apprehensions, sometimes crying out, "This time, I'm not going to make it!"

But, of course, I do find the way through. If a concept occurs to me, so must its creative development follow. Therein lie instinct and intuition; solving is the natural tendency of writers. Yet, to paraphase T. S. Eliot, between the idea and the reality falls the shadow. In the shadow, the woman working lives. In the shadow, she finds life long enough and worth the time. In the shadow, she recalls, reconstructs. I create. I am the shadow.

This, then, is not a play-pretty to be held, soft and cuddly, in the hands of the child. My fictions for children, young people, descend directly from the progress of black adults and their children across the American hopescape. Specifically, they derive from my eccentric family, from that Perry progenitor—Grandpa Levi Perry. Levi's hand burned shut from a fire in a gunpowder mill where he slaved, three dollars a week. And the rest of his life, this hand was a fist raised high, scars hidden in its closed palm, so that the child I was might swing on it, squealing with delight. For me, ever after, the raised black fist was my Grandpa Levi holding me on high, lifting me, higher and higher. At one time or another, it held all of my brothers and sisters on high. All of us, held high, until our legs were long enough to reach the dust where we stood on our own. And Grandpa Perry *is* John Henry and High John de Conquer. He is inextricably bound in me with the myth of the self-made, and the closed fist of burn scars, hidden.

I believe in what I write for young people, that its call is important—the call being the essence of the people's lives it depicts—and the depiction is necessary, as well as art. In truth, I write for myself in the sense that what I write is what I care about and what pleases me, whether I make a living at it or not. I write in the hopes that my own children will have something of value and that I will have given all children something I can be proud of.

I am convinced that it is important to reveal that the life of the darker peoples is and always has been different in a significant respect from the life of the majority. It has been made eccentric by slavery, escape, fear of capture, by discrimination and constant despair. But it has held tight within it happiness, a subtle humor, a fierce pride in leadership and progress, love of life and family, and a longing for peace and freedom. Nevertheless, there is an uneasy, ideological difference with the American majority basic to black thought.

A British critic wrote about this woman working: "There is a difference in the furniture of her writing mind from that of most of her white contemporaries: dream, myth, legend, and ancient story can be sensed again and again in the background of naturalistically described present-day events" (Townsend, *A Sounding of Storytellers*, 1979).

That difference is directly derived from my heritage. It is the dream of freedom tantalizingly out of reach that makes the difference. A dream juxtaposed with the myth and historical truth of our proud and ancient kingdoms and their highly developed institutions and arts. Thus, our collective unconscious is set apart. And we have two consciousnesses: one, contemporary, and one, ancient. We are American black and we are African, to say nothing of the European strains. We infer the African; we know it was and no longer is. But we wish for it; we are bound by it, and it is hauntingly imagined again and again throughout our folklore and literature.

Echoes of long past times serve to feed my imagination. They may sound of African dreams or my own family truths. Most often, they are of family. Poor we were and isolated, deliberately, surely, into clans of relatives in a remote corner of Ohio. My own family group must have been encompassed by a dream out of a Faulknerian night. We were all refined daydreamers. I was a sophisticated "nightmarer" like my father. My old man, the kind, sensitive musician, had spectacular, dangerous, also comic nightmares that shot him out of bed and nearly out of the window with a howl and roar that could wake the lifeless. Farmers close enough to be awakened by the noise blinked a couple of times and then went back to sleep. They were my uncle Willie and uncle King, who realized it was Dad still trying to catch his ship that had come in.

That was Dad's favorite expression: "I'm waitin' for my ship—li'l

1 0 5

black-hulled beauty with white trim." The nightmare commenced with Dad reaching the dock on the day of the ship's arrival, just in time. But Dad would be waylaid by the Faceless One, who pursued him throughout his hallucinatory sleep. Dad's imaginary pursuer never caught him that I know of; yet it caused Dad to miss his ship each time. The reason why, I suppose, my dad was a musician, composing rink-a-tink mandolin tunes and classical melodies at dawn.

I inherited the pursuer, and it's a shame that Dad never learned my trick of maneuvering out of its way. I rose above it. When the Faceless One appeared out of nowhere, I flapped my arms and, miraculously, floated over its head. The thing must have comprehended defeat, for it did not last long in my sleep, perhaps a year of recurrent nightmares. I worked my arms — such will and determination that took! I didn't see a ship that had come in, but there was an immense golden sun wafting serene on the night as I lifted off, flapping my arms. I was a child of the sun and I became a writer, I suspect, at the moment my imagination saw to rise above the pursuer.

In the use of imagination, I am a practical working woman. My regimen is not strict; I have none of the angst that is the complaint of so many writers. Something occurs to my imagination just about every day, and so I work each morning until tension develops inside me. Then, I know it's time to do something else. I take care of things here at home; and, I take care of Mother, who is eighty-eight and feisty.

It surprises me, though, that most of the time I think about making books only when I'm at the typewriter. The rest of the time I'm living, and maybe that is the key. The woman working is the woman living her life. The life energy — the humdrum, the exciting moments, the trials and tribulations, memory, knowing, imagining — serves as enrichment of the work the woman finds she is compelled to do. I work no more than five hours at a stretch. The required energy and the concentration does not last for a longer length of time.

A book, working, is hard. Yet, it is marvelous work, surprising in that it has its own dynamism. I may begin with a fairly clear concept of story, but somewhere in the midst of it, the story no longer belongs to me. It is taken over by the characters who must live it, who are individuals who change and shape it according to their own will. The created characters have their own power of intent on the page and I may not alter it to suit myself. In the early work, I did tend to exaggerate physical traits or quirks of characters. Think of Zeely Tayber's (from *Zeely*) six-and-a-half-foot height, her thin, beanpole body. Or Mr. Pluto (*The House of Dies Drear*), his lame leg and green eyes. Or Junior Brown (*The Planet of Junior Brown*) drowning in his hugely fat body. These grotesqueries seemed necessary in order to shed light on the characters' inner life and condition. But now, my characters have few manifestations of this type, since they are constructed from the inside out from the beginning. Emotions and how they act upon them tend to reveal who the characters are. Jack Sun Run (*Arilla Sun Down*), bare chested and golden, riding his horse, is a still shot, an old sepia print, and a revelation of Jack's commitment to being Amerind.

In the more recent psychic fantasy books of the Justice Cycle (*Justice and Her Brothers, Dustland*, and *The Gathering*), the extrasensory ability of telepathy and telekinesis the children have are not mere peculiarities, but represent a majestic change in the human race. Moreover, they symbolize the author's style as a signature of belief that change is what is worthy of one's concentrated effort; that the only certainty is uncertainty. Thus, the work is continually growing, changing its entertainment as the woman working grows and changes. Changing woman, working.

My daily life does not often enter into my working. It serves better as the center of me within myself. I enjoy my life extremely; yet I live it with a sense of melancholy, which has its origin in black history and life in America. The melancholy sense is an inherent quality of the work, inseparable from the lives of the characters. It pervades the fictional hopescape with a reality: Black life is at once better and worse than it has ever been. Better for some, worse for most. This is not bitterness, it is truth.

The challenge for the woman working is to deal with the truth through youth literature with an evolvement of a fiction of compassion, love, hope, and humor. It is beyond question that as many of the young as possible should appreciate and share in the truth. For it is not mere subject matter that occasionally turns grim. It is the history of a people and their life at present. What can be shared of it is its depiction as serious entertainment through the art of children's literature.

Within the life force of black history and traditional lore are boundless possibilities for creative work. I mean not to perpetuate a literature of despair, but to present to youth an indication of a people's range and unique capacity for living. It sounds more difficult than it is. But it is subtle work and cannot be accomplished as simply as other kinds of work with less historical grounding. On the surface, the stories are simple and straightforward. But beneath, there may be more than one meaning introduced at once. Children should not concern themselves with "understanding" the fictions in a hard and fast sense. I suggest that the best way to read is to open the mind and enjoy. Allow fiction to happen to the senses and find happiness. I do.

CORETTA SCOTT KING AWARD
ACCEPTANCE SPEECH:
Sweet Whispers, Brother Rush

Given at the American Library Association
Conference, 1983

*T*HANK YOU. I'd like to thank Mrs. Rollock and members of the
Book Committee of the American Library Association's Social
Responsibilities Roundtable. It's my pleasure to be here and to accept
the Coretta Scott King Award.

I also bring you greetings from my husband, Arnold Adoff, who
is unable to be here. John Steptoe lovingly and perceptively illustrated
Arnold's book, *All the Colors of the Race*, and received an Honorable
Mention in the category of Illustration for the Coretta Scott King
Award. Arnold wanted me to express his grateful thanks to the Book
Committee.

Over the years we both have attempted through our books to present to young readers something of value to their lives from a somewhat
unique and different perspective.

I consider myself to be a student of history as well as literature, so
much so that most of my books have an historical aspect that becomes
an integral part of the fictions. It would seem that I cannot write a
book that takes place in the present which does not in some way evoke
an atmosphere of a generation or two preceding that present.

We carry our histories, our pasts, around with us in the present through states of mind, family history, and historical fact. I have lived most of my life with the intimate knowledge of a rare hereditary disorder called porphyria. For perhaps a third of my life, I have attempted to dispose of my superstitious fear of the disorder by the means most available to me — through my fictions. But it wasn't until 1980 that slowly the seeds of a fiction began to grow in my mind, using the metabolic defect of porphyria as a plot-motivating device. I have always utilized my background and my family history as a jumping off point for fictional reality. *Sweet Whispers, Brother Rush* was written as honest entertainment, in memory of past ghosts finally put to rest through the creative process of the Known, the Remembered, and the Imagined.

My personal history is black African/American history. No other source is more specific to, or symbolic of, my writing than the historical progression of black people across the American hopescape.

I became a student of black history at the age of thirteen after I read Shirley Graham's *There Was Once a Slave*, a biography of the life of Frederick Douglass, a book that literally changed my life and thought. But I had a propensity for history probably much earlier. I grew up in an eccentric community in Ohio, in a region steeped in fugitive slave and abolitionist history. My knowledge of the American Civil War Underground came to me practically through osmosis, from individuals whose knowledge of subjugation and flight was often firsthand. My father was a student of history and literature as well. His love for both can be traced to his enormous respect for W. E. B. Du Bois, the great black scholar and intellectual. One of Dad's relatives was married to a Du Bois cousin. My father knew Du Bois slightly, I believe; he subscribed to the *Crisis* magazine, the official organ of the NAACP, of which Du Bois was editor. The *Crisis* came into our house periodically. And Dad would tap the editorial page with his finger and command me to read. I don't recall one single editorial. But when I came to write a Du Bois biography years later, so much about the man seemed to be there in my mind already.

But it was just my good luck to have descended from a slew of talkers and storytellers—plain out-and-out liars at times—who did not merely tell stories, but created them when they forgot parts of real stories or family history, who in effect, created who they were and where they came from and what they would become through acts of imagination. My dad and mother often told the same stories over and over again. Sometimes, they would change the tales, sometimes not. And it is because of them that I am a storyteller. Their persistence in telling, in influencing me, is why I keep writing story after story in an attempt to discover where the truth begins or even where it is. There are as many truths, I suspect, as there are ideas for books. What is so marvelous about the creative process is that one may get at the truth in an entirely new way each time one writes.

I have mentioned influencing. Yet, it must be that I write to in-fluence, just as my parents told aspects of black history in order to influence me in this way:

Dad told about Jack Johnson, about Blind Lemon Jefferson and Florence Mills. He told about the vast campground of American Indi-ans in Canada and the northern United States, which he was privileged to see at the time of their waning, before they disappeared forever. He told about not being able to perform, of being barred from the concert halls of this country. He was a mandolinist and an extraordinary one, who had played in mandolin clubs and performed on radio. But he could not join a musician's union because he was black and he was, unfortunately, made bitter. My mother told about her dreams of fin-ishing college, which unfortunately, also, she was unable to do. But I knew from that one story what was expected of me.

From the hundreds of letters I receive from young people, I am aware that my books have influenced *them* in special ways. If a young person finishes one of my books knowing more than she knew before reading it, I am pleased. If she learns respect and tolerance for other ways of life, a respect for language and literature, then I feel I have done the best I can do. I don't think I actually set out to influence. But my writing does influence, there can be no mistake about that. There is a great deal to think about when one attempts to write a fiction. One doesn't think consciously about changing minds and hearts. But it happens that minds and hearts are changed by words. I was changed by Shirley Graham's rendering of the life of Douglass. My own father was changed and strengthened by the writings of the great Du Bois. So was I changed and educated by Du Bois. The man's writing should be required reading for all Americans. This seems a fitting opportunity to quote him—one small quote, on his having become a teacher and his search for a school in which to teach in the rural South:

> I learned from hearsay (for my mother was mortally afraid of fire-arms) that the hunting of ducks and bears and men is wonderfully interesting, but I am sure that the man who has never hunted a country school in the South has something to learn of the pleasures of the chase. I see now the white, hot roads lazily rise and wind and fall before me under the burning July sun; I feel the deep weariness of heart and limb as ten, eight, six miles stretch relentless ahead; I feel my heart sink heavily as I hear again and again "Got a teacher? Yes." So I walked on and on—horses were too expensive—until I had wandered beyond railways, beyond stage lines, to a land of "varmints" and rattlesnakes, where the coming of a stranger was an event, and men lived and died in the shadow of one blue hill.
> (Du Bois, *The Autobiography of W.E.B. Du Bois*, 1968)

Through his ability to write, Dr. Du Bois transformed his truths into forms of art. The fiction writer starts with artistic forms and directs her efforts toward the possibility of truths.

The making of fiction is foremost a self-viewing. One begins with the view from inside oneself. If the view is certain and true, then what is made of it in terms of language will become a positive force for life and living.

The making of a fiction is always a surprise. I am as astonished sometimes by what comes from the self-view as anyone. For a finished fiction is always somehow greater than the elements of fact, memory, and imagination that go into creating it. I can tell you the story of *Sweet Whispers, Brother Rush*, and none of the telling will have quite the impact of the created story as written. A book is always more than its parts or its telling. There is a life it has that goes beyond what was put into it. The fiction stands independently from the self, more profound, more magical than anything the artist may have experienced, And it is amazing that one actually does get it all done and that it all comes together and has form as well as content.

I am a weaver of dreams, in a sense, and I believe in the magic carpet of words. The miracle of language is the extraordinary magic to be made by putting down words to form meanings.

I believe in living a responsible life and all of the good connections to such a life. I believe in the validity of the thousands of ways people thread their lives with possibilities and come to terms with themselves. It's the weaver's work through the making of literature to prove and to foretell the nexus, the link between one way of life and another, between him and her and you and myself. We are all one race, after all, and that is what I have always had to say.

I am happy to accept this award. It's meaning for me is that I have been held accountable and found responsible. In my own way I hope to continue helping to advance among the young the cause of literacy and understanding and the cause of freedom from bigotry and prejudice, in the spirit of Dr. King and Mrs. King.

Thank you very, very much.

THE SPIRIT SPINS:
A WRITER'S REVOLUTION

*Given in 1985, in Kent, Ohio, this is the first lecture in the Virginia
Hamilton Lecture series, which quickly expanded to become the
Virginia Hamilton Conference, the longest-running event in the
United States to focus exclusively on multicultural literature
for children and young adults. The conference is held
each April at Kent State University. Four pages of
the speech are missing, as is noted in the text.*

T HANK YOU very much and good morning. It is indeed an honor
to be here. When Marilyn Apseloff, who was then professor here
at Kent State in the Department of English, first contacted me on
behalf of the Virginia Hamilton Lecture Committee in December of
1983, proposing an annual lecture in my name, I was astounded. After
all, I had been scribbling away down there in southern Ohio, weaving
my tales, and I hadn't suspected at all that folks up here were watching
so closely. Needless to say, I happily accepted the honor. Moreover, I
was and am most grateful that the honor was bestowed on me while
I am still among you to enjoy it. It isn't always the case, and such
forethought on the part of all those concerned is deeply appreciated.
I want to thank especially the local committee, professors Anthony L.
Manna and the esteemed professor emeritus Clara Jackson, and Ann
Hildebrand and Robert Rogers, also professors in the Department
of English, for their perseverance and hard work in the endeavor to
gather and rally the diverse forces in children's literature to the cause
of the Virginia Hamilton Lectureship. I am moved by the caring of

all involved and also I am well aware of the toil that has gone into the project.

It has been a long way from where I started. It was never my design to come so far. When I started, there was no strong intent on my part, no specific direction. I had a powerful sense that I wanted to write. I thought it somewhat amusing that people would buy what I had done for free for so long. I was fortunate to meet at the start a serious, kind, perceptive editor, head of the children's book department of a major publishing house, who apparently saw something in me that I had not fully realized was there myself. I learned from the very beginning that nothing that is significant is ever too difficult to be accomplished.

What I remember about the growing-up years in Yellow Springs, Ohio, is that I was free. Whether that is a true memory or a necessary fabrication is beyond my knowledge. But what I recall is that I was free from work, free from pain. I knew no hunger, no sadness. I was free to think and to play. If I needed rules, I made them up myself. Be home before dark. Through fall and winter, study hard, don't miss school, read, listen. Write everything down.

In summer, get up by ten o'clock in the morning. Please don't slam into the wet sheets flapping in the breeze on the clothesline as you run from the house. Go pick berries or greens with Marlene, my cousin. Sell what you pick to neighbors and our mother's missionary lady friends. The missionary ladies were a church auxiliary. It was a joy stepping into the half-light of silent, perfectly neat front parlors in the early afternoon. Out of the heat of a hot day. Backs of sofas, the arms of easy chairs, protected by lace doilies. The gleam of polish on the floors and the dining table. The slow, sweet ticking of the grandfather clock. Watching the stooped back of Miss Wing, a very elderly missionary lady, as she rummaged through her purse, over there at the breakfront, finding the right amount of change. I remember Miss Wing and her formal gray silken dresses. It is fitting that the essential family in *Willie Bea and the Time the Martians Landed* should be Wings, too, to keep the memory of Miss Wing final and secure. I do that quite often. I keep memories safe by crystallizing them within a fiction. The form of

115

a memory is altered but it will maintain the texture and color of the original experience from which the memory is kept.

But as for rules, what my parents did, perhaps without fully realizing what they did, except to know that it was their way and, therefore, right, was to allow me to grow up believing I had made my own rules. I know I couldn't have, but I hold to the belief that I did, and it is a belief I cherish. It is the belief which has allowed me to find my own way in the literature I create. My rules, which come about from a lack of concern for rules, of proper ways of doing things, allow me to deal in fantasy while not writing fantasy in particular. In this way, I am able to go beyond realism. I am often able to make my own reality, which I discover is not like other realities. For what I conceive of as my prerogative is to aim the realism of a fiction beyond itself.

At once a narrow vision comes to mind. A typical Ohio scene. A tightly nestled farm — farmhouse, barns and outbuildings, and the proverbial silo. The farm is isolated, surrounded by golden fields. For it is winter. The color of dormancy of winter is golden in sunlit Ohio. The sun gleams on the farm buildings weathered silver. Suddenly, the silo is spotlighted. It is made to glow in the earth's turning light of sun. It is . . . no longer a silo, but a ship bound for space. And it's not my doing, but it amazes that the definition of a silo is "an airtight tower in which green fodder is preserved" and also, "a large, underground structure for the storage and launching of a long-range ballistic missile." A silo is a tower, is a ship, was a missile, long before I thought to look up its definition. Here, the silo transcends itself. Or our knowledge of it is beyond our experience of it and is transcendental.

Aunt Leah states this accurately in *Willie Bea and the Time the Martians Landed*. Quoting: "But that *anything* can happen. Anything under the sun. One night you look up, there's a monster, it's a combine, it's a monster. One time a spaceship lands right there on the Kelly farm. And who's to say it can't! Who's to say it didn't? And why that radio play just then on this night in this world?"

Old mystic Aunt Leah. She defines the way I thought about things in that book and the way I think generally. To my mind and in my fictions nothing is exactly as it seems. *Willie Bea* is based on a sleight of hand—martians into farmers, monsters into combines. It is as natural for me to write the English language in its literal sense, which for example, incredibly defines all coin currency as silver and as *change*. I do with words what is already a construct of the language. A human being is a person, is a man or woman, is Adam and Eve, is me, a writer, a mother, and so on.

My very first memory of seeing myself is that of seeing an image of myself. I was a small child, and I was staring into a mirror and knowing that what I saw was not actually me. I thought of the image: Why *is she sad?* Not me, not why am *I* sad, but *she*, why is *she* sad. By seeing an image of myself, I forever changed myself, I, and the image "she" as well. *She* was sad. I did not apply sad to *me*. Never have. For if *I* were sad, I could at once project sadness away to *her*.

Therein lies the point of pause between writer and character. She was sad. It was I who thought that. Any image of myself that I could see, therefore, was not me and not sad. I had thus separated the image I saw from myself. Right at that moment transpired the delay into which the transformation of feeling entered, as the writer created and observed the character "she."

What I learned in beginning writing courses in college was that one must write from one's own experience. That truth is limited. It holds true to a certain depth and for a certain period of time. But really what is necessary is that one experience the image and not the actual living through an event for the character to separate from the writer. I did not have to experience what it must feel like to be old Jackabo, the "island mahn" in *Junius Over Far*. The book followed from one simple image of an actual Ethiopian septuagenarian who was the grandfather in an Ethiopian family newly settled in my hometown after Haile Selassie's death and during the revolution.

The grandfather came to town to visit his family. He was used to walking long distances. And in the dead of winter, he wore nothing but a sand-colored cloak draped about his ancient body and sandals on his feet. He leaned on a tall bamboo staff. He was often found in

neighboring towns, having taken a nine-mile hike in search of . . .
who knows what? Once he was discovered hopelessly lost and wandering the outskirts of Dayton, some twenty-five miles removed from
his point of departure. I saw the old gentleman just twice before he
disappeared from the town for good to go back to his homeland. But
I will have the image of him in my mind forever. To my mind, he was
the Ethiop, transplanted to my familiar, snowy village corner. How did
he get there, in that snowbank, his ebony skin a gift to the blinding
winter white? What was he doing there? How extraordinary that he
should suddenly enter my life that way and change it. He was forever
transformed for me out of his real time and place. My image of him is
that of every transplanted black being walking the world. How easily
he transcended my reality, which is after all the only reality I deal with,
to become the island mahn, Grandfather Jackabo, forever longing for
that which is beyond the present, in the past or in the future, or in
dream. Quoting from *Junius Over Far*:

Old Jackabo dreamed he rode a leatherback sea turtle weighing a thousand pounds. How it made him laugh! Ahhh! Hee-
hee! He could feel the massive reptile sway its half ton beneath
him as it cruised just under the water's surface. He dreamed he
sat in a saddle on the turtle's spotted yellow shell in a sea up
to his waist. Jackabo's protruding belly, shining like a cooking
pot, was in the lead through the turquoise ocean. It hurt!

"Slow down, mahn, Nulio," Jackabo called to the turtle.
Nulio was its name. "You go make me two Jackabos in no
time, son."

"Got to be goin', Grandfahtha," said the leatherback. "It
time for school, dontcha see?"

"School? Where school, turtle-mahn?" asked Jackabo.

"School which goin' down," Nulio answered.

"Where be school which goin' down, son?" asked Jackabo.
He spoke in rhythm with the leatherback's swaying through
the sea swells.

"Be home." Nulio turned to look at Jackabo. Then he dived, dived into the wavering, soft light of the silent ocean deep, carrying old Jackabo with him.

I will drown, was Grandfather Jackabo's last thought. In the dream he could not swim. The salt sea stung his open, staring eyes. It pressed hard against his eardrums. He held tightly to the lanyard made of strong cord that was hooked inside the turtle's beak. He couldn't let go. He breathed deeply his last of waters he called the Caribbee Sea.

There is nothing quite like the sight of a giant leatherback turtle in turquoise water. The first time I actually saw one, I gave it the name Nulio. Jackabo's dream of conversing with the harnessed turtle allows the writer to reveal certain aspects of Grandfather Jackabo's thinking. We know that his grandson, Junius, is on his mind, because Nulio speaks in the same island accent and rhythms as would Junius if he had been there. Nulio calls Jackabo Grandfahtha, just as Junius would have, and talks about going to school as Junius would. So without ever mentioning Junius, we understand that Grandfather is separated from him but still has Junius on his mind. Both Grandfather Jackabo and Nulio exist in the fiction far removed from the two first impressions or images that caused them — my actually seeing the Ethiop out of his place and time and the chance sighting of a giant leatherback turtle, after which images came the pause, in which Grandfather Jackabo and Nulio were created.

But I think we have to believe that the strands that make a book can't always be unraveled. Even if they could, I don't think we would want to or need to separate them. A fiction is made in order to bring together distinct irreducible parts of the writing process for the reader's entertainment. And by entertainment I mean the coherent consideration of imaginative ideas.

What I see changes me and what is seen by me as well. The Ethiop into Grandfather Jackabo. The leatherback into Nulio. And me?

I have a young friend at the Cooperative Children's Book Center,

University of Wisconsin–Madison. She is K. T. Horning, who probably knows as much about the writer Virginia Hamilton as anyone. She had written to me while doing a paper on my books for one of her courses. Not long ago, I was in Madison at the university and at one point in a long day I was autographing books with K. T. at my elbow. She was staring at me and continued staring. Finally, after careful consideration, I asked her what was on her mind. One does not ask that question lightly of K. T. And she said, "You keep changing. Just when I thought I knew what you were about, you changed again." She had recently finished reading the galleys of *Junius Over Far*.

That is the writer's key, of course. Once something is created, it is new and the writer is made new as well. Having written *Junius Over Far* I am not precisely the same person I was before the concept of it flourished into fiction. So it is with all my books, with *Willie Bea* and *The Magical Adventures of Pretty Pearl*, and so on. Writing a book, I often feel as if I am lifted, as though I am spinning out through the time and space that is confined in the fiction's construct. Writing then becomes a spiritual experience. Not a religious experience, but an intellectual one that is characterized by the ascendancy of the spirit. And by spirit I mean the life principle, the thinking, insightful feeling part of the self. It is this turning, this spinning motion of the spirit around the center of the self that is my motivation. When the motive that is me — that inner drive, impulse, or intention — has completed its spin and spiral, there will be, perhaps, a finished cycle of creative, fictional events that suggest this writer's revolution.

I think it was Nina Mikkelsen who wrote that children's fantasy novels based on African traditions, with Afro-Americans as major characters, simply did not appear to exist before the publication in 1983 of *The Magical Adventures of Pretty Pearl*. If that is so, it is surprising but understandable. More than time fantasy, as is found in the Justice Cycle books, *The Magical Adventures* is historical fantasy that uses the body of Afro-American experience in an amalgam of black American folklore from myth through conjuration, on to the call and response toning of old Africa. The book came about because it occurred to me in the middle of a sunny afternoon that there were no black female folk *her*-oes, as opposed to *he*-roes, other than Harriet Tubman. Then, thoughts of John Henry and John de Conquer naturally led to the creation of an in-kind female protagonist to counter those two. And she would be two in the form of Mother Pearl and Pretty Pearl.

Pearl. There is a long association in me with Pearl. I have an Aunt Pearl. My mother's aunt. Huge, silken, lightish-skinned lady. Spoke rapidly, Canadian sound in her voice, as have many members of my family who rested for a generation or so in Calgary, Alberta, Canada, before settling finally in my corner of southwestern Ohio. Aunt Pearl impressed me with her speech and her tiny gold earrings. Her mothery manner. The fact that her hugeness seemed to surround the child I was. Such first impressions appear to be stamped indelibly on my sensibilities. The memory of Aunt Pearl embodies both her and me in a tight circle of caring. Thus was formed long ago the idea for both Mother Pearl and Pretty Pearl as one self. No creation has changed me more than the forming of Mother Pearl and Pretty. No book has given me more satisfaction than the writing of *The Magical Adventures*. Sometimes, long strands make a generous weave and a perfect braid. I will always think of *The Magical Adventures* as my most perfect entertainment. That doesn't mean that anyone else has to think that or even that it is true. And not to say that there aren't any knots in the braid. Perhaps the dialect of the book is off-putting, difficult for children as well as adults. So it may well be, but it is the proper language for this book. I'm absolutely certain of that. It is important to me that I pass along the knowledge I have about certain aspects of black culture and heritage. No, it is essential that I do that, whether the knowledge is lore or fiction, or whatever else.

When writing the god character John Henry—for in *The Magical Adventures* John Henry is the brother god of the best god, John de Conquer—I wrote him in the style of narratives written long ago. I used the language that depicted him as you find it in early books that describe the John Henry legend. Everything I wrote about him was created by me new, but it has the sound of all other narratives about John Henry that have gone before. Quoting:

> I weighted twenty-five pound eleven when I be born. I is now big like a giant . . . I got a new red suit in my git bag. I got a three dollar hat with a red hatband. I got new shoes. I got a red scarf. I got de blues. I got bad ways and good times. I got a big heart and a bigger mouth.

There is in me a large amount of the Du Bois concept of the talented tenth. Du Bois believed that one-tenth of blacks could manage their own education and would need to pass on what they had learned and teach the nine-tenths less fortunate than themselves. I do believe that I have an obligation to pass on what I know to those who may not know. And I am not the only black writer who feels that need. John Edgar Wideman, writing in the third book of his Homewood Trilogy, entitled *Sent for You Yesterday*, states, and I'm quoting, "Past lives live in us, through us. Each of us harbors the spirits of people who walked the earth before we did, and those spirits depend on us for continuing existence, just as we depend on their presence to live our lives to the fullest." It is truth that I might also have written, for it expresses my belief and concern almost entirely. But I would extend the Du Bois concept further to say that the passing on of knowledge is necessary not only for the minority group, but it is essential for the majority as well.

But it is for reasons of history and heritage, long lineage and continuing existence that the prose that ends *The Magical Adventures of Pretty Pearl* read this way, and I'm quoting Pretty Pearl speaking of the best god, John de Conquer, who always carries a side drum called a hypocrite:

> John de Con-*care* live in de southern soil. Him albatross, him manlike and him best god of Mount Kenya. Anytime we need him hard, he hit that hypocrite. *Ta-ta-tum*. Teachin',

'Know him by de Conquer, secret root. *Ta-ta-tum.* Him comin'
home to us, hold us safe. John de Conquer!

"Yea, Lawd," the folks murmured, and sat there, satisfied,
enjoying themselves.

So it was that Pretty Pearl came down from on high. Yes,
she did. Say it was one long time ago.

And by saying that, "Say it was one long time ago," we connect
the past with the present storytelling. All of *The Magical Adventures of
Pretty Pearl* becomes a telling for those living now, about those living
then. It's similar to a concept in song that the great bassist Charlie
Mingus wrote called "The Fables of Faubus," which begins, "Tell me,
Daddy, of the Fables of Faubus and Marcus Garvey." That's Governor
Orval Faubus of Arkansas who prevented black students from entering
Little Rock Central High School in 1957. Garvey needs no explana-
tion. The meaning of "The Fables of Faubus" song is fantasy, is that
hard times have passed and become lore and fable. Thus, *The Magical
Adventures* is historical fantasy — "Say it was one long time ago."

I think of myself as a humanist. I believe that writers must, through
their writing, help young people become advocates for their own human rights. Somehow, our children's literature seems to have become
removed from the young themselves. The slim presence of minority
literature, or the lack of that presence, would give the impression that
large groups of minorities do not exist in this country. Minority young
people are essentially voiceless in the struggle for their own welfare. I
wrote the novel *A Little Love* with the concept of voiceless young people in mind. Young people who never have enough words to express
how they feel. The way Sheema Hadley speaks to us in *A Little Love* is
contemporary, realistic, and termed *black English* by some. I know her
language derives from her working class background. The first sections
of the book take place in a large vocational school in the Midwest. The
young people who attend the school are tough and quick to strike out
with the fists rather than to use words. They read some magazines;
they read with difficulty if at all.

123

Will the young people about whom this book is written ever read it? Are they capable of reading books or do they care to? I can't allow myself to think about that question too hard. What I must always remember is that if there is a young person somewhere who wants to know what is in that book, who wishes to extend his or her comprehension of others unlike him or her, or simply, to find something between the covers of a book that reflects his or her personal struggles, or to find a new sort of entertainment, then the book is there for reading. It is also there for me. When the question of making a book about someone like Sheema Guidama Hadley occurred to me, I felt compelled to shape her within the novel form. When I want answers for myself and when I want to share them, to entertain with them, I compose a fiction.

Writing as I do from a minority perspective in a majority society, and indeed that is often a whole other world, far different concerns enter into the fictions. In my mind are new insights from the recent Jonathan Kozol study titled *Illiterate America* (1985). If truly one-third of all adults in this country are illiterate or nearly so, and 44 percent of black adults nationwide are illiterate, where does it leave black children and me? If the printed word shifts to the side and no longer is the center of our knowledge, what happens to those just now beginning with learning, to which books have no central meaning. Even with television, my seventeen-year-old son's generation grew up knowing that books were far more important than the flickering images on the tube. My son may love MTV, but his knowledge still comes essentially from the printed word. Probably not so for the next generation, who will have more difficulty reading as the glut of videos and computers find more room in their consciousness.

A Little Love was an attempt to bring another class of black American into young adult literary consideration, besides of course the entertainment of the fiction. There are classes of Americans that never quite show up as features in our literature. Sheema Guidama Hadley and Forrest Jones and Granmom and Granpop are four such features.

I love them dearly, especially Granmom and Granpop. A scene in the book that is so close to me is this one:

> Granmom turned to face them. She was grinning from ear to ear, her eyes shining at Granpop. She began to dance. The prettiest little dance Sheema could remember seeing. Just a one-two-three, kick one way and a one-two-three, kick the other way. A whirling, holding the dress out on either side. A tiptoeing forward and then back and then a side-to-side swaying. Oh, it was nice.
>
> "Granmom!" Sheema whispered. "You sure somethin'!"
>
> But Granmom only had eyes for Granpop right now. And slowly, Granpop got to his feet. Pushed back the chair. He was small and wiry, very compact. He hadn't gained a pound in forty years. He wore yellow suspenders and gray work trousers. A gray shirt open at the throat. He looked neat, like a farmer who had come into town on a Saturday. His hair was gray, cut short. He had a bald spot in the back the size of a rubber ball. The bald circle was shiny and had a crease in it that he said happened to him in 1918 when he was fifteen. He never did say how it happened or what caused it to happen.
>
> Granpop grunted and did a couple of knee bends to get himself started. Then, with great dignity, he began to shuffle a counterpoint to Granmom's dance. Eyelids half closed, he held his arms out from his sides and dipped, then surged forward on the three-count of Granmom's "one-two-three, kick."
>
> "Hee, hee," laughed Granmom, watching Granpop's moves. Then Granpop swooped near her and took hold of her about the waist, standing well back from her kick to one side and the other. The touch of his circled fingers, thumbs on her waist was so delicate, Granmom could freely move and sway. Granpop swayed with her. Respectfully, he nodded at her, smiled at her. The dance went on to a silent music.

"You remember that?" Granmom murmured. "You remember?" She smiled at Granpop.

"Yea," he said. "It was 'Bye Bye Blackbird,' and I come dancing in the ballroom." But his breath was short.

"And I saw you, too," Granmom said, remembering, wheezing slightly. "I saw you come dancing—'Bye Bye Blackbird!' and that was it." She sighed happily.

"You smell like beer!" Granmom said, huffily, shoving Granpop back. That broke the mood. And, soon, they stopped the dance. The silent music, the distant time, was gone as if it had never been. Both Granmom and Granpop found their way back to the table. And between them, they finished the beer. They slumped heavily in their chairs, breathing hard.

"Whew!" Granmom said. "Beer sure do taste!"

I read that about the old folks, Granmom and Granpop rather than a section about Sheema for several reasons. One is that I cannot separate young people in my books from those older persons who love them or who affect their lives. I want young people to understand that those who love them are a gift to their lives. Granmom, Granpop, Grandfather Jackabo, Aunt Leah are gifts in the lives of the young characters. They are presents out of the past to be opened and held and loved. Another reason I wanted to read this section is that it in a sense specifies some of my own loved ones. All of it is my own imagination except for the "Bye Bye Blackbird" part and Granpop dancing into the ballroom. "And that was it," Granmom says. That according to my own parents was how they met. My father being a marvelous ballroom dancer. It was in Calgary, Alberta, Canada, that the ball took place. Black people were quite fond of balls. Kenneth Hamilton came waltzing in his own inimitable style into the ballroom. Etta Belle Perry was there. He waltzed right to her and took her in his arms. And as Mother always said, "That was *it*." Well, that's a fine romance. Whether the truth is not so important.

I've cherished that story all of my life. It appealed to some romantic sensibility within me and it seemed fitting that it should be given over to Granmom and Granpop to continue a loving tradition. A good tale begs to be shared.

Speaking of good tales, I am fond of folktales and I'd like to read from a collection of mine which will be published in the fall by Knopf. The collection is called *The People Could Fly: American Black Folktales*, told by Virginia Hamilton and illustrated by Leo and Diane Dillon. The Dillons will contribute the jacket art and forty drawings. I have told twenty-four tales from the large body of American black folktales, mainly from the plantation era.

Folktales carry us back to the very beginning of people's lives, to their hopes and their defeats. American black folktales show us people most of whom long ago were brought from Africa to this country against their will. They lost their origins as they left the past, the family, the social group, and their languages and customs behind. It's amazing that the people could ever smile and laugh, let alone make up riddles and songs and jokes, and tell tales. But tell tales they did. And many kinds of tales told long ago were passed along to us and are still told today.

The People Could Fly collection is divided into four categories of tales. They are Animal Tales; Tales of the Real, Extravagant, and Fanciful; Tales of the Supernatural; and Slave Tales of Freedom. One type from the Real, Extravagant, . . .

[MISSING CONTENT, FOUR DOUBLE-SPACED, TYPEWRITTEN PAGES]

We might now talk about what I do and how I do what I do. All writers have their own how. The why is a mystery full of need to know, to question, to symbolize, to portray, to grow, to evolve. Buffy Sainte-Marie sings in a song, "Little wheel spin and spin; the big wheel goes around and around." That's a very Indian concept, one that I made use of in the fiction *Arilla Sun Down*. I will, of course, continue to make use of my society, my environment, the world of children and young adults I know, the turn and spin of my own mind, to create that which interests me and to question and answer. The books I am doing now seem hard and I don't really know why that is, except perhaps that I am revolving again. Writers go through periods of growth, I suppose. Sometimes it feels like retreating.

But I hold to the Kozol ideal that literacy represents "some sort of answer to a universal need for vindication and for self-perpetuation." People need to read and enjoy reading materials that are meaningful to them. Kozol calls them "oral histories which they can learn to transcribe, keep, and share with their children."

I put together the folktale book *The People Could Fly* as a way of keeping an important part of the black past for everyone, not just for one minority or for only black children.

Although I appreciated the recent good review of *Junius Over Far* in the Sunday *New York Times*, I resented somewhat the reviewer saying that the novel had the "clear intention of enlarging black people's awareness of their past." The assumption seemed to be that black people's awareness alone needed enlarging. I think nowadays the majority of black people are quite aware of their past. That past, of course, needs keeping and saving and revitalizing and reintroducing to new generations. It is a constant struggle to keep the culture of the past present. But it is some of the majority society apparently who believe the black cultural heritage should be enlarged only for blacks, that it offers little by way of instruction of knowledge to whites.

We cannot afford to separate ourselves, one group from another. We do, but we do it at great psychic expense and risk to humanism and democracy. Whatever art I possess is a social action in itself. For I have always maintained that fictional people live within a social order. And mine live in a largely black social order, not because I believe in some sort of racial separatism, but because I have been attempting for so many years a certain form and content to express black literature as American literature and to establish a pedigree of American black literature for the young. Having to prove an identity over and over again is a condemnation of a society that will not readily believe in it, a society that recognizes me most clearly when I write about blacks in social-conscious ways that are familiar to them, which reaffirm the assumption that black people are just like white people. However, some of the classic depictions of individual uniqueness among my books are at present unavailable in paperback—*Zeely, Arilla Sun Down*, the Justice Cycle books, *The Planet of Junior Brown*. But that is a whole other story that might well be examined sometime under the heading "The Silent Censorship."

When I write about situations as found in *Arilla Sun Down*, in the Justice Cycle books, and in *The Magical Adventures*, that is, in cultural-conscious books, I sense the nervous smiles and the peculiar silences. I used the science fiction mode in the Justice Cycle to express the past, present, and future of a race, part of which is at war with itself, simultaneously through four individuals with different and extraordinary powers. What I attempted there was generally misunderstood or, worse, passed on with little comment. The Justice Cycle books are unique beyond their black science fiction adventure mode—unique in language, in portrayals of the black social-action experience. They are also found by some to be difficult to read.

I'm aware that a large part of what I attempt to do in books for the young is considered too hard for them and often has not been tried before. American children bear the burden of relative ease in their lives. They have many choices beyond to read or not to read. They are often lazy readers. What I attempt is not too hard and not too difficult for them. But it may be true that they must first familiarize themselves with the degree of difficulty that results in our comprehending one another when our society allows the separation of its groups culturally and socially from one another. And again, writers must contend with the large problem of national illiteracy generally and black illiteracy particularly. Illiteracy hurts the writer from the minority most directly. And the minority writer must contend with the new phenomena of resegregation. Little Rock Central High School is again today almost totally black, which tends to perpetuate one group's misunderstanding and misreading of another.

But quite often, nice things do happen cross-culturally and racially. A white woman told me the story of her experience of reading *A*

Little Love first before giving it over to her teenage daughter with the comment only, "I think you will find this interesting." The daughter read the book and liked it. "But didn't you find the black English difficult?" The daughter said, "What black English? Mother, that's the way everyone talks."

Well, we know that everyone doesn't talk like Sheema Hadley. But there is a hipness among American children, which comes from emulating the young star and rap culture. What the daughter meant was that all teenagers, to some extent, speak the same language, more than the adults speak one another's language. If you go to a Midwest vocational school and any city school and a lot of small-town schools of America, you will find that the kids all talk alike, no matter their color or heritage, and they will use the same inflection with key words. It is often a rich language teenagers use, which I am developing into a book on which my son, who is sometimes a delicious writer, and I might collaborate.

But the forms I use in writing new material will change as I discover new ways to express the content I seek to reveal. Experimentation comes over me in waves. I had been on a wonderful spin for a few years, wonderful book ideas that seemed to write themselves. I thought it would last forever. But I suspect that for such ease to last forever might mean that I had ceased to grow.

Before I close, I wish to announce my intention at the invitation of Kent State University Libraries to house a significant number of my manuscripts and supporting memorabilia in the Department of Special Collections. I hold on to the manuscripts for a long, long time and give them up reluctantly. However, it seems fitting that they should settle in a place in time and in tune with the lectureship, so that those attending the annual lecture can naturally browse among the manuscripts if they care to. I have never given a page away anywhere.

And last, I'd like to thank everyone again. It is truly a privilege to be here. I can tell you that the writer's revolution continues, little wheels spin and spin, and the big wheel, slowly it turns. Yet still, it turns.

CORETTA SCOTT KING AWARD ACCEPTANCE SPEECH:
The People Could Fly: American Black Folktales

Given at the American Library Association Conference, New York City, 1986

I HAVE BEEN a student of American black folklore for many years, but it hadn't occurred to me to collect the material in book form until Janet Schulman, editor in chief of Random House and Knopf Books for Young Readers, thought of it. "Virginia, I just had a fantastic idea," she said over the phone one day. "Only you can write it, and only the Dillons can illustrate it." Only Janet could be so certain. In two seconds she convinced me as well. So it is she we have to thank for a remarkable thought and, too, all of the people at Random House who took such special care with this book. Also, many thanks to my splendid editor at Knopf, Frances Foster, who was clear always as to my intent, both with the tales and the commentaries, and as to where I was headed with the project, even when at times I was unsure.

The People Could Fly idea became a reality, and the parts—illustrations, text, and in-house bookmaking—came together in a most qualitative fashion to produce a work that has proved appealing to readers of all ages. When the work was published, I felt that those fugitives depicted flying away in Leo and Diane Dillon's dramatically stunning, magical jacket art were free at last. So, too, was the book in its entirety, free to find its own level of readership. I am happy to say that *The People Could Fly* has soared to capture the imaginations of readers everywhere. An author can ask for nothing better for one of her books.

Therefore, tell me a *tell*. What was it like when you were my size? Tell that one, you know, about Grandpa and what he did. The age-old request first heard at our grandparent's knee. Tell me a story. Not "read me a story." That would come later. But tell me, in the bonding sequence from elder to young one. Make images, sights, and sounds out of thin air using the tones of the voice. That is what "Tell me a story" means, truly.

Through words we learn and know about ourselves. Literature gives us images with which to think. Those images are composed of a creative process of documentation, recollection, and imagination — I call it the known, the remembered, and the imagined — which I use every day to make my literary efforts come alive in seeming (reading) and in sounding (telling).

Wherever there are people, there is spoken language. And wherever we live together, people use language to tell stories. Each of us is a storyteller, for the most fundamental form of tale telling is that quintessence of chatter, that most perfect manifestation of rumor and idle talk — gossip. "Have you heard the news?" "He told me that she . . ." "But did you hear what she said about . . ." "Then, I said I wouldn't be caught dead . . ." "Believe me, honey, when I tell you!"

The delicious story of our lives told in daily episodes. Think of the soap opera as a simplex form of gossip. We've all listened to it and retold it. We are all tale tellers, some better than others. It has been said that when gossip grows and becomes large enough to transcend its time and place, when it is handed down from one time and place to another and changed and polished, it then becomes the folktale.

I am a tale teller, a folk teller who writes her stories down. My ability grew from a similar source, that of family tales and gossip. Thus, we have my own grandfather, Levi Perry, three quarters of a century ago gathering his ten children about him, saying, "Sit down, and I will tell you about slavery and why I ran, so that it will never happen to you." Told in so many words to me by my mother, Grandpa Perry's eldest daughter.

Levi Perry's life, or the gossip about his days, has elements of mystery, myth, and folklore as well as the three elements already mentioned. It is from hearing such family tales that I became a student of folklore. The result, of course, is my own *The People Could Fly* collection of verifiable folktales.

You see, the slaves — those former Africans — brought, chained, to this continent had no power, no weapons to aid them in overcoming their oppressors. So it was that they used the folklore they created here to comment on their lives of servitude and to give themselves comfort and strength through endless hard times. Some of these tales are absolutely unique in the folktale genre. But how were they told — and where — is the question I asked myself again and again.

There could not have been any easy way for these tales to develop over time. There was no safe place where, and no condition under which, the slaves could sit down and simply tell stories, except in the safety of the forests. Most of the Southern country was forest. Plantations had been carved from them and were surrounded by them. In the hot, humid months of summer, the owner and his family and servants left the plantation for the summer home built in the cool forest. The forest was forbidden to the ordinary slaves who were not house servants — for obvious reasons.

But in those months when the owner was away, some slaves found the courage to make a secret place for themselves in the great forest. Here they gathered under cover of darkness to pass gossip and to discuss what was beyond the forest. Some had heard about an extraordinary land on the farther side. But which side was that, and how far was far? Their meetings were so secret they dared not use their own names for fear the names would somehow reach the ears of the overseer. They

1 3 3

dared not touch one another, lest the mere touching give away an identity. They put on their tale-telling voices. Wryly but firmly, they questioned one another in the dark upon entering that secret place:

"That you, Possum?"

"Yay," Old Possum would answer.

And, "That you, Sis Goose?"

"Ayay, hits me," whisper the Goose. "And you, Bruh Bear?"

"Yayo, it's me."

On around in the dark. "That you Bruh Rabbit?" A voice would ask.

"Nobody else but," say the Rabbit.

"What you got to tell us tonight," asks Bruh Deer.

"Aye, me," says Sis Deer.

"And the allagatuh right by her," says Bruh Allagatuh.

"Well," the Rabbit says. "I come to tell you a *tell*. It my dream, call it free-dom or war."

"Well, which?" Allagatuh asks.

"Don't know somethin about which," Bruh Rabbit says. "I just got to tell some of both."

"Wait," Sis Goose says. "First, we not all here. Where be the Fox? We not hear um say good evenin just yet."

"Bruh Fox," Old Possum say, way low in his throat, "he gone."

"He gone?" they ask at once.

"Yay, heard tell Fox done flew the coop," says Possum. "He fly over the forest high as you can go. Fox gone and gone the long, long gone."

"Ayay. Ayay."

Therefore, I imagine that this then began the time the animals talked that is mentioned so frequently in the literature as well as the beginning of the tale-telling time. In the same way, when slaves escaped, the idea of literal flight took hold, and the people who could fly were born. It could have been. It is an explanation of the way slaves disguised themselves even from themselves, taking on the names of animals as protection. And a good explanation of why the animal tales seem so right and so perfectly developed. With *The People Could Fly*, my hope was to make a tantalizing book to read and to create a metaphor for the modern-day struggle and achievement of black Americans. I hoped to meld the spoken with the written word in a language that would seem a language of commonality that would in turn reflect the dreams of all Americans.

Black people continue to rediscover their own history—to say nothing about nonblacks only now discovering important areas of the same history as an integral part of larger historical patterns. Individuals have told me that *The People Could Fly* changed their lives. We tend to think that everyone is like ourselves, involved with the printed word. It is always a marvel to discover that there are people who live quite comfortable lives while reading books only very occasionally. A book such as *The People Could Fly* makes a profound impression on, and is a revelation to, the intermittent reader.

Working in the area of black materials and experience is exciting and thought provoking. I've not found the research in black heritage and culture a cause for despair, however sorrowful some of the areas might seem. Many times one feels like an explorer, tracking along the "hopesteps" of beings dead and gone. Following trails of dogged courage and will beyond imagining across dangerous entrapments.

With this book I've tried to present a rounded primer in the artistry of the American black folktale. To neglect our folkloric past is to no longer remember the verbal word and its emotion and sound of meaning. It is to lose the sense of ourselves talking to one another. I hoped to evoke that feeling for language and exquisite sense of story that fine tale tellers of old had who devised these wonderful tales out of the good and bad experiences of their lives.

Black folktales, I believe, allow us to share in the known, the re-membered, and the imagined together as Americans sharing the same history. How the tales sound when spoken and how they seem when read implies the listener and the reader. From teller to reader is the unbroken circle of communication. We all contribute to a construction made from mere words. We are all together. That is what language does for us. That is what *The People Could Fly* may do for us. To say, from one of us handed down to the other, you are not alone. Thank you for this very American award for my American book.

ON BEING A BLACK WRITER IN AMERICA

Speech from the proceedings of the Children's Literature Section
of the Forty-Eighth International PEN Congress,
New York, January 14, 1986

I WRITE FOR young people in part because my rural childhood was filled with light, openness, and time for my imagination to soar. I keep wonderfully clear memories from that period. And as a novelist, I am able to transform that which evolves from my own experience of living into a coherent fictional form. This may be the fundamental meaning of self-expression: the discovery by the author of new ways of expressing real sources of living that are particularly hers. Thus, writing over a period of time does indeed stand for what she has lived and what living has meant to her.

I have written twenty books for young people starting from the read-alone age to young adult age, so that now a brand-new generation of young is acquainted with them. I consider myself a fictionist, although I have written biographies of the great baritone Paul Robeson and the fine scholar W. E. B. Du Bois. Over the years, I have attempted through my books to bring to children and young adult readers something of value to their lives from the unique American black perspective, as well as to shed light on the real concerns of young people in a world in which survival becomes for them increasingly more difficult.

Through character, time, and place, I've attempted to portray the essence of a race, its essential community, culture, history, and traditions, which I know well, and its relation to the larger American society. I endeavor to demonstrate the nexus the black group has with all other groups, nationalities, and races—the connection the American black child has with all children—and to present the best of my heritage.

I consider myself a student of history as well as literature. My books generally have a historical aspect that becomes an integral part of the fictions. A novel taking place in the present will often evoke an atmosphere of former generations. We carry our pasts with us in the present through states of mind, family history, and historical fact. No one source is more specific to and symbolic of my writing than the historical progression of black people across the American hopescape.

Historically, Americans have thought of themselves as egalitarian, aware at least of a constant assertion of the equality of all. We proposed a unique concept: that the young have the right to books reflecting their cultural and racial and spiritual heritage. Cultural democracy was to be the giant step on the way to equal education and the first principle to the attainment of human equality. We assumed as a human right that all people have free access to information about themselves and their pasts.

While many of us hold to the same beliefs, others attempt to censor what American young people will read by removing so-called controversial books from library shelves and, more subtly with books by and about blacks, by simply not making them available, by not purchasing them.

In some cases, works by and about blacks are said to be too sophisticated, too high art for the young. Books like my own, which are occasionally mildly experimental—with subject matter having to do with mental dissociation, graphic imagery of nuclear explosions, Amerindian and black survival in a hostile majority society, children alone and hungry for love and companionship—are said to be, and often by those adults who should know better, only for the especially gifted child. It is rather interesting that the awards some of my works have received often contribute to the apparent suspicion that the works are "art" or "literature" and therefore too difficult or too special for the usual or ordinary child. These adults would keep the young at a safe and quasi-literate level, where their response to life and to the world remains predictable and manageable. The way I counteract such backwardness is by keeping fresh my awareness of young people's keen imaginations and by responding to their needs, fears, loves, and hungers in as many new ways as possible.

Whatever art I possess is a social action in itself. My view is that black people in America are an oppressed people and therefore politicized. All of my young characters live within a fictional social order, and it is largely a black social order, as is the case in real life. For a score of years I've attempted a certain form and content to express black literature as American literature and to perpetuate a pedigree of American black literature for the young.

"If a race has no history, if it has no worthwhile tradition, it becomes a negligible factor in the thought of the world and it stands in danger of being exterminated." So goes the warning given by the Afro-American historian Carter Woodson. The truth of that statement has been made chillingly clear. Whenever individuals are denigrated because of their ideas, color, religion, speech and, further, because they are poor and deprived and black, you can be sure those individuals are in danger of becoming nonbeings and less than human.

I write from a love of creating and fabricating. It is also very important to me that I speak to the history, culture, and traditions that I grew up with. I am informed by black educators that American black and white students entering colleges today have little knowledge of our literature and only generally know our *her*-oes and heroes such as Mary Bethune, Rosa Parks, Phyllis Wheatley, Harriet Tubman, Paul Robeson, W. E. B. Du Bois, and, yes, even Martin Luther King Jr.

In my most recent work, entitled *The People Could Fly*, I have developed the black folktales from the plantation slave era as a metaphor for the present-day struggle and accomplishment of American blacks. I believed that the folktales would further demonstrate that storytelling is not merely a thing of the past, but a continuing cultural imperative. The tales illuminate the triumphs of talking and telling among the people in the present and reveal the connections of this ethnic group to its historical self. I wrote them in a language that I felt echoed the language of early tellers, and which would be understandable to today's readers. Readers would discover therefrom that people have always found ways of keeping their courage, their pride and talent, their imaginative consciousness. All of the tales in the new collection were formed and polished in that very worst of times.

A black writer in America skates between two allegiances, the one of being black and the other of being American. This duality Dr. Du Bois called two separate hearts. When I begin a book, the question arises, to what degree is this book an American book and to what degree is it a black book? How the same and how different? The answer changes. What America means is a conscious choice that I seem to make according to the subject matter each time I write.

What being black means is a constant in myself and my work. It is the belief in the importance of past and present Afro-American life to the multiethnic fabric of the hopescape and the necessity of making that life known to all Americans. It is the belief in the preservation of the life and literature, the documentary history in schools and libraries for succeeding American generations. It is the imaginative use of language and ideas to illuminate a human condition, so that we are reminded then again to care who these black people are, where they come from, how they dream, how they hunger, *what they want.*

THE ZENA SUTHERLAND LECTURE

Presented May 2, 1986; sponsored by the Chicago Public Library
in cooperation with the University of Chicago, honoring the late
Zena Sutherland, who edited the University's Bulletin of
the Center for Children's Books *for nearly thirty years*
and wrote the textbook Children and Books

INTRODUCTION
OF VIRGINIA HAMILTON

BY BETSY HEARNE

W HEN I FIRST met Virginia Hamilton, it was in 1974, right after she won the triple crown — the Newbery, Boston Globe–Horn Book, and National Book Awards — for her novel, *M. C. Higgins, the Great.* She asked me, in all innocence, I presume, what was so different about her books. It was a justifiable question, since all the starred reviews said her books were different. I fumbled toward something about imagination and originality, but it wasn't a very satisfactory answer, and I've thought about it a lot over a score of years as I've read each of her books. Although imagination and originality are always rare commodities, other writers of children's literature do have them. There's something more specific about Virginia's work which, if

I can finally define it, I would call a joining of the traditional and the innovative to make strong new literary structures.

Her Jahdu tales use words in rhythmic patterns of folkloric storytelling that are renewed to fit and follow the small roving rascal who dares to come from a mythical past, even as far as the streets of Harlem — Jahdu, whose favorite word as he runs in and out of trouble is *Woogily*, an exclamation that will stand by any child in times of trouble. The heroine of *Zeely* assumes the image of a Watusi queen who seems to walk out of an African past into the present, just as a mysterious figure in *The House of Dies Drear* emerges from the days of slavery into the lives of a Midwestern family. *Arilla Sun Down* explores a girl's African American and Native American roots in a stream-of-consciousness narrative. *The Magical Adventures of Pretty Pearl* blends mythology and history with a god-child's wandering from Mount Kenya, where she lived with her brother John de Conquer, down through the world and woods of the American South, into hiding with black and Cherokee refugees, into the company of the giant hero John Henry himself. *Willie Bea and the Time the Martians Landed* returns to the dynamics of an extended family on a specific night — Halloween of 1938, during Orson Welles's famous broadcast. The protagonist of *M.C. Higgins, the Great* struggles to unite a legacy of hill-country music and community with commercial invasions that loom in a slag heap over his future. *Sweet Whispers, Brothers Rush* materializes a family ghost to help a child understand her neglectful mother and dying brother. Even the realistic novel *A Little Love* connects the relationship of a young couple with that of grandparents, so that the sense of personality as history is never lost. *The Planet of Junior Brown* deals with the sorrows of children who have been cut off from their roots, the bare emotional survival of those who must substitute peer for generational support. Hamilton's complex biographies of Paul Robeson and W. E. B. Du Bois strengthen young people's understanding of parallel conflicts in their society's past.

Virginia Hamilton's recharging of tradition with currents of creative energy and untried techniques carries literature from the past through the hands of the living present into a lasting future. What child can resist this cumulatively cadenced retelling from *The People Could Fly: American Black Folktales*? Like most of her writing, it will sound both deeply familiar and strikingly new:

Little Daughter was outside the fence now. She saw another pretty flower. She skipped over and got it, held it in her hand. It smelled sweet. She saw another and she got it, too. Put it with the others. She was makin a pretty bunch to put in her vase for the table. And so Little Daughter got farther and farther away from the cabin. She picked the flowers, and the whole time she sang a sweet song.

All at once Little Daughter heard a noise. She looked up and saw a great big wolf. The wolf said to her, in a low gruff voice, said, "Sing that sweetest, goodest song again."

So the little girl sang it, sang,

"*Tray-bla, tray-bla, cum qua, kimo.*"

And, *pit-a-pat, pit-a-pat, pit-a-pat, pit-a-pat*, Little Daughter tiptoed toward the gate. She's goin back home. But she hears big and heavy, PIT-A-PAT, PIT-A-PAT, comin behind her. And there's the wolf. He says, "Did you move?" in a gruff voice.

Little Daughter says, "Oh, no, dear wolf, what occasion have I to move?"

"Well, sing that sweetest, goodest song again," says the wolf.

Little Daughter sang it:

"*Tray-bla, tray-bla, cum qua, kimo.*"

And the wolf is gone again.

The child goes back some more, *pit-a-pat, pit-a-pat, pit-a-pat*, softly on tippy-toes toward the gate.

But she soon hears very loud, PIT-A-PAT, PIT-A-PAT, comin behind her. And there is the great big wolf, and he says to her, says, "I think you moved."

143

"Oh, no, dear wolf," Little Daughter tells him, "what occasion have I to move?"

So he says, "Sing that sweetest, goodest song again."

Little Daughter begins:

"*Tray-bla, tray-bla, tray-bla, cum qua, kimo.*"

The wolf is gone.

But, PIT-A-PAT, PIT-A-PAT, PIT-A-PAT, comin on behind her. There's the wolf. He says to her, says, "You moved."

She says, "Oh, no, dear wolf, what occasion have I to move?"

"Sing that sweetest, goodest song again," says the big, bad wolf.

She sang:

"*Tray bla-tray, tray bla-tray, tray-bla-cum qua, kimo.*"

The wolf is gone again.

And she, Little Daughter, *pit-a-pat, pit-a-pat, pit-a-pattin* away home. She is so close to the gate now. And this time she hears PIT-A-PAT, PIT-A-PAT, PIT-A-PAT, comin on *quick* behind her.

Little Daughter slips inside the gate. She shuts it— CRACK! PLICK—right in that big, bad wolf's face.

She sweetest, goodest safe!

Virginia Hamilton.

LECTURE:
HAGI, MOSE, AND DRYLONGSO

I T   I S   A N   H O N O R to be here to give the 1986 Zena Sutherland Lecture. There had to have been an occasion when I first met Zena Sutherland, for it was the time I was beginning in my field and had gained some attention for my first book. Thus, I was being shown around and found myself at a festive gathering that included Mrs. Sutherland.

Yet, it is far easier for me to believe that I have always known her than to recall our being introduced. There are persons who affect one significantly. Zena Sutherland has been for me a constant guardian, wisely giving advice most often by means of her subtle reviews of many of my books. The best critic, in my opinion, is the one who teaches. I have studied her reviews of my work as one takes a course in "How to Build a Fiction." Lesson number one: Never paint the *would* until the *could* is nailed. The reviews have been consistently enlightening. It is through educators such as Zena Sutherland that we writers are able to face our weaknesses. Some of us admit, in a moment of weakness, to having them. We trust best the objective, cool hand. At least I do. I recall the last line of Zena's *Bulletin* review of *Arilla Sun Down* in November 1976. She thought that what was outstanding about the book was the characterization and "the dramatic impact of some of the episodes." Now, if the author has any sense, she will key in on the word *some*. She will march right back through the book and ferret out the *other* that may not have had dramatic impact. *Some* does imply *other*. Thank you, Zena, for all that you have taught me over the years.

I will tell you some of the reasons I do my work the way that I do. A novelist writes carrying a single idea, high above her head, like a big stick, over months and months. I have carried a somewhat abstract idea about the fundamentals of writing around for years. Beings, humans, are the long and short of things. Nothing is beyond the evidence of the senses of beings. That which is being will become, and becoming is everything in terms of the fiction I write. What is lasting and what is permanent is change. That is why novel writing is my fulfillment. Novel writing for young people, as opposed to adult novel writing, presupposes becoming and change. Our young protagonist begins ill-defined, but begin she or he must, whether or not she or he has definition. We observe, reading, as this being changes to become the very embodiment of growth, development, and definition.

A fiction is still a lie, and character, a being, or protagonist in a fiction, is still a setup, a proof in the air outlined by the imaginative use of language. A fiction doesn't necessarily reflect a real world. It, itself, isn't real. It is a closed system of the author's own creation in which the author "be's" the creator, something of a god-person who must always stand away, out of sight and out of mind as the creation works its way around the undefined being.

The creation encloses the being character in its own unreal world, which for us readers, of course, becomes the only reality. We can't get out of the unreal real world until we put the book down, until the undefined being totally becomes, breaking the bubble, the skin of the creation, of the lie, and we are let go.

The best search for becoming that I have done as the writer, and the best unreal world that I have created is the world and characters of *The Magical Adventures of Pretty Pearl.* I say "the best," because writing the book did best for me what I demanded of myself. I had a picture of a would-be world that I wanted to have become a real world. I wrote as near to the picture as I could. So *The Magical Adventures* begins as one thing and ends by becoming another. The merging of being and becoming is here as close as I've ever written. The novelist working within this fiction *fragments* herself into separate *entities* or qualities that become creators of the unfolding fiction. High John de Conquer and John Henry, existing as they do ready-made in black myth and lore, are two sides of a gold coin kept spinning in the same way that the totally imagined Mother Pearl and Pretty Pearl are two sides of another coin. Here is a whirling, blinding balance of natural forces.

The Magical Adventures is at once my most fun and most serious work. It is an organic whole coming as it does from the depths of the author-creator. There are mistakes, of course, errors of judgment and choices—all of my books have them. Perhaps all books have them to some extent. The dialect or speech is off-putting for some black people, particularly, and for high-school-age students who, having less historical perspective, misread the colloquial speech of *The Magical Adventures* as stereotypical black English. If I had a second chance, I might think about doing the language differently. But aesthetically, I think the language is true within the confines of the would-be world of the book.

A really first-rate lie that passes itself off as a fiction should reveal a clear face-to-face stand between illusion and reality. I think of illusion as the art of the impression of being. The art of fiction or literature is the illusion of reality. The magical effects that change Pretty Pearl into Mother Pearl are the art of illusion at work on character, atmosphere, and place.

Reality can be thought of as time, movement, action, *becoming*. Reality is change inside the illusion of reality. Perhaps all is illusion after all. This kind of thinking reveals that our very words become illusive. Our language — *all is illusion after all* — becomes ephemeral. The perfect book would be one in which each word vanishes as it is read. This mental exercise, a kind of intellectual striptease, often brings me insight into some fiction I'm working on. I want us to rid ourselves of any set, easy pieces we may have and allow our minds to open and our feelings to rise.

When I finish a book, I get rid of most of the imaginative residue and real research by simply putting the residue out of my mind, forgetting it, and by laying aside the tangible evidence. Presently, the tangible evidence, including drafts of a book, becomes the Virginia Hamilton papers and is shipped off to Kent State and Central State Universities in Ohio, which keep my papers for scholars and students. When the material of a book is laid out from beginning to end, it can be a revelation to researchers, other working writers, and even to me — how bad a first draft was and how it finally evolved into something decent. When I look at this material again after many years, I don't remember what my thinking was when I wrote it. But once I start reading, I can get back into the imaginative processes fairly easily.

Although my involvement with *The People Could Fly* is over, I am holding on to much of the research, at least the pieces of it, the flavor, place, and time, in order to maintain the same mental state of the plantation era for another project I'm attempting. This involves a time period one hundred and thirty years ago, and we can call it a *do-cunovel*, something based on factual material and historical incidents, but with blank areas that can only be filled with fiction.

At the same time, I am working on a contemporary young adult novel in which the black female protagonist idealizes her newfound friends, a nitty-gritty young white couple whom she actually nick-names "A White Romance," which is also the title of the book. Again, in the abstract, it is a story of illusion scraping against reality that demonstrates further the act of being and becoming. However, I do not write in the abstract, although I think in it, and this book is writ-ten on a very down-to-earth level to reveal a young black woman seeing a white world, a white romance, in her own cultural and racial terms.

The People Could Fly was one of those thoroughly pleasurable proj-ects that one comes upon occasionally. The book wasn't my idea. It was my publisher who said to me, only you, Virginia, can do this project justice and only the Dillons can illustrate it. I was convinced in less than two seconds that this was absolutely true. It was a project that I could work on maybe eight, ten hours a day without really feel-ing that I had left the swing and the playground. If I discovered a clue to something, I couldn't stop until I had tracked down the solution. And it didn't feel like work; it felt like an exploration of my own heart and being.

My initial plan for the book was like a puzzle. I could work at it in parts and then put all of the parts together. The title and the title story, "The People Could Fly," were with me from the beginning. This tale came to mind when the project was proposed to me, and it became my barometer and the yardstick by which I measured the atmosphere and depth of other tales and how they might fit into the whole scheme. If a tale didn't fit easily into my puzzle with "The People Could Fly" as the centerpiece, then I decided not to use it.

Now that the book is out there in the real world and all of us who worked on it are long since finished with it, I feel as though *The People*

Could Fly is truly free at last. It has found its own level. It has soared. It appears to have a very broad appeal, and a writer can ask for nothing better for one of her books. So much is lost, thrown away over and over again in our society. Maybe this book will become a bridge from one time to another.

Black people themselves continue to rediscover their own history. I have had people tell me that *The People Could Fly* literally changed their lives. We tend to think that everyone is like ourselves, continually involved with literature and history. It is always a marvel to discover that there are people who live in this world only reading books very occasionally. A book like *The People Could Fly* makes a profound impression on the intermittent reader.

Working in the area of black history and experience can be sobering at times. It is always thought provoking. It is often exciting. I have never found the material of black heritage and culture a cause for despair. One feels like a detective many times, tracking along the hopesteps of beings dead and gone. Following trails of dogged courage and will beyond imagining across dangerous entrapments.

One never knows what one will discover alone at night, steeped in the research. I do start working very early in the morning. By nightfall, if the world is really evolving—that is, if my mind is working—I may cease to feel as though I am body. I become mind and idea, response and feeling. I am free of my time and place. I am one of the long-gone beings come back to life there in my study, which itself expands into a road, a path, a darkness, a world. Cunning, desperate, beyond alertness, I am *being* this hearing-intense individual, all-seeing in the dark.

One night I took a side trip, following a mere mention of a group of African Americans who escaped hard ground together. In the dark they ran, some thirty of them, mostly adults and strong male children. They went a long way, long time, and I followed. The first one held tightly to the hand of the second, and so on. There was no leader. There was just the first, the second, on down the line. Long, long time, and finally, they crossed a great river. They were free. They had

149

hidden so well, had run into no other humans, had made their way over weeks and weeks without speaking more than a few words to the fugitive behind or in front.

At last, they straggled out of hiding. They saw people. But sadly, they could not understand a word spoken. Evidently it happened that, in their confusion of days and nights of wandering, they had got turned around. They'd crossed the wrong river. This was not the Ohio River. For the place was Mexico, and the river turned out to be the Rio Grande.

What an extraordinary tale for a collector of tales to stumble upon. Perhaps some of you know about this historical incident. That account that I've told you is all that I've found. I made note of the incident and put it away. Then I neglected to note where I put it away. Then I neglected to note where I put my reminder of the source material, carelessness which is typical of me when I'm distracted. Oh, I'll remember, I tell myself.

But what happened to those people? What year was it? Did they all survive? What, where, when? Sometimes it's hard to let something like that go. I think about it at odd moments. I don't go looking for the material. Maybe someday there will be time for that special hunt.

The period of slavocracy and abolition, masters and servants, rivers and runaways, and bounty hunters and rendition, stays with me because of my work on the new docunovel and because that period of history always gives me new insights. Sometimes, the research takes me back beyond what I actually need for my story. Often, it is necessary to divine what is in a name or a song or a saying. Figure out why these bonded ones were so certain that there was a time when animals talked, for instance. One finds very general references in the research for such a time, just as one finds fragments about flying and flying Africans and empty fields in which the farm tools continue to work with nary a hand to move them.

Perhaps Hagi knew of this, and Mose, and that the time was Drylongso. A long time ago, imagine you could be there on the cleared land, perhaps a thousand acres surrounded by the miles-wide band of impenetrable forests. The dead silence rises from the clods of earth as a condition of dreadful soundlessness.

The heat surrounds everything, smothering like a shroud. The stench hangs above the heat shroud, spreading like a curse. It is the odor of decay and animal and human waste, of climatic inversions that hold the putrid smell of the unwashed who have sweated, slaved, slept, sweated, awakened, sweated, and gone unwashed for days and weeks and months. The stench is a bitter taste, settled down in the soured lunch pails, eaten and swallowed by the hundreds of the slaving in the endless rows as the sorrowful nourishment of their days. There are too many of these blacks, finally; there is too much cotton and the price too low, too much heat and stench. Only the bonded can withstand such heat and the diseases that rise out of it. At any given time in the heat months, a fourth of them are sick. Who is there to remark on their being born and dying? Only they, themselves.

The owners are gone from the plantation. They have taken to the forests—lock, stock, and slave guards to watch their children, and servants to prepare and hand them their food. They will stay among the cool forest trees in their summer dwellings for the duration of the devil months, to return when the weather breaks around harvesttime; the only whites remaining to watch over the fields and the blacks are the overseers.

Overseer turns red, angry from the broiling sun. He grinds his hate through the rawhide whip slashes at black shoulders. The driver remains as well, for he and his family, if he's got one, are the only black elite allowed on the plantation, with his home away from the other slave quarters and next to the overseer's.

The little-known driver, the overseer's right hand, was always a black man, the strongest and baddest—John Henry would have made a typical one, if he'd got knocked out of him his tender heart. The driver was able to handle rawhide even better than the overseer. Caught in the middle between slaves and masters, he was perhaps the first one called Mose, feared by ordinary slaves more than they feared the overseer who was the man's substitute. The driver was made to dress

1 5 1

differently from the slaves, so that he could always be identified with the overseer, the stand-in man.

If the driver turned on the stand-in man, then the overseer would, in turn, turn on the slaves. But if the driver turned against his own kind, then he had done the dirty work for the man himself. And if the driver could relent and fool the stand-in man, then, he would. But if he could not, the driver would do what he must to those of his kind and to himself. No slave was ever more alone and hidden inside himself than was the driver, at once victim and the victimizer. In that great tale, "The People Could Fly," in the end, it is the overseer who tells about the flying Africans. It is the master who says it is all a lie and a trick of the light. But it is the driver who keeps his mouth shut.

Driver blows his horn or rings a bell after all hands have eaten the evening meal. "Oh, yes! Oh, yes! Ev'body in an' the doors locked," he hollers, signaling from the quarter to the overseer the end of both the slaves' labors and the quick moments of time available for the family and the social life on the slave street (Van Deburg, *The Slave Drivers: Black Agricultural Labor Supervisors in the Antebellum South*, 1979). Driver is responsible for so much—for sweeping the neighborhood for runaways and for the nightly verbal report to the overseer of the day's accomplishments and failures. He might lose his position at any time if he didn't do well, to end a beast of burden back in the fields.

See how overrun the fields are with this bent-low, squat-low humanity? They are better than cattle or horses, for they know how to straighten and ease their spines. They know how to laugh and sing, how to hold back the fear and the crying, and how to pick and pluck in unison. The more of us be, the quicker we work, they once thought. But why work quick, they learned, when there is no pay for anything? And if *They* find out there's no work for us to do, we'll get sold. Then where will we be? No one knows how bad a new owner, worse than one we have.

The women in their own cotton field, endless rows. The men in separate fields, hour upon hour. All these are the ones who labor on down to earth. These are the sorry ones who do not know the magic, that special African mystery. They cannot fly, cannot flee. They have no idea where they are, save that it is never home. It is called Partee Plantation, or Boyntin. They don't know where to run. See the blackness all around, and how far is the far over there where the horizon meets the forests? Only the owner and his tribe may enter the forest, so he says. But old Hagi and some of the others know better.

Hagi watches. Hagi, the granddaughter of an old driver, ancient herself now. Her work is valuable, although less each year. But she is ready with the tools of her trade, pieces of towels, some clear water for the brow. Sure hands and healing roots. A knife for cutting what must be severed. If a woman looks to fall with a borning child, Hagar is quick to scrape a hole over which the pregnant one will crouch and drop the babe. But right now, all is calm. Hagar, called Hagi, straightens her coarse sackcloth.

She stands, shields her eyes, looks off into the unending paleness of the sizzling light. Up there in the blinding blue shines even brighter the one called Hannah, that burning being sun.

"Huh," Hagi grunts. Shielding her eyes, she purses her lips and whistles in a piercing scream that is like a soul lost on the air. All others in the fields pause as the whistle screams by them, then ceases. It is a signal, and the sound of Hagi's voice now rises on the stillness.

The field hands, as little as one-fourth hands, boys and girls of thirteen; half hands, older youngsters; three-quarter hands, young, strong women; and whole hands, either one man in his prime or a man and his woman—they sway with this ancient formula of bringing life: Hagar's song.

153

> *Blow winds, Blow winds blow,*
> *Wind, blow winds, blow.*
> *Oh, won't you go down Hannah,*
> *Sunlight*
> *Drylongso, Drylongso!*

Strong Mose, grandson of drivers and cousin to old Hagi, is there in the field with the men. He catches the whistle first. Listens for the incantation. Hears it and takes it up, carrying it deep inside, and brings it forth again in his male strength to the other men: "You go down, now, Hannah, Oh, Hannah."

Hagar's lament was a message, telling all who cared where they would meet in secret. For it was forbidden for more than five of them to meet together. Absolutely forbidden that they enter the forest. Never would they murmur or even think their own names or the names of those who would gather.

But "Hannah go down," was the key phrase. Sundown brought darkness and darkness was the forest. *Drylongso* was the word.

They did meet way in the dark deep in the forest trees. And the password was given, barely whispered. "Drylongso." And answered, "Drylongso." Right there in the dark, where one could not see another, where there was safety in invisibility. And they would ask of one another:

"That you, Possum?"
"Yay," Ol' Possum would answer.
And "That you, Sis Goose?"
"Ayay, Ayay, hit's me. And you, Bruh Bear?"
"Yayo, it's me, it's me."
And on around in the dark. "That you, Bruh Rabbit?"
"Nobody else but," says the Rabbit.
"What you got to tell tonight?" asks Bruh Deer.
"That you, Deer?"
"Aye, me, and Allugatah right by me."
"Well," the Rabbit says. "Come tell my dream, call it war or free-dom."
"Well which?"
"Don't know, but just got to tell."
"Wait," Sis Goose says. "First, where be Bruh Fox?"

"Bruh Fox," Old Possum says way low, "he gone."

"He gone?"

"Yay, Fox done flew the coop. He done run the run. Fox gone and gone the long, long gone."

"Ayay. Ayay."

So, therefore, begins the time the animals talked. A brief docu-drama. This, then is the beginning of being and my being. Now we surmise, we infer how and why the animals talked and how so many animal tales came to be. The slaves deliberately took the names and personalities of the animals of the plantation as a cover to protect themselves even from themselves during those dangerous, clandestine meetings by which they passed along plantation knowledge, knowledge of the world, of the forest and beyond, where they told tales and truths about matters that concerned their survival.

Conjecture rises from the actual source material like a mist. The people I create move through the mist, dignified, dramatic, isolated, universal, forever made different and the same, yet always human and always changing.

I imagine that Hagi, as they called her, overheard the mistress say something to the effect that "Mistress believe the rain done dried up, the world be dry so long."

Now Hagar heard these words, exactly as they were said—dry so long. But she knew *drought* in her own words, her own language structures handed down, from near myths handed out of old Africa, from the bowed humanity in the holds of slave ships. She could smell *stepney*, they called drought and hunger, in the very air, years before it came. And stepney slowly became for her drylongso. It was black people hungry and thirsty. Drylongso had been lived with and dealt with for as long as anyone could remember.

When the anthropologist John Langston Gwaltney published his self-portrait of Black America entitled *Drylongso* in 1980, one of his contributors said this about herself:

1 5 5

I know your mother must have told you what mine told me: "The tongue is steel, but a closed mouth is a shield."

You know, I said that to the child and she got out her little book and wrote it down. I like that child because she's what I was when I was young. I don't mean I look like her. The truth is, son, I have never been the kind of person people would turn around and look at on the street. I'm just, well, what you might say drylongso. Neither ugly nor pretty, just drylongso.

Drylongso came to mean ordinary, the way drought was not news in Africa or in America. It is only natural that those driven by drought should become one and the same with it. Ordinary. Drylongso.

Clarence Major's *Dictionary of Afro-American Slang*, published by International Publications in 1970, designates *drylongso* as three separate words and defines it as a 1940s expression meaning dullness or fate.

I have studied enough black dialect and true narrative to know that slang expressions existing in the forties were likely current in the thirties and collected in WPA projects. Much of the narrative was related by actual former slave informants or their immediate descendants. I find it remarkable that drylongso is in current usage. Just as are Hagar and Mose. Hagar, or Hagi, being the archetypal, mythic black elder woman of the so-called American black nation. The character Hagar is a key figure in Toni Morrison's *Song of Solomon*. Mose has been always the prototype for the ordinary or common black male. He is the former driver or his descendant who, by his bravery and caring, has fallen from the governor's grace to the level of the ordinary field hand.

The Dictionary of Afro-American Slang defines Mose as simply "A Negro." Gwaltney calls Mose the archetypal "straight" black male. The typical Mose in one of my books would be Black Salt from *The Magical Adventures* or perhaps Silversmith from *Sweet Whispers, Brother Rush*.

The Black Salt character is at once ordinary and extraordinary. Of the people, he has the driver's leadership ability as well as the patriarch's desire to protect and lead his kind. Silversmith is a protector, also, for young Teresa Pratt, a father figure with the common touch.

The younger female or the young woman of the black nation has numerous names. Pretty Pearl and Mother Pearl from *The Magical Adventures* are typical of the variations on the theme of the black woman. To cast pearls before swine is a provocative idea and perhaps lies as a submerged thought in my naming of these characters.

A *diffy* in the black idiom is a streetwalker. A *sediddy* is one who is overly sedate; a *peola*, a light-skinned black woman; *Aunt Jane*, a female Uncle Tom. A *band* is a woman, a *banana* is also a light-skinned female. A *Banta issue* is a pretty black girl. A young woman is also a *bantam*, and so on. But the most common names are Hagi, Jane, and peola, terms still in use.

The lore and literature, the myth and conjecture, and the factual history of the past are at all times present in me. I write from the black experience for an audience as free and as large as I can find. I write from a love of creating and fabricating. I write in disguise in search of truth. I develop black folktales from the plantation era as a metaphor for present-day struggles and accomplishments of American blacks. These folktales demonstrate that tale telling is not merely a thing of the past, but a continuing cultural imperative.

I see black literature and the literature I create as a social action. Black people are an oppressed people. There is little black writing that is not socially conscious and race-conscious writing. There is no other way but this way for a black writer to be considered a writer of truth in this society. The very substance of our thinking is of struggle, becoming, and change. There is thesis and antithesis in search of synthesis. All of my young characters live within a fictional social order, and it is largely a black social order that is characterized by tension, insecurity, and struggle. The final analysis is one of growing consciousness. There is what history teaches us, or should.

I believe in the preservation of life and literature, the documentary history of the struggle in schools, in colleges and libraries for coming generations of Americans. Imaginative use of language and ideas illuminates for us a human condition, and we are reminded again to care who we Americans are. In this instance, who are these black people, where do they come from, how do they dream, how do they hunger? And we are reminded to value what we have and to know always what we want.

I am pleased to have this opportunity to share some of my reasons for being and my words with you.

Thank you.

THE SPIRIT SPINS:
A WRITER'S RESOLUTION

Speech reprinted in the ALAN Review, Fall 1987;
original audience unknown

A VERY GOOD morning to everyone. It is a pleasure to be here. I want to begin this morning by having you listen to the voice in your head. Good advice, I think. Also, "Listen to the Voice in Your Head" is the title of a poem from a work in progress entitled *Teenage Heartbreak Blues*, by Arnold Adoff (Actual title upon publication was *Slow Dance Heart Break Blues*, 1995). I have been given special dispensation to dip into the *Heartbreak*. I'd like to read "Listen to the Voice in Your Head" to you now. It is dedicated to the adolescent within each of you and to young adults everywhere:

> You will never be tall
> You will never be slim
> You will never have a chest, male or female variety /
>   That will cause excitement.
> You will break out with a huge
>   pimple on your nose the afternoon
>   of the Big Game
>   The Evening of the Big Dance.
> You will break out / You will break out
>   No one will ever love you and the world will turn /
>   Its great equatorial back on you and you / will live

159

In a swamp of defeat and self pity and even your   ·
   Mother
Will stop making sandwiches
   And
You will never be tall / You will break out forever.

That was my adolescence. Oh, how I cringe, remembering it even today. Oh, how I suffered through it and for it. Oh, how I cried over it and loved crying, looking at myself in the mirror at my pale, pinched face—I always found it lovely—and trembling lips, and loving the awful, delicious sadness of my dying for love, for wanting this *guy* I could never quite get who was on the varsity. Oh, my aching heart, my moans at being so skinny, flat-chested (believe it or not), too self-conscious to cross a room without tripping over my own bobby sox and falling on my face.

Who doesn't have vivid images of adolescence? It's amazing that any of us made it through. For then, we were earth's aliens. We, who mutated at puberty into these out-of-bounds, screeching/painfully shy, overbearing/underachieving, maniacal/angelic, poor, wretched teensters of the human condition.

To think it will and/or has happened to our own children is enough to cause an international ban on mother- and fatherhood. Ban the bombs. I know what I was like. I could sleep sixteen hours at a stretch and be mystified why my mom refused to make me a grilled cheese sandwich. I could stare immobilized out of the window without blinking until my father came home and demanded that I do something, anything. I could eat two chocolate sundaes, drink a milkshake, eat a Mars bar before the movie, and two bags of popcorn inside during the movie, and a large pizza with everything after the movie, and drink two Cokes along with it. "The waitress forgot our water, get some water." "Can I borrow your comb?" "Who's that with *her*!" And later laugh for days hysterically at the slumber party gossip over hot dogs and fries. Wake up at four AM on the floor and get sick in Agnes's bathroom. And be refreshed by one PM the next day in time to get home and have four hours to get ready for the big game that night.

My adolescence was far tamer than that of my kids. Theirs could be dangerous, and it was. Wild parties, car crashes that split the peace and tranquility of small-town Saturday night. Good friends died. Or big, dark cars *cruising* the neighborhood kid hangouts, selling nightmares, worse. My young adults grew up wary of strangers, knowing never to leave one house for another without calling home or telling a friend, and so on. They grew up, not quick to smile, almost angry that we had given them a world of danger, terrible weapons, little wars. They are slow to trust, but finally, are trusting and smiling. They are perceptive young people. They knew what they wanted to be at an early age, as I did and as their father did. That, our generations have in common. They grew up, avoiding the alienation from their parents that I and their father experienced with our own. I wonder why that is. What did their father and I do that was right, or did we have anything at all to do with it? Our young adults told us more than we sometimes wanted to hear. Perhaps they drew closer to us because their world was a tougher place; they needed to hold on longer to what they knew and whom they could trust. Yet, it's wonderful, those long conversations we had late at night sometimes, that told us their fears and their dreams in their own words. What I have learned from my young people and, yes, from observing their friends, has lifted my spirits up high and made my head spin, *changed* who I am and revolutioned the manner in which I live and think and work.

Long ago, I knew that when I had children they would be such and such a way. I would teach them this and that. They would of course want thus and so. Oh, they would want exactly what I had planned for them. I wouldn't make them do anything, but knowing what was best for them, I would definitely lead them along the righteous way of their lives.

You know, all of us parents think like that, to some extent. We *do* believe we know what is best for our children.

161

We say, "Kid, I don't think those are the kind of young people you should be associating with."

Or, "Mary, why don't you try working on the school newspaper. You know, your writing is really wonderfully special, so like poetry, dear."

Or, "I think you should really consider becoming a lawyer. The papers you wrote on the American Revolution are like law briefs. Let me talk to Tim Donaldson, the lawyer, maybe a part-time job at his law office."

"Un, would you tell Michael not to call here after eleven o'clock, please, dear."

"And just suggest to Allan, please, not to go into my refrigerator like he owned it. Don't any of these kids ever eat at home? Why must I supply ten gallons of lemonade for the soccer team?"

"I have to drive how many to the state orchestra auditions. Where? But that's one hundred and fifty miles away. You have to be there at eight o'clock in the morning?"

Mine are two beautiful, headstrong, stubborn young people. They pay attention to everything I tell them and then turn right around and do precisely what they know is best for them. They have minds that they created, a condition, I think, that surely they inherited. Son Jaime is the youngest. Daughter Leigh is the oldest. Once, I thought to ask Jaime what he would be if he could be anything in the world. I expected him to say a seven-foot-tall basketball player or a millionaire or both. He said, "If I could be anything in the world, I would be born first before my sister."

Only in his later adolescence did Jaime resolve the conflicting emotions he had squaring his macho teen boy image with the fact that his sister entered the world four years ahead of him. For him, having Leigh for a sister was serious business. She was tall, willowy, talented, outgoing and manipulative, lettered in sports and sang like a bird. He was too short for his age, plump, nonverbal, never smiled willingly and was steadily argumentative.

It took them years to work it out, to become friends. The spirit spins, the revolution in Mom and Dad is the way they learn to let things be. They learn hands-off, the philosophy of allowing the pain and holding back the comfort. Let the kids figure out how to comfort each other a bit, how to respect themselves.

In our family we believe in talking things out. And somewhere the muse, the art came to them. Somehow, the recognized talent for the wonderous possession that it is. They seized upon their artistry, recognizing it at an early age. And it became for them that bridge to knowledge and maturity. Not all young people are artistic, but most of them have sensitivity and are sensible, finally, concerning themselves.

I write for the adolescent and from adolescence and to it because I have seen its metamorphoses; I have witnessed this arch of destiny in countless young people carrying them from uncertainty to triumph as they learn to discover their selfhood.

It is a challenge for me as a writer to explore the often brave ways in which young people face themselves and one another and the adult world they must enter. Looking out from their junior and senior high-school years, it must seem frightening, out here where we are. "If I can just be like you, Mom," they might say, "if I can just be successful." "Oh," they say, "I'll never be anything—will I? Will I? I can't do anything. Where will I go? College is so big . . . too small. Too far away. Too close. I won't know anyone. No one will like me. Will I get in? Will I have friends? Who will I date? What will I wear? How much stuff do I *take with me*? I will never sleep in a noisy dorm with strangers. What will I do? *Do my own laundry?*" Now these are the kinds of fears that the successful, college-bound students invariably have. Imagine what sort of voiceless dramas go on within the students not so successful.

It is truly a long way for all of them from where they begin, on through their young adulthood.

It has been a long way, also, from where I started, perhaps farther than I would have dreamed, certainly farther than my own young

163

people will have to go. I don't think I was designed to come this far. I am your garden variety, farm-bred overachiever. Early on, I had a powerful sense that I wanted to write. And later, it was amusing to me that people were willing to pay me for what I had been doing for free.

Freedom is very important to me. What I remember most about growing up as an adolescent in Ohio was that I was free. Whether that is a true memory or a necessary fabrication is beyond my knowledge. But I took it upon myself to make regular visits, my cousin and I did, to my mother's friends and relatives who were old enough to be my mother's mother. These were missionary ladies of the church auxillary, and I found them fascinating. They seemed to me to have lived in another time and were merely passing through my own. For me and my cousin Marlene, it was a joy stepping into the half-light of silent, perfectly neat front parlors with blinds drawn against the heat in the late afternoon. The back of the sofa and the arms of easy chairs were protected by lace antimacassars they'd crocheted themselves. Polish gleamed on the oak floors and the dining table. I remember the slow, somnific ticking of the grandfather clock. "Why were there no grandmother clocks?" I wondered as I watched the stooped-back Miss Wing, an elderly missionary lady, rummage through her ancient calfskin purse, over there at the breakfront, hunting up the right amount of change. And finding it, holding it between delicate thumb and finger out to me, she would speak, "Dear, take this to your mother, if you will. Etta put in for me last Sunday when the plate came around, as I'd forgotten my money."

"Yes, ma'am, Miss Wing," I would answer and gingerly take the change, blackened by time. I remember Miss Wing in her formal gray silken dresses down to her ankles. And it is fitting, I think, that the essential family in a book of mine, *Willie Bea and the Time the Martians Landed* should be named Wing, too, in order to keep the memory of Miss Wing final and safe.

It is my habit to crystallize memories important to me within a fiction. The real Miss Wing was a tiny, birdlike woman, softly wrinkled and yellow in skin coloring. I adored her. The fictional Wing family has the same coloring, but their service to the fiction is much harsher in tone, in character and content, than the real Miss Wing would have been. What remains constant, I think, is the point of view from the real experience into the fictional portrayal. I saw the real Miss Wing through steady, vibrant, adolescent eyes. One views the fictional condition through the same eyes. If the portrayals seem at all vivid, it is because the extreme clarity and vitality of youth, that extraordinary young energy, *is* the seeing eye.

If I may return to freedom for a moment, I think what my parents did for me without realizing it was to give me the sense that I was free to *create my own mind*. It is a belief that I cherish, that allowed me to bring to my own young people that same belief for them. And it further allowed me to find my own way in the literature I create. What rules I go by have come from my lack of concern for rules or proper ways of doing things. I feel free enough to deal in fantasy, for example, while not writing fantasy in particular. In this way, I am able to go beyond realism to aim a fictional world beyond itself.

I am most successful at this in books that are classified as adolescent, young adult literature. *Junius Over Far* and *A Little Love* fall into this category. *Sweet Whispers, Brother Rush* does not quite; and yet, I see it as sort of a pretrial for *A Little Love*, and I will have something to say about it a little later. *Junius Over Far* is an adventure romance; *A Little Love* is a "love" romance. *Junius* adheres closely to the formula, "Boy meets girl, boy loses girl, boy wins girl." But the love angle is hardly central to this story. The adventure plot is more significant. But more important than either is the marvelous journey that the character Junius must take and which is essential to any traditional romance. In the novel, Junius and his fater, Damius, begin a journey to find out about the trouble Grandfather Jackabo is having. There is a generational test, or struggle, and all three male members of the Damius Rawlings family—the son, Junius; the father, Damius; and Grandfather Jackabo—seem to be warring with some inner turmoil.

In the end, they will return to the point at which the journey or inner struggle began. The traditional reality romance is aimed somewhat beyond, in the sense that the book's main characters are black and the predominant speech is West Indian, and the traditional locus or setting is the black milieu of a Caribbean island.

The romance of the novel *A Little Love* is traditional in the "love" romance sense. The love is symbolically related to spring and spring green, new growth, and beginnings. Sheema Hadley's ordeal will be overcome by a happy ending. But not before she embarks on a journey in search of her missing father, which symbolizes her search for selfhood, definition, and maturity. In this book, the boy meets girl formula is altered in that from the very beginning, Sheema has someone who loves her. The young man, Forrest, never falters in his love for her. By the end of the book he loves her more, enough to ask her to marry him. And, by the end, our heroine will be victorious in her awareness of her own value and acquiring the tools she needs for a better life.

Sheema Hadley from *A Little Love* is not a traditional romantic heroine. She is overweight; she is not particularly pretty. She is black. She is poor and speaks a street language that adults would find offensive. But Forrest Jones loves her. Her grandmom and grandpop love her without qualification. She doesn't know why anyone would love her, since she sees herself as totally unlovable.

I love Sheema, too. I created her and it's my fault that the world seems stacked against her. But my own quest was to make the reader love her without qualification as well.

The Sheema Hadleys of our society are not often subjects for serious young adult fiction. They do not fall into Western acceptable norms for romantic matter. That is why I choose them as my subjects. They are the forgotten whom I will not forget, and I hope you will not forget.

Now I would like to substitute the novel, *Sweet Whispers, Brother Rush*, for *Junius Over Far* in forming with *A Little Love* a kind of literature triptych with a third romantic novel. First, *Sweet Whispers, Brother*

Rush is not exactly a young adult novel; its subject matter is at times difficult and complex. There is a young man who, let us say, is love literate. There are two young people who are largely on their own. Teresa Pratt takes care of her older brother, Dabney, who is retarded and physically ill. But the romantic formula boy meets girl is altered here to the strong affection between a loving brother and sister. Boy loves girl because sister loses brother when Dabney dies suddenly and tragically. Teresa is so upset by his death that she plans to run away, perhaps to find her father who she remembers only vaguely. But she does not run away, yet thinks that maybe someday she will go off on her own. We know that in the middle book of the triptych, *A Little Love*, Sheema Hadley does take the romantic journey in search of her father. *A Little Love* was meant to be a sequel to *Sweet Whispers*, but then I realized that Sheema was older, different, and both she and Teresa were really individuals in my scheme of teen romances.

The third book is entitled *A White Romance*. It is a traditional love romance, but again with large exceptions to the romance formula. Here there is a dual love angle. The central characters are black and some are white. Here we have genuine friendships. And the traditional romantic love, usually only suggested in the romantic novel, is quite clearly consummated in *A White Romance* as it is in *A Little Love*. The formulaic boy meets girl, boy loves girl, boy wins girl is again altered to girl meets boy, girl loses boy, but finds a different perhaps better boy. The quest or adventure is present, but here it is rough and dangerous and takes place at a heavy metal rock concert in a huge arena in the Midwest.

The traditional narrator is almost nonexistent in this novel. And there are few orthodox transitions. Except for the beginning, the book is almost totally dialogue. We are plunged into the world of a magnet school seen through the eyes of one main character, Talley Barbour, and we are gripped by her vibrant and vivid young adult psyche.

Again, my aim is to have the reader pay attention to and have sympathy for nontraditional characters and lifestyles through patterns of the traditional romance. These characters and their lifestyles are a metaphor for the real world. We Americans need to consider all of us essential to the total fabric of our society. This concept of humanism, the belief in the welfare of us all as one world, is central to my writing.

Our young adult literature tends to remove from the young adults themselves. The slim presence of parallel culture literature would give the impression that such large parallel cultures have no presence and do not exist in America. I wrote *A Little Love*, *Sweet Whispers*, and *A White Romance* with the concept of voiceless, somewhat hopeless young adults, who never have enough words, money, love. Before they are out of their teens they seem beaten, dispirited, characterized by unease.

Will the young people about whom my triptych books are written ever read them? Are these young adults capable of reading books; do they have the mental ease to concentrate long enough; do they care to read?

Most of the time, I avoid such questions. What I must remember is that if there is a young adult somewhere who wishes to extend his or her comprehension of life and lifestyles, who wants to find something between the covers of a book that reflects his or her personal struggles, dreams, or even to find a new sort of entertainment, then these three books will be there for the reading. They are also there for me. Because somewhere deep within, the Sheemas, the Teresas, the Talleys have long since touched me with their special magic.

My son's generation of young adults grew up knowing that books were more important than the flickering images on television. He may love MTV, but he and his friends know that knowledge still comes from the printed word. This may not be true for the next few generations, who may have more difficulty with reading as the glut of videos, computers, and cassette tapes finds more room in their consciousness. It is hard for me to conceive of a world without writing and reading at its center. I hold to the Jonathan Kozol ideal that literacy represents "some sort of answer to a universal need for vindication and for self-perpetuation." And, yet, three-fourths of the world does not have food to eat, and in terms of that deprivation, reading does seem elitist, if not meaningless, and self-perpetuation seems doomed to failure.

American young adults bear the burden of relative ease in their lives. They have endless choices beyond to read or not to read. Moreover, the writer must contend with the large problem of national illiteracy, and black illiteracy in particular. Illiteracy hurts the writer of the parallel cultures most directly. But quite often, nice things do occur cross-culturally and racially. A woman who is white related to me this story of her experience in reading *A Little Love* before giving it to her teenage daughter with a single comment, "I think you will find this book interesting." The daughter read *A Little Love*, enjoyed it.

"But you didn't find the black English difficult?" asked the mother.

"What black English?" said the kid. "Mom, that's the way kids talk."

Well, we know that all kids don't sound like Sheema Hadley. But there is a kind of American hipness among our young adults which comes from following trends on television, in magazines, music and concerts, favorite young stars from a variety of culture stations. All teenagers speak the same language to a great extent, more so than do we adults speak one another's language. Go into a city school, a Midwestern vocational school, any American high school, really, and you will discover that young adults use the same symbol words and sign words no matter what class they come from or what their color. They will inflect key words in the same manner. Young adults all over the country speak of "dweebs" and "wusses" and "nerds." "Chill out" is a watch phrase. One will say, "Jerry is taking Terry out and she's not *even* pretty" with the emphasis on *even*. As teachers of English, you might find my acceptance of colloquial speech simplistic. But young adults use a rich, expressive language. The hope is that they will know standard English and its value, but continue to create their own minds, so to speak, which is expressed through creative English. It was from

169

listening to my son and his friends that I first got the idea for *A White Romance*. They are keen observers of the young adult society and eager participants. They touch me with their honesty and integrity. Jaime has a friend, Chris, who is a wonderful guitarist, who loves most heavy metal music, his choice for himself. He attends, as does my son, any heavy metal concert within a hundred miles of home. I wanted Chris to hear the new cassette by one of my favorite pop singers. He listened to a cut, respectfully, and then struggled with himself as I asked him, "Well, what do you think of it?" Poor young man. Here was Jaime's mother, this writer, asking him something about pop music. He struggled; I could see it on his face. But finally, his sense of himself shone in his eyes. He would tell me the truth and he said, looking me dead in the eye, "I'd rather listen to nothing, *loud*."

He just gave me one of the best lines I'd heard in a long time. My mind couldn't have created that sentence. His did.

We come now to the part of the breakfast talk set aside for the writer's announcements. I have written a sequel to a book entitled *The House of Dies Drear*, which I mention because it is a two-part Wonderworks (PBS) telecast. The sequel is entitled *The Mystery of Drear House*: *The Conclusion of the Dies Drear Chronicle*.

Also I'd like to announce a work in progress, rather like a tragic romance, part fiction and part fact, that takes place in 1854. I believe it is pertinent to the present. It is a slave-rescue case taking place in Boston; it became a famous national cause of the time. I mention it because the past for me is always present. I write largely from the black experience, for an audience as large and varied as I can find. I am not only a black writer for black people, rather I am a writer for people. I believe in the decency of us all. I write from a love of life and fabricating, in search of truth. Sounds silly to say it, but there it is. And to say one thing about the folktale book, *The People Could Fly*. Young adults often enjoy having the tales read out loud to them. I had good results reading to kids at a local college not long ago. These folktales I developed as a metaphor for present-day struggles and accomplishments of parallel culture. These folktales from the plantation era demonstrate that tale telling is not merely a thing of the past, but a continuing cultural imperative.

People of the parallel culture are an oppressed people. There is little American black writing that is not socially conscious or race-conscious writing. In it is thesis and antithesis in search of synthesis. My young adult characters live within a fictional social order characterized by tension and struggle. The final resolve is for awareness, growing consciousness. History teaches us that the progress of civilization is for the growth and refinement of human consciousness, or so we hope.

Imaginative use of language and ideas illuminates for us a human condition which we all share, which reminds us to care who we Americans are. Who are these black people? Who are these white people? Who are all these people; where do they come from; how do they dream; how do they hunger? We are then reminded to value the young—young adults—and to understand what they desire and dream.

Those are my pronouncements. I am awfully pleased to have this opportunity to share some of my reasons for being with you.

BOSTON GLOBE–HORN BOOK
AWARD ACCEPTANCE SPEECH:
Anthony Burns: The Defeat and
Triumph of a Fugitive Slave

Given in Sturbridge, Massachusetts,
on October 24, 1988

I AM VERY HAPPY to be here and to accept this Boston Globe–
Horn Book Award for *Anthony Burns: The Defeat and Triumph of
a Fugitive Slave*. If the nomenclature is significant that describes works
in which individual freedom is the greatest good, then *Anthony Burns*
is best expressed as a narrative of historical reconstruction and a study
in liberation literature. Neither a total life study, nor entirely history
or fiction, it is nevertheless my contribution to the memory of a coura-
geous and humane, gentle man.

If this were the life of any ordinary individual not of a parallel culture who had become enormously famous toward the end of his life,
the factual chronicle of his whole life would have been sifted through
and the empty places investigated, filled where possible and duly recorded. But because Burns was born a slave and grew into a kindly,
self-effacing server in bondage, no one seems to have had the inclina-
tion to look behind the extremely sketchy biographical material of his
early years once he became famous. Nothing more was ever added to a
few facts repeated again and again.

For years, this problem stymied me in the writing of his life. Some of the notations were: Burns was born a slave. He was hired out from the age of six or seven. He traveled to the hiring ground, which was actually a system of slave rental, in charge of several nameless slaves. His father was said to have been a captured freeman taken south into slavery. The father died. Anthony, whose mother was a breeder woman, was a favorite of Master Suttle, the elder, and later, of the younger Suttle. Anthony learned to read and write secretly, sometimes with the help of white children. His desire for freedom gained strength when a fortune-teller prophesied that he would go free.

The development of the man's struggle over time, from childhood to his death, was more important to me than the limitations presented by the lack of historical records of his early life. Thus, for example, taking the slim piece on the prophecy, a scene developed this way:

One day, when he, Anthony, went into the employer's kitchen to eat, he met there the black woman other slaves called a "two-head"—she was a seer. Everyone knew her as Maude Maw.

After introducing himself, he asked, "You can read all what ain't be yet, for true?"

"Done seen behind me, all-time," Maude Maw said, and paused a moment before she went on. "Now can see before me when it please me."

A two-head for true, Anthony thought. "Yessum, well, will it please you to see before you to where I might stand?" Anthony asked.

She stared at Anthony a long time. In a moment it felt as if heat came to him out of her gaze. He felt slightly dizzy and his eyes began to tear, as though he cried. Yet, he felt utter calm inside himself. . . .

"Wings over Jordan," she said. "Never fear. Wings over Jordan."

Meaning of course that he would go free.

But most of the book concerns itself with the thoroughly documented and interpreted latter third of Anthony Burns's life—about nine years. Unfortunately, in the documentation of his escape, capture, trial, and rendition back to Virginia and his ultimate release from bondage, Anthony became lost in the sea of events, in the worthy lives and actions of famous white men, and the convoluted dealings among the infamous. In the past, that was the way his life was portrayed, as significant only in terms of the great cause, the abolition of slavery, or the efforts of great men, as revealed in this scene:

> "When I heard of this case and that Burns was locked up in the Court House, my heart sunk within me." Wendell Phillips bowed his head. . . . "If Boston streets are to be so often desecrated by the sight of returning fugitives," Phillips continued, "let us be there, that we may tell our children that we saw it done. . . . Faneuil Hall, is but our way to the Court House where tomorrow . . . the children of Adams and [John] Hancock are to prove that they are not bastards. Let us prove that we are worthy of liberty," Wendell Philips finished.

Those were Wendell Phillips's words, all documented, given at the Faneuil Hall public meeting of Burns's defenders, May 26, 1854. I don't mean to diminish them in any way. The great words and deeds of men like Phillips are what I consider part of the liberal and often radical heart of this country. The abolition of slavery and the abolition of the Fugitive Slave Act were liberal causes of free and independent citizens in search of radical solutions to federal government conservatism and Southern and Northern racism. The whole time period intrigues me because of the parallels to the present I discover in it.

But my call was to bring the struggles, the hopes, and concerns of the brave soul who had started it all—the fugitive slave—into the light and to center the narrative upon Anthony Burns.

I make choices about whom to portray in writing books of history and liberation. I act as a witness, not only to hear and to know by visualizing and perceiving the past as objective reality. I bear witness, by documenting the evidence of another's suffering and growing awareness of self in the pursuit of freedom.

Liberation literature frees not only the subject of record and evidence but the witness as well, who is also the reader, who then becomes part of the struggle. We take our position then, rightly, as participants alongside the victim. We become emotionally involved in his problem; we suffer and we triumph, as the victim triumphs, in the solution of liberation. Thus, past and present are revealed as one through freedom of the individual.

Sometimes, one writes and feels disquiet for a long time after. But my experience writing *Anthony Burns* and my long involvement with the material seems to have settled me down. Afterward, I was calm. Whatever Burns meant in my life had come to a final and comfortable rest.

Thank you for your acceptance of this work. I'd like to thank Janet Schulman, editor in chief of Alfred Knopf and Random House Books for Young Readers and Stephanie Spinner, associate publisher of Alfred Knopf, executive editor of Random House Books for Young Readers, and my editor on *Anthony Burns*. Stephanie is an editor with exacting sensibilities. When I would want to give up on a difficult scene full of complex ideas, she would urge me on, gently insisting that surely just a little longer and I would find the proper words.

It seems a long time ago that Janet Schulman first spoke to me about doing something "historical" that would be pertinent to today's times. Indeed! So writing the life of Anthony Burns, while a serious experience, also gave me this very pleasant association with people who cared considerably about bringing some of the history of the parallel culture and the truth of the past into the lives of modern young people.

TAKE YOUR TIME

These remarks were made at Travelers in Time: Past, Present, and
to Come, *CLNE at Cambridge University, Cambridge, England,
in 1989. It appears in* Origins of Story: On Writing for Children,
*edited by Barbara Harrison and Gregory Maguire and published
by Margaret K. McElderry Books, 1999. A version of "Take
Your Time" also appeared in* Travelers in Time: Past,
Present, and to Come, *published in 1990 by Green
Bay Publications in collaboration with
Children's Literature New England.*

I AM A PRODUCT of Midwest America. The mighty Ohio River,
some sixty miles from my home, forms great loops in my imagination as it does actually on its snake-and-wind through rich borderland.
Time, in such rural places of America, moves slower than in other,
larger places. No huge shopping mall has descended upon the populace overnight, forever changing the rural landscape. No McDonald's
or Burger King to mar the rural north entrance into the village. The
one Kentucky Fried Chicken franchise, located to the south out of
town and on the highway to Xenia, the county seat, took years to pass
stringent rules of the zoning, planning, and priority boards.

My mother, now ninety-six years old, was born in Yellow Springs.
Her father came there as a fugitive from injustice. The story of Grandpa
Perry's journey from the slave state of Virginia to Ohio defines the

parameters of my creative writing. That I am named Virginia can be no accident. I am the only one of generations named for a state. Serendipity. If I have the aptitude for making desirable discoveries by accident, and I do, time and time again, so, too, did my mother, at least once. By naming me Virginia she made me ever aware of my legacy and my responsibility to history as it relates to my historical past. Ancestry. I am of two minds within my writing, to say nothing of the female force of gender.

I begin a book with a character. I find I write against that character. There is often the stability of tradition and traditional life—timelessness—which is the character's background in opposition to the transient and unstable modern urban life—and time—usually represented by another more worldly character. The power of these opposites is dealt with in separate ideas—past and present, light and dark, staying and leaving, natural and supernatural, tradition, superstition, and enlightenment. Somewhere between the opposites is a synthesis or balance.

My characters have contradictory desires, as do I. Tradition and at least the slowing down of time is likely to win out in my books, but with a profound feeling of sadness and loss.

My being part of a parallel culture—of a minority group in a sense in opposition spiritually and societally to the empowered American culture—adds, I think, to this sense of opposition in my characters. They want to be American; they are black. They are uncertain of their position in society. They move through life and time with *dis*ease. They seek some relief from the conflict. They know that any moment of time and in any place the American dream can become a bad dream and may well become their nightmare. This then is their reality. My grandfather fled slavery toward freedom. But did he find it? My characters search for happiness; does this search cause them to move, to run?

Time is of quality. Remember the time? A grand time was had by all. Once upon a time. In the beginning. My time is your time.

Time to leave. Time to be born. Time to live. Time to die. There is no time.

Time is of quantity. I spent all day. Time hangs heavily. I have time on my hands. His shoulders were bent, were weighted by time. She let time dribble away.

What does happen to time in a book? Whose time is there in a book? What happens to the writer's time; what is its significance, its definition? In a fiction, several kinds of time seem to be at work simultaneously. The real time of the author ceases to exist as she becomes immersed in the time and place of a fiction or nonfiction and within the intensity and time-beat of characters. What begins then is the time of the novel, and the march in time of characters, within which time expands and contracts as if it were a living entity.

In my most experimental work, entitled *Arilla Sun Down*, I use all manner of literary devices to expand, bend, and contract time. My main idea for the book was my observation that we all carry our pasts around with us. Some of that past is conscious, but a good deal of it remains steeped in childhood or the layers of the unconscious. Nevertheless, we respond to that past as though we remembered it, through mannerisms, tone of voice. We reflect the looks of mothers, grandparents, and so forth. We have character propensities that sometimes are unfathomable to us, but may seem perfectly reasonable to a relative who observes biological evolution in action. "Son, you walk just like your granddaddy. You never knew him, but you walk and sound just like him," a relative might say.

My thought was to give the past and present in *Arilla Sun Down* a feeling of simultaneousness by alternating different time frames and focusing as though both were there in the present before the reader's eyes. The protagonist is a teenager but the book opens when she is a small child. The language of the narration is stylized to reflect the distortion in time and the otherworldliness of unknown memory. The child would not remember her early years. So the author uses poetic license.

From chapter one, page one of *Arilla Sun Down*:

Late in the big night and snow has no end. Taking me a long kind of time going to the hill. Would be afraid if not for the moon and knowing Sun-Stone Father is sledding. Way off, hear him go, "Whoop-eeeee!" Real thin sound, go "Whoop-eeeee!"

If Mother could see me, she would say, *What you doing up? Get back under the covers. Catching your death.* But Mama sleeping on. I can slip on out to the moondust snow. She not seeing everything I do, like she say.

Now hurry to follow all of the tracks going deep in the snow. Knowing there is some big hill where all tracks of children go. Downhill is deep in a moonshade and ends at a cliff. Only Stone Father can stop a sled in time. I can't stop it. Jack Sun Run wouldn't care to try. I am smallest, knowing nothing for sure. But I think my brother, Jack, is a horse.

Jack Sun Run still sleeping. He is bigger. But I am who slipping away.

Arilla finds her father and persuades him to sled with her down the dangerous hill at the bottom of which there is no fence, only a deep gorge. Her father tells her:

"Arilla, now hear me. . . . If the creeps come over you, don't let loose, or I'll never catch you in the present time."

"Knowing that for sure," I saying. Downhill ends at a cliff. Over the cliff is another time. Having seen no one go over or coming back. They say three people have gone. Two boys and an uncle, so they say.

In Arilla's and her father's lifetime cycles, death is not the end of time, but simply not the present time. It is described as "another time," all things in their cycle of life being equal.

By the second chapter, we are back into what can be thought of as present time. Arilla is no longer a child. But let her speak and you will see how she sounds in her present:

For sure, my Birthday would be a disaster. I mean, worse than the time they tell about when that Learjet piloted by some rock-and-roll star-boys crash-landed in Wilson Onderdock's Black-Angus pasture a mile outside of town. Knowing something about Black Angus and Onderdocks gives a clue to what kind of engagement went on in that cow pasture for half the night. Even if one of the star-boys was bleeding all over the place, Wilson Onderdock said *nobody* was getting any blood transfusion and an ambulance ride until his prize bull hanging in little chunks on the fence was paid for.

My Birthday was shaping up to be the same kind of for-real bust. I would be surprised if there wasn't a little blood and guts somewhere in it, too. Because any event that had me at the edge of it when I was supposed to be dead center, and had Jack Sun Run at the center when he shouldn't've been there at all, was doomed any sixteen ways you wanted to look at it. It was just that with my brother being the Sun, if the day didn't naturally revolve around him, then it couldn't happen.

The power of the sun. We reckon time by the earth's rotation around the sun, and so, too, do Arilla and the whole book actually revolve through the time of this fictional world around Jack Sun Run Adams. Between the time of the child, the first section that I quoted from *Arilla Sun Down*, and the section about Arilla grown to teenhood, lies time and its passage, change over years, parts of which Arilla may actually recall. But she cannot recall all of it. A gentle Indian man by the name of James False Face whose secret name is Talking Story has profound influence over her development; so that, by the end of the book, when he, through a shadowy, ghost, or dead time—he, himself is dead—reveals to Arilla her secret name, she is already aware of it, and knows she is the Wordkeeper:

> *Wordkeeper?*
> *"Hearing you, too."*
> *Think of a time, any time, and I will be with you.*
> *"But you going now?"*
> *Yes.*
> *"Can't I going with you?"*
> *Yes, if you want to.*
> *"Is it far—going?"*
> *It is only in a circle.*
> *"Then you coming back again?"*
> *I am here and now, then and there, in all things.*
> *"You just going around?"*
> *Yes.*
> *"Then I thinking to stay here."*
> *Stay, then. Live with honor. And Wordkeeper?*
> *"I hear you."*
> *Remember who you are.*

Time as a circle is an ancient concept. Think of Cronus devouring his own children, the offspring of time itself. It is also an Amerindian concept and that of countless other peoples. Ashes to ashes and dust to dust.

Because of the stylized language of this section, the psychic distance is not distracting. In fact, the psychic distance between the characters and the reader is almost nil. The reader feels that she or he is somewhere there between Wordkeeper and Talking Story, who is himself speaking softly either in Arilla Wordkeeper's head or in her ear. Stylization and a close-up psychic distance enables the author to avoid sentimentalizing Arilla's profound sense of loss because of James False Face's death. We can use all manner of distancing to present events in time. "It was Saturday, Arilla Adams stood waiting." (That's one distance, rather remote and somewhat formal.) "Arilla hated being on a horse." (That's a closer distance.) "Lord, the smell of the horse made her ill." (Still closer.) "The rain seeped down her neck, it covered her hair, freezing, turning her lips blue." (Very close, indeed, we're right up front.) Psychic distancings are moves of a camera. Books usually begin with remote or medium shots, and as we focus in on the protagonist, we are close up and intimate or personal. The mind created the camera, and as we see our characters in action, in time, place, and space, we see in terms of the camera eye.

I would guess that I am intimately involved in this Wordkeeper section I've quoted. The symbolism is great here. James False Face is a veiled reference to the Paul Laurence Dunbar poem, "We Wear the Mask."

> We wear the mask that grins and lies,
> It hides our cheeks and shades our eyes—
> This debt we pay to human guile;
> With torn and bleeding hearts we smile . . .
> We wear the mask!
> (Dunbar, "We Wear the Mask," 1896)

James is my father's middle name. It is certainly true that the exchange between Wordkeeper and Talking Story is somehow a farewell to my deceased father. It is I, the author, saying, "Never fear, what you desired all your life for yourself and was thwarted will be carried on by your children. There is a keeper and the keeper protects the flame through her time, and passes it along."

ADDRESS TO THE 1990 GRADUATING CLASS OF BANK STREET COLLEGE OF EDUCATION

New York City, 1990

*T*HANK YOU President Shenker, distinguished alumni, members of the board of trustees, members of the faculty, administrators, friends, parents, and the 1990 graduating class. I gratefully accept the honor graciously bestowed upon me. I am proud to be a member of this 1990 graduating class, and optimistic, or it is better to say that I am certain, that whatever awaits you graduates will challenge you to give of your intelligence and your abilities to the highest degree. This celebrative day is about happy endings and rather uncertain beginnings. It is about what you have accomplished as education master's students and what you will accomplish as educators. We are in agreement in that we are partners in goals aiming toward the literate society. The literate society is under siege. Our children fight to learn, fight to read, and fight for schooling that will teach them how to progress in a democracy that supposedly values them as aspirant individuals.

And I would like to speak to that literature connection between us, parents and professionals, and them. When we talk about literature in terms of children it sounds a bit high-minded. But as an author who has written some twenty-five or more books for young people, books that are read by Japanese children in their language, by German children in theirs, by Czechoslovakian, Swedish, British, African, French, African American, white American, Chinese, and Latin American young people, one travels to the heart of rather profound language, literature, and societal matters. I believe all children are our treasures. I believe we have buried large portions of our treasures through disinterest, disassociation, neglect, mind abuse, lack of recognition and caring for all of them equally as children and as treasure.

We made the assumption some time ago in this country to advocate not only the fundamental right of all children to read, but also their right to books that reflect their cultural and racial heritage. This is a unique if not a stunning concept for which numbers of nonwhite and white Americans have worked hard to make a reality. That all children have the right to books that reflect their concerns, their needs, and their ethnicity, that all children need to be exposed to other cultures and other races in a real sense and in terms of literature are ideas few countries in the world have responded to positively.

Yet we, ourselves, have not lived up to our own suppositions. Now it is time, I think, that we reassert the assumption and that we rediscover the treasures, dig them up, take a soft cloth to use on the hard labor of commitment and understanding; look at them anew, smooth them so that they shine in the reflected light of our respect for them, our young people.

Literature, like justice, begins on a simple, human level. Such as paying attention, listening, answering questions, seeing the problems, and sensing that our understanding, our kindness, serves a good purpose.

I had a friend, Danny, who some years ago was in elementary school with my son. Danny was very proud of me. He didn't know much about my relationship to the world, but in my hometown I received a lot of attention, and he knew I must be somebody. Since he was in class with my son, Jaime, and they were friends, then he was somebody, too. Danny would sometimes come home with Jaime and he would take time to visit with me. Clearly I had become one of his favorite attractions—the somebody. But then, I believe his concept of me changed, to puzzled curiosity about what I did, the making of books. We talked about that one day. I told him that a book had to have a start and a finish. And in between there had to be something going on, something that would hold the reader there inside the book. "You have to mess around in there and keep things going," I told him.

"You mean like a fight?" he asked.

"Maybe a fight," I answered. "At least, you have to have folks doing things that get them upset and confused and maybe trying things out on one another sometimes."

"You can do that?" Danny wanted to know.

"I can do anything I want to the folks in my books," I said, "and nobody can stop me."

Well, he thought about that. "You're the boss in there," he said. I could tell he liked that. But I was aware he wanted to ask me something very important to him and was having a hard time. Danny stared at me a long time before he, finally, blurted it out: "But where do you get all those different words?" he asked. Well, I was speechless for a moment before I realized that Danny probably had never read a book. And he thought a book was full of words, no two of which were the same. Think of that, think of the fear in Danny, defeating himself, creating failure before he'd even started.

I informed him that I used almost all the same words over and over again in every book. "I don't learn a whole volume of new words each time I write," I said. "For example," I told him, "I use 'the,' 'is,' 'it,' 'he,' 'she,' 'open,' 'close,' 'inside,' 'outside,' 'grass,' 'car,' 'tree,' 'sky,' hundreds of times in books. I only know a certain number of words."

Telling him that seemed to make things a lot easier for him.

But isn't it curious what young people will imagine when they are afraid? And yet, although my young friend wasn't a reader, somewhere along the way he understood the importance of books and reading.

I talk to many young people in and outside of this country, young people from age seven or eight to sixteen and seventeen, and I have never spoken to one of any age who did not know somewhere inside that books and reading and writing were of enormous importance. Even those who weren't readers knew how important reading was. How did they know this? Well, I believe always inside of them as they grow and go to school is that knowledge gleaned from educators like yourselves who serve them, most of whom have served them well. Often it is children's well-kept secret that teachers have truly taught and profoundly influenced them. So that when I enter into their world, I become significant, too. They're amazed that I'm alive, that I'm real. For some strange reason that I'm not quite sure of, they think books are written, I believe, by dead people. That's about as close as I can come to what goes on in their minds when they see me and shout, "Look! It's Ms. Hamilton, she's alive! She's really here." What they are saying really is: "You have come to see us; therefore, we must be important." What occurs is much the same as happens when teachers pay attention to the unspoken yearnings, the feelings of children. The child responds, believing that if the teacher shows a caring, then the child has to be someone of value.

Young people do create enormous problems for themselves. Reading and writing are often not a natural process the way they should be. Reading is made so much easier when it is done simultaneously with writing.

Before 1910, every child who went to school started with a slate and a piece of chalk, and writing and reading were never taught separately. But somewhere in the decade between 1910 and 1920, the slate became a symbol of rural poverty. It was taken away and the process of reading became visual. Human hands as the entry points into a child's brain is not a new concept; it has just been forgotten. Educators have pointed out that children begin intuitively to write and the child's hands are a powerful instrument of learning. When there is sound-symbol connection, the child can learn quickly to put sounds on paper. When a child tells a story, the child learns just as quickly what words mean and what language is.

California educator Lynn Landor founded Children's Own Stories, a literature-based language arts program of which she is program director. It is designed to aid, to complete, or to complement a teacher's curriculum. The program helps young persons to express themselves orally and to write the expressions and read them, which expression come from their own experiences, from the day they start school, Ms. Landor states, and that continue throughout life. In other words, through the use of their own language skills, their own narrations, the young are empowered. They are given authority, they are authorized, they are permitted to progress and grow.

Quoting Ms. Landor: "I wanted them to understand that behind all books—especially the children's books written for them—are people who create stories from their life experiences, real and imaginary." Children are people is the final word from Ms. Landor. They have a right to expect our respect for what they know and say.

I did not start out writing books with a cause in mind. My purpose as a novelist, biographer, and compiler of stories was to entertain myself and others, to write well, to tell good stories and to introduce readers to the joys of literate language. Moreover, I hoped to make a living. All of the above are still my purpose and my goal. But I suppose that which is my heart and soul will out. I've further attempted to portray, not so much the reality, but the essence of a people who are a parallel culture community in America. Taking a worldview, I do not call black people a minority. I've attempted to mark the history and traditions of African Americans through my writing, and to bring readers strong stories out of the parallel culture, past and present, and memorable characters who live near to the best they know how. I involve myself with expressing through fiction and nonfiction the qualities that created characters and real historical individuals bring in empathetic experience to today's children and young adults.

In the nonfiction work, which I find is as significant to me as

1 8 7

my fiction, I've documented the deeds, the defeats, and successes of talented and important individuals who are black, relating their lives and works to the times in which they lived. Young readers may then comprehend, rather painlessly, the idea that society can be of their own making, expressing their needs, which are fundamental to their existence as citizens. If there is a message here, it is that, by doing, they themselves can effect change. The young reader as a responsible part of society is never far from my thoughts as I write.

By no means do I write for one single ethnic group over another. My characters are usually black. They want to be American; they don't always feel that they are. They are uncertain what *American* is and of their position in the American society. They move through life and time with *dis*ease, often. They seek some relief from the conflict, as the great black scholar Dr. W. E. B. Du Bois wrote in 1903 in *The Souls of Black Folk*, a black American has a double consciousness, as "two souls, two thoughts, two unreconciled strivings; two warring ideals in one dark body, whose dogged strength alone keeps it from being torn asunder." I and thou, me and society. Furthermore, there is a contemporary black conscious as well as an ancient one. My parallel culture is American black as well as African, to say nothing of the European strains. We infer the African and make it our own. We aspire to it and we are bound by it; it is hauntingly imagined again and again throughout our folklore and literature.

My characters reveal the double-consciousness born out of Africa and slavery that Dr. Du Bois wrote about so well. At any moment of time and in any place the American dream can turn into a bad dream and may well become their nightmare. This, then, is what I project through my literature as the essence of one parallel culture's reality.

What I write, then, and what children tell us through their own stories is much the same. On many levels it is liberation literature. Through the struggle inside us and outside of us, we and our young people bear witness to our own growth and power, to the passing of time and of history. Little more than two hundreds years have gone by since stories and novels have been published in quantity, developing from the fifteenth-century invention of moveable type.

However, myths, legends, and folklore come to us from an ancient tradition of tale telling. They go back to the very beginnings of the communal existence of hopeful peoples. It is imperative that we tap into this old tradition in teaching our young. For what children say is often what they are feeling, told more clearly than we imagine. I collect and rewrite myths and folktales because I know how close they come to our feeling hearts. Through my tellings, others may retell this age-old lore to suit themselves, which may in turn help to stimulate the telling about their own family cultural heritage.

Telling, writing, reading, learning are a dynamic in which certain expectations are satisfied. Telling gives us an idea about how stories begin and end. Writing teaches the shape of words and their orderly march to logical thinking.

Reading shows us that we are constantly changing our minds and revising our opinions as we read in the very way a writer makes revisions and choices as she writes. I am convinced that when I become excited or moved by a particular passage or scene I am writing so, too, will the reader, at the same point in the story.

The joy is that through books, through reading and writing, our personal self-interest comes to mean an interest and a better understanding of our collective self. We the people have so much in common. We have more in common than is apparent from our differences, and the ways we seem bent on separating ourselves one from another.

To the graduates I would like to reiterate that ahead of you lie educational challenges, really life challenges—for education is life—that when openly and honestly met, will help free our children and thus ourselves from racial and class divisions. The primary educational assumption can be carried along a good deal of the way through artistic and creative processes that you as educators know best how to relate to the young in your charge.

I would end here by again quoting Dr. Du Bois, who revolutionized the thinking of blacks about themselves as well as the thinking of non-blacks about them. Eighty-seven years ago he wrote, "The problem of the twentieth century is the problem of the color line — the relation of the darker to the lighter races of men in Asia and Africa, in America and the islands of the sea."

I am ashamed that we of the twentieth century must hand this sad legacy to you to carry forth into the twenty-first century; 2001 begins your time, you who are graduating today. It is shameful that we have carried such divisive concerns — prejudice, discrimination, injustice — through our children, on through generations.

As educators, you are challenged to help us all out of our past to make things right in your future.

Thank you for your attention. I wish the graduates luck and prosperity. May you have what you need while you earn what you want. It has been my pleasure to share with you what I value most.

REGINA MEDAL
ACCEPTANCE SPEECH

*Given in 1990; the Regina Medal is awarded annually
by the Catholic Library Association "for continued,
distinguished contribution to children's literature
without regard to the nature of the contribution."*

THANK YOU very much. I am so happy to have been selected as the thirty-second recipient of the Regina Medal award for the body of my work or, as the letter to me from the executive director of the Catholic Library Association announcing the award states, "for a lifetime of creating outstanding books for children." I hope I have done that. It isn't what I set out to do. For I had not looked that long or that far when I began.

But I know that if I have accomplished anything, it is because librarians, teachers, and educators have been beside me, also reaching out to give to young people. You are their constituency, as you are mine. Many times, it is because of your careful introductions that my books are placed into young and hopeful hands. I want you to know I am aware of that and I am ever grateful to you.

When I am away from home, which is often, traveling, speaking, my dear mother is mentally right with me. She is one of our elder elderly and in a care center in our hometown. She is not ill; she is old, ninety-seven to be exact, and when I am away a part of my mind is always concerned with her well-being. I know Mother cannot live forever, and it is as if I evoke parts of our past together in order to keep her life with me in spirit. Mother was always so proud of my success over the years. And whenever I could, I made sure she shared in it. When I won the Newbery Medal, the local library had a reception in my honor. All of my relatives came as did friends and colleagues, all day long, even though it poured rain the entire time. Folks greeted Mother first, as was respectful, and then me. I wish everyone could have known her in her prime. Not five feet tall and round, she most resembled Mrs. Santa Claus. One of my cousins at the reception mentioned later that he wasn't sure who was being honored, or who enjoyed the occasion more, me or my mother, she beamed so with pride.

I think I have learned best how to live every stage of life by observing the great dignity and, yes, good humor, with which my mother has entered and gone through the aging process. Naturally, from my observations has come a book. Entitled *Cousins*, it will be published this fall. It is about five cousins, but the eye of it, the resounding spirit of it, focuses on the distance, on the background, where an elderly woman lies quietly through her days in a care center waiting for her eleven-year-old granddaughter to visit.

I wanted you to know that I do not stand alone, but rather as the result of the careful nourishing of my family.

My purpose as a novelist, biographer, and compiler of stories has been to entertain myself and others, to write well, to tell good stories, and to introduce readers to the joys of literate language. Another purpose in my writing did not come early on, but developed slowly as I began to realize my writing had a certain depth. And that has been to portray the essence of a people who are a parallel culture in America. I do not use the term *minority*. In my opinion, it is a deceptive term. *Parallel culture* describes better, I think, the multicultural communities of America. I've attempted to mark the history and traditions of African Americans, a parallel culture people, through writing and to bring readers strong stories and memorable characters living the best that they know how.

My books are rarely planned in note or outline form. I write, usually from a simple and limited thought or idea. But each day thereafter I am involved in expressing through fiction and nonfiction the qualities that created characters and historical individuals who bring an empathetic experience to today's children and young adults.

In the nonfiction work, which I find is as important to me as my fiction, I've documented the deeds, the defeats, and successes of talented and significant individuals, relating their lives and works to the times in which they lived. Young readers may then comprehend rather painlessly the idea that society can be of their own making, expressing their needs, which are fundamental to their existence as citizens. By doing so, they themselves can effect change. The reader as a responsible citizen is never far from my writing process.

Furthermore, in nonfiction writing, truths as facts are placed within a literary system by means of time as history, which historical period is then transformed through the experience of a historical personage into a form of art. In fiction writing, one starts with artistic forms that portray a created character within a time frame and a place, and the literary purpose is directed toward the possibility of truths.

I have said many times that, for as long as I can remember, I've wanted to be a writer. But secretly, I would have given anything to have been a basketball player like my oldest brother, who was a high school basketball star in Ohio in the late 1940s. Oh, he would never do now as a star because he is less than six feet tall. But then, when speed was everything, well, my dad and I would listen to the regional and state contests over the radio and thrill at my brother's daring as he dashed down the court. "There goes Hamilton, stripped the ball right out of Gaber's hands," the announcer intoned. "He's alone. He's up." There's a long pause, an excruciating silence, and then the screaming crowd and the announcer, saying, "That's all folks! K. J. Hamilton Jr. has done it again. Little Yellow Springs has won the regional."

Yes, to be a star like my brother, I wanted that. I settled for cheerleading and girls' basketball, a very different status for women of the 1950s. I wanted to be a singer and was, for a while, in Ohio, Pittsburgh, New York City. I never considered myself a true musician. Singing happened while I was on co-op jobs out of the liberal arts school Antioch College. I moonlighted at night from my day job working for Community Services (the Community Service Society), Harlem, New York, branch, or the Urban League of Pittsburgh. I lived at inexpensive settlement houses or commons, exchanging room and board for a contribution of hours of working with young immigrants, Puerto Ricans, or other ethnic groups. On special evenings, I wore tea-length pink gowns for singing performances, which gowns I thought made me look terribly sophisticated. That I might look ridiculous had not occurred to me at that time.

However, I soon realized I could not present my whole self before the public as a singer must do, whether she felt like it a certain evening or not. Singing was not for me. But all of this time I was a writer, or rather, posing as a writer.

In New York in the middle and late fifties, as an artist, style was everything. I lived in the East Village and later in Greenwich Village, working part-time as a bookkeeper and cost accountant—a day job at which I looked properly businesslike and serious. The rest of the time I was an aspiring artiste. I lounged in coffee shops, wore velvet slacks and a black velvet beret, and read the Sunday *Times*. I smoked cigarettes through a silver cigarette holder. I shudder at the thought. Yet still, looking ridiculous had not entered my vocabulary.

But I was young and frightened, I think. "What if" was entering my thoughts. "What if I can't be a writer?" I worried. "Then what will I do?" Ever so slowly the fear of failure climbed into my being. Who would I become in that enormous city of millions of people? Did they all want to become some great success as I did? In order to be a writer, I would really have to work hard. First I needed to find out how one went about getting published. I hadn't a clue.

But the saying was that if you lived in New York long enough, no matter what your field of endeavor, you would meet all of the people you needed to know. There was another saying repeated again and again: "There are fifty thousand musicians in New York City, all looking for an arranger." Something similar might have been said about writers, "all searching for a publisher." But finally meeting whoever you needed to meet was first the myth and then, as I found out, quite true. Today, my daughter, who is graduating from the master's program at Manhattan School of Music in opera training, has been meeting conductors, managers, and coaches at auditions who she needs to know. It happens. But sometimes it would seem to take forever.

So it was that back then in the late fifties, my serious blue-and-worried period began. I stayed home nights. I shunned human contact; I thought that was the way to become profound. I stayed in my cramped East Village apartment and wrote and wrote, and took novel-writing and short-story courses. Other writers out to become famous also were a revelation. So were the professors, who had a coterie of well-dressed admirers who seemed to follow them from course to course. One novel-writing course was taught by the executive editor of Random House. You see, slowly the romantic who calls herself writer gave way to the realist whose name was worker. Mr. Hiram Haydn of Random House took an interest in my work, was most encouraging. I was his student when he, Michael Bessie, and Alfred Knopf Jr. formed Atheneum Publishers. I so wanted to be published by them, but it wasn't to be.

Being a published author happened quite by accident. A college chum of mine had gotten a job as an ad writer for Macmillan Publishing. "Whatever became of those stories you wrote in college?" she asked one day. "I think they'd make a great children's book." "What's a children's book?" I asked.

She proceeded to explain that there was a field of writing devoted to children's literature. In fact, the Macmillan company had an entire department and support departments of advertising and art production called the Macmillan Children's Book Division. She persisted, trying to get me to take one of my college stories (I had majored in

195

writing at Antioch) and develop it into a book, which I stubbornly refused to do. But finally, to satisfy her, I typed up the original story and let her submit it to this editor she knew.

That twenty-page story called "The West Field" became the finished 127-page book entitled *Zeely*. The editor who loved it from the first was Richard Jackson, who went on to create Bradbury Press. And the editor in chief who went on to publish a number of my works and who taught me an enormous amount about writing for children was Susan Hirschman, whom many of you probably know. My college chum is Janet Schulman with whom I still publish, although at a different publishing house, titles such as *The People Could Fly* and *Anthony Burns: The Defeat and Triumph of a Fugitive Slave.* She is now editor in chief and vice president of Knopf/Random House, Juvenile Books [today it is called Random House Children's Books], and my oldest friend. We are both so busy that we don't get together often. But when we do, for lunch or dinner, or at some quiet breakfast together at an ALA meeting, we cherish the moments, thinking we've come a long way.

I have published twenty-five books in twenty-three years since 1967. I have written twenty-seven; two will be published this fall. I am at work on a companion book to *The People Could Fly* for Janet at Knopf and an omnibus collection of my Jahdu stories plus four new Jahdu stories to be published by Harcourt Brace Jovanovich and illustrated by Barry Moser. Both books are due to the publishers by June 30. I will work night and day for the next few months, which I don't mind.

I call myself a writer, as I have since my college days. Not a children's book writer, not a woman writer, not an American writer, not a black writer. Not a black American woman children's book writer. But a writer. Novel writing has always been my forte. But nonfiction writing is a kind of special love of mine. I don't execute those works often. But when I do, I become deeply involved in the process. As far as I am concerned, there is no other way to proceed with such work. Through the written word, one has to become a part of the real person that one is attempting to make come alive, just as one steeps one's self in the created characters of fiction writing.

Fiction is the creation of reality. The primary subjects of fiction are emotions, beliefs, and human values. By the age of four or five, we have experienced everything we need to write fiction—love, rage, boredom, loss, guilt and fear, and even death. There is personal experience as well as the experience of observation, and both can elicit profound emotional responses in the would-be writer.

As a child, I knew both kinds of memorable experience, and the memory of them feed energy into my writing to this day. The uncle who is killed in a car accident in *Sweet Whispers, Brother Rush,* who is Brother Rush of the story, was a real person, my mother's brother. He was actually killed in the way described in the book. I was the favorite niece he had been bouncing on his knee moments before his death. Of course, as I was an infant, I did not experience the actual event of my uncle's fatal accident. But I heard the story so many times growing up that the depth of it became an experienced event in my imagination.

The heart of any book is the making of its time, place, and story. One begins a story with character, but all characters are shaped by their movement through time shared in one special place. There is the reality place of the author's true existence in real time, and there is the fictional time and place that is a limitless frontier. The reality place, the civilized place, lies next to the fertile, unexplored frontier. The author crisscrosses the border between the two. Hearing the call of the imagination from the frontier, she deciphers the urgent message, as it were.

Often a story of mine will relate to my historical past time. I make the mind-and-time leap back to my ancestral continent and oral narration forward to America and folk telling, on to my hometown time and place and storytelling. From there, the work I do and the way that I do it becomes more abstract, involved with education, critical analysis, research, experience, and imagination. But the time line is unique

197

to each author. The reader comes to believe that the subject and its artistic form have not been presented before, that the reader is having a new experience, something she or he couldn't have imagined. This storytelling feels like the stuff of life. It combines all of the elements of fact and memory, feeling and imagination, to evolve finally into something greater than the sum of these parts.

Place and time are indeed at the heart of things. Place has much to do with the manner in which I create character and plot. I am a product of Midwest America. The mighty Ohio River, some sixty miles from my home, forms great loops of living experience in my imagination, as it does actually on its snake-and-wind through rich border and valley land.

Time in such rural places of America does move slower than in other larger, more densely populated places. No huge shopping mall has descended upon the populace overnight, forever changing the rural landscape. No MacDonald's or Burger King, for instance, to mar the rural north entrance into my hometown.

My hometown has been a village for nearly two hundred years. Five generations of my kinfolk grew up there. Today, the single Kentucky Fried Chicken franchise, located to the south, out of town and on the highway to the county seat of Xenia, took years to pass the stringent rules of the zoning, planning, and priority boards.

Mother was born in the village of Yellow Springs, Ohio. Her father came there as a fugitive from injustice. The story of Grandpa Perry's sojourn from the slave state of Virginia to Ohio defines a parameter of my creative writing. That I am named Virginia can be no accident. I am the only one of my family out of generations named from a state. Serendipity. If I have the aptitude for making desirable discoveries by accident—and I do, time and time again—so, too, did my mother, at least once. By naming me Virginia, she made me ever aware of my legacy and my responsibility to history as it relates to my historical past. I don't believe it an accident that I have written a documentary history about a fugitive, Anthony Burns, from the state of Virginia. The choices I make in my writing subjects often have a lot to do with my ancestry, whether I am aware of it at the outset or not. Also, I am often of two minds within the writing, to say nothing of the female force of gender.

There can be tension in these cross-purposes that allows me to use a technique of opposition. The fabric of my fiction many times becomes a force against itself. For as I begin a book with character, I find that I write against that character. There is a stability of tradition and traditional life—call it timelessness. This represents the character's background in opposition with the transience and unstable modern urban life, which I think of as time-present. Time-present is represented by another more worldly character. The power of these opposites is dealt with in separate ideas—in past and present, in light and dark, in staying and leaving, in natural and supernatural, in tradition and superstition. Somewhere among the opposites is a path for synthesis or balance.

My characters have contradictory desires, as I do. Tradition and at least the slowing down of time is likely to win out in my books, but often with a profound feeling of sadness and of loss. Take the novel, *M.C. Higgins, the Great*, looking at M.C. and his opposite, Lurhetta Outlaw. There is finality in the fact that M.C. uses his great-grandmother Sarah's gravestone in order to strengthen the land against the tearing loose of the spoil heap left over from strip-mining, which heap is swollen by rain and poised precariously above his home. Quoting:

> He [M.C.] made a rectangle large enough and Ben [his friend] fitted the stone in. M.C. shoveled dirt over it and all of them helped Ben pack it in.
>
> "Sarah, good-bye." [M.C. is thinking]
>
> All of this time, the day stayed gray. Sarah's [mountain] was gray. But as the afternoon wore on, the mist rose into gathering clouds from mountain to river. They hung low, crowding above the high steel of M.C.'s pole.
>
> M.C. never looked up, but he sensed the clouds massing.

He knew his work was urgent.

"Lurhetta, good-bye." [Again, M.C., thinking]

"Good-bye, M.C., the Great." [Lurhetta, saying in his thoughts.]

There began to take shape a long, firm kind of mound. The children fed it. M.C. shoveled and Ben packed it. In the immense quiet of Sarah's Mountain late in the day, they formed a wall. And it was rising.

That's the end of the book. The end passage suggests a world wheeling through time and quiet. We sense the immediacy and urgency of time and experience.

In his thoughts, M.C. says good-bye to Lurhetta Outlaw, who as you may remember, wandered into the hills of his home and changed him forever. And in his mind, she says good-bye to him. That is to say that whatever is to be M.C.'s fate will continue to be shaped by the mountain, by his father and mother's regard for past and time and place. Tradition wins M.C.'s heart, but with a new wisdom, with a longing now for risk, modernity, other places, Lurhetta—all, at the moment, beyond his reach and will to know.

My being a part of a parallel culture, in a sense in opposition in some ways to the empowered European parallel culture, adds, I think, to this sense of opposition in my characters. They want to be American; they are black. They are uncertain of their position in society—thus, M.C. swings precariously on his pole.

They move through life and time with *dis*ease. They seek some relief from the conflict. But they know that at any moment of time and in any place the American dream can become a bad dream and may well turn into a nightmare. This, then, is their reality.

My grandfather fled slavery to freedom. But did he find it? By some measures he did, certainly; he obtained land through hard labor and he prospered to some degree.

My characters search for happiness; does this search cause them to move, to run? Two separate thoughts give them strength and unity of definition when at last they do define themselves.

My protagonists are loners, but they are also leaders. They have their own minds, things happen to them and around them. Often, they are the instigators of events. I think of Teresa Pratt, Arilla Adams, Sheema Guidama Hadley, Talley Barbour, Pretty Pearl. You have to admit, they have interesting names! Junior Brown and Buddy Clark in the novel *The Planet of Junior Brown* might be two sides of the same coin. Or mirror images in which one reflection is oddly distorted. But all of these characters define themselves through their own actions.

Characters come to me unbidden. They somehow create themselves out of the needs I must have to define the conflicts of my own nature and imagination. They often present themselves having names, dressed a certain way, and in motion. They are born into my consciousness with conflicting emotions and desires. Once they are visible to me, I execute conscious choice to define and establish them within a plot structure, time frame, and place.

My mode of operation is to capture you entirely from the first sentence, as in this section from *Cousins*. I believe in reading to an audience wherever I go. Next week I will read for RIF [Reading Is Fundamental] in Washington. But here is a taste of the novel which is all of eighty-nine pages long. I read from an early draft of *Cousins*. I believe there is room in the text for the reader to come in and imagine part of the story. We read and fill in the spaces. We begin to notice patterns, a sense of structure, a banding of feelings, and we slowly begin to make sense out of our reading, to recognize a kind of system of signposts which make us feel comfortable as we find out way through.

Reading is a dynamic in which certain expectations are satisfied. While reading, we constantly change our minds, we revise our thoughts in the very way an author makes revisions and choices as she writes. I am convinced that when I am excited or moved by a passage, a scene, so, too, will the reader be.

[PASSAGE SHE READ HERE IS UNKNOWN.]

Ernest Hemingway thought it very bad for a writer to talk about how he writes. "He writes to be read by the eye," he said, "and no explanations nor dissertations should be necessary." Well, that may be so. But from experience, I know that the audiences who hear me always want to know how it's done. And that, of course, is the question of all questions. The answer is adequate at best. But Mr. Hemingway did say something that I do agree with. He said, "Read anything I write for the pleasure of reading it. Whatever else you find will be the measure of what you brought to the reading" (Hemingway, *The Paris Review*, Spring 1958).

I can say at last that writing is a joy for me and I hope reading me is the same for you.

Thank you.

TOGETHER:
VIRGINIA HAMILTON
AND ARNOLD ADOFF

This presentation was given in South Carolina at the annual Writing Improvement Network Literature Conference in 1992. It is representative of a joint program occasionally given by Virginia and Arnold, including a conversational skit between them highlighting the differences in their writing approaches.

GOOD MORNING, everyone. We're very happy to see you and to be here at the Annual Literature Conference of the Writing Improvement Network. It's our first visit to Charleston. However, I'm familiar with the historical preservation here. In fact, South Carolina is one of the richest sources for folktales and legends in this country. Why is it y'all had such unique stories to tell? I don't know, but you certainly did.

Our speaking as a team is fairly unusual, although we've been doing this now for a few years. Now that our children are grown, we can travel together. I usually start out doing the talking. Many of you know Arnold. Being a poet, he is known to write short and tends to talk long. As a novelist, I usually write long and talk short. So I am the designated intro presenter. We've divided our presentations today into parts. We've tried to have some of every part of interest to all writers, teachers, other authors, and so on. The first part is a statement concerning what has become our theme, since we're on the road so much—"Looking For America," which might also be called "Literature and Democracy" or "Multiculturalism as a Way of Life." The middle part has us performing a short skit that demonstrates the differences in the thinking and writing processes of a poet and a prose writer. In the last part, we each will read from our writings and share with you some of the results of the work we do.

Arnold and I travel quite a lot, looking for America. We always find it; yet, it's never the way we think it's going to be. We find that we can never say "This is America." This is the way it is. Because America changes; it's not you, him, or me, alone. America grows before our eyes. It's always somebody else's America, too. And we find we have to keep looking for it the way its people change it. In our writing, we have to rediscover and redefine it time and time again. It seems like only yesterday, but the two of us have been making multicultural literature for over a quarter of a century. Multicultural America means that we, all of us, are many ethnic groups, who are in turn parallel culture societies.

Do I need to say anymore that multicultural America means white people, too? To use my term *parallel culture*, rather than *minority*, is to put us all on the same level. We've made the assumption in America that young readers as well as old have the right not only to read, but to read about themselves, about who they are and what they want. My books entertain, and they also express my feelings about the equal worth of us all. I am a woman, a mother, a sister, an aunt, a daughter, a cousin, an African American, an American, an author. I was once a child, and I know how to write from any of these positions. I create stories through the use of language in which characters become real readers. It's no accident that I love reading and writing and the English language. English is the most flexible and versatile language any writer could hope for. All of my life I've had teachers, mainly teachers of English and literature, who then taught everything, too—reading, writing, math, spelling—who loved what I loved. And they took me seriously, that I wanted to write. In all of my life, I never had a teacher who didn't encourage me.

Some people say that is unusual. I hope not. I hope teachers realize their power and the importance of kindness and fairness as well as firmness. The encouragement I was given went a long way to leading me right here. How one mixes the magic potion of the creative process, heritage, ethnicity, place and time, and language, makes the magic of words and writing. When I sit down to write, I think about all of the things I know about that affect my life. I am a mother, a woman, a sister, an aunt, an African American, a cousin, an American, an author, and I know how to write about all of these . . . positions. While writing, I ask myself: What is important about the characters' lives? I am always aware that the imaginative use of language and ideas can reveal a human condition. I want the reader, the child and the adult, to care about who the characters are. I want readers to understand and feel for the Native American characters or with the white characters. With each book, I hope to create a world in which the characters become real to the reader, with real experiences just as in real life. The creative process for any writer involves heritage, place and time, sociology, psychology, and many other "ologies" and "isms." How one mixes this potion makes the magic of writing and brings the written, created world into sharp focus in our real world.

SKIT

VH: Arnold and I have been married now for thirty-two years, since 1960, and we're still trying to get it right. Living together and writing separately, and for the most part, doing both pretty happily.

AA: [*expand*] And for the lesser part, argumentatively. We disagree a lot. That's because I'm essentially a poet and you are signficantly a fictionist-novelist.

VH: [*eyeballing*] Right.

AA: There is a difference you know, since poetry is the highest art form. [*expand*]

VH: He really believes that. But I think I do know how we are different; that is, we think really differently. Remember that time downtown with the horse?

AA: Oh, don't tell that old story again.

205

VH: But that's it, that story is the key.

AA: What's the key?

VH: I'm about to tell you the story. It's an oldie but goodie, and it is very revealing of the difference between this poet and this novelist.

AA: Really?

VH: I'm sure of it. Are you ready?

AA: Do I have a choice?

VH: [*V. smiles sweetly to audience*] Arnold loves taking walks from our house into town, which is about a mile each way. But now that he's had surgery on his knee, he walks that distance only occasionally. Everyone knows him, and he often stops to talk to friends along the way. Never send the poet for a much-needed stick of butter or a carton of milk—he could be gone for hours. But good books of poetry do develop for him out of this simple exercise of walking, seeing, thinking. One day, he came home from such a walk all excited. "Guess what I saw?" he said. "Don't bother me, I'm working," I told him, from my prone position on the hammock on the patio. Those of you unfamiliar with novelists' work habits please note that daydreaming from the prone position is a sophisticated although neglected technique of the writer's craft which I highly recommend. Ignoring my admonition, the poet continued:

AA: I was downtown and there was this guy on a horse, no saddle.

VH: "Yeah?" says I.

AA: And something spooked the horse. It lit out down the street.

VH: Yeah?

AA: Yeah, and this guy, blond, with this long, ponytail—

VH: Yeah, he wore his hair long, like you do, huh?

AA: But listen, the guy is clinging to the horse's neck, and the horse, tearing down the street like a streak from hell. This guy's ponytail, streaming in the breeze, golden. The horse's tail streaming out, all golden. Both of the tails like sun flags, waving in the breeze.

VH: "No kidding, sun flags," I said, taken by the picture. "What happened?"

AA: Huh?

VH: Well, what happened? Did the guy get thrown off? I bet the horse knocked over Dale Kuder's garden-fresh vegetable stand, right?

AA: No! I don't know what happened. What difference does it make what happened? You always want to know what happened. It was just this guy with the ponytail. His hair streaming back and that horse's.

VH: Do you realize that most of the time you don't make sentences?

AA: [*Ignoring V*] Fantastic! That hair streaming back . . .

VH: Yeah, I get the picture. Just golden.

AA: Fan-tastic. [*eyes shining, staring off at the sunset*]

VH: And that's it, that's the difference between us. The poet's idea of a good story leaves, for the novelist, much to be desired. I am always telling Adoff to make a sentence when he tells me something. In vain, I search for a subject and a verb.

AA: It's true, impressions are my first concern. I stop to frame what I see. An impression doesn't have a history or a time. It just is.

VH: While that which *is* for me starts before the present, maybe at *was*, and may evolve into *will be*. A novelist figures out what is going on and on. Where there's a beginning, there's a continuing and a resolving. Things in my books unfold and in the nonfiction works as well. One uses the same novel process for them, also. Ideas, thoughts begin, progress, and finally end. Thesis, antithesis, synthesis.

AA: But I'd like to stress the similarities between us, particularly, in our backgrounds. My father came from Europe in 1912.

VH: My grandfather Levi Perry was born a slave in Virginia and came to Ohio as a fugitive and freeman in the late 1850s.

AA: I was born in New York City.

VH: I was born on a small truck farm in Yellow Springs, Ohio, and went to college in my home state, to Antioch College and Ohio State University. I was born a female, of course, a hetereosexual writer, American, and African American.

AA: Finally, a poet with an emphasis on inference and implication and that moment of image and impression.

VH: A prose writer interested in and excited by the English language and its uses in narrative, which presupposes the passage of time.

AA: Time for me is the element of rhythm or music in my vertical poems, poetry.

VH: I see time as a vertical through space. Like an infinite spiral attached to an invisible arrow. But on the page, time is a horizontal that begins and ends.

[Arnold begins his approach, talking about the making of a poem: vision and revision . . . and revision again. Unlike Virginia, who carefully wrote out her part, Arnold spoke extemporaneously from notes, which have since disappeared.]

HAMILTON'S APPROACH

My purpose as a novelist, biographer, and compiler of stories has been to entertain myself and others, to tell fine stories, and to introduce readers to the joys of writing literate language. I also want to portray the heart of a people who are a parallel culture community in America. I would prefer that everyone use the term *parallel culture* rather than *minority*. Parallel culture gives equal footing to all societal and ethnic groups that contribute so much to our democracy. I've attempted to mark the history and traditions of African Americans through the writing of the black milieu and by introducing memorable characters who live the best that they know how.

My approach to writing and creating prose means dealing with memories from childhood that do eventually fit within a creative process. That process of imagination is then woven into the fabric of a fiction. I've come to believe that the need to fabricate is my way of solving problems of experience and memory. It is the way I retain the essentials of my heritage perhaps for future generations. My fictions all have a basis in some reality of a small or large experience, although they are rarely wholly autobiographical. I therefore use storytelling through writing as a way to share in community, as my parents did and as did their parents before them.

My family used telling story to define the boundaries of our living. I learn new ways of storytelling all the time. Sometimes words are an obstruction and sometimes they are a revelation. Sitting around the fire, telling stories is a common image and common knowledge. But we don't always realize that peoples use story as a means for keeping their cultural heritage safe and also keeping safe the very language in which the heritage is made symbolic through story.

Interestingly, the Africans who were the first generations of slaves in the plantation era here in the United States saved something of their history and ancestry by putting their African languages within the newly learned English language. Black folktales of that era have many homeland or Mother Africa images and longing. To American ears Afro-English words in the Gullah speech and Geechee dialect can sound strange or foreign as they are rendered in such tales as "Bruh Alligator Meets Trouble" in *The People Could Fly* collection. In that story, there is the Gullah expression "He yeddy but he ain't shum," meaning, "He hears him but he doesn't see him." The Gullah speech was meant to give power to the teller and to save some aspect of the home language.

Often the words met magic, as in "A Wolf and Little Daughter" in the same book collection when Little Daughter sings, "*Tray-bla, Tray-bla, cum qua, kimo.*" The wolf even asks his would-be victim, "Little Daughter, sing that sweetest, goodest song again." And as if to ward off the bad wolf, she does and is saved. Coming into the cave or the hut for early peoples must have meant coming into the warmth around the fire, coming inside, out of harm's way. Stories of hunts and escapes meant getting away and coming inside to safety. Inside was being *with* rather than with*out*. Being safe in order to tell fearlessly about danger.

My father, Kenneth Hamilton, was a natural, a fine tale teller. He told me wonderful stories of past times—of the last great gatherings of the Northern Plains Native Americans for example. Sitting there in

209

the firelight and safety of our home place, he and my mother taught me how a story began and how it ended by just the way they told and retold and recast their lives in terms of what they had seen. Using the gift of his warm Midwestern voice, Dad often told about Canada, where he traveled from Quebec to British Columbia while working as a pullman porter on the Canadian transcontinental railroad.

He might begin a tale: "Did I ever tell you about the time . . . I discovered this bear hunter in Calgary, Alberta?"

"No!" I exclaimed, "Was he lost?"

"I'm still undecided about that," Dad said. "But I found the bear he was after before he did!"

And off he'd run with the story, a bit too long to tell here, although it is fairly short. It can be found in its entirely in my introduction to the "World Folktales and Fables" section of the new *Elements of Literature, First Course*, published by Holt, Rinehart & Winston.

My mother, also a fine storyteller, had a honey-sweet voice all her life. She would start a story with, and I quote: "I remember something about that . . . let me see . . . It reminds me of the time all of the ivy fell from Mrs. Pinkston's house." "All of the ivy fell? All at once?" I'd say, incredulous. "Well when did that happen?" And Mother would be off and running with the tale about "the day the ivy fell." It can be found in its entirety, part true, part fiction or fancy, part tragic, in my novel *Sweet Whispers, Brother Rush*.

They learned storytelling from their mothers and fathers, as I learned from them. And something else I learned: I learned that accounting, narrating, made me feel secure. There was always great comfort and satisfaction in the telling. I feel more comfortable in writing my stories down rather than telling them out loud. But to this day, when I sit down to write, I feel very calm and safe. My blood pressure actually goes down, and I am comforted by all those generations of tellers who enriched my blood with their accounts of themselves and their wishes and dreams. Putting one word down after another in narration, in accounts of events, shows the passage of time. Words in progression take us where we want to go without placing our fragile beings in jeopardy.

I create and re-create my own experiences through memory and imagination formed into a creative process. My ideas are translated at once into characters. Created characters are my way of reaching out from inside myself to the reader. It is how we meet in understanding and community. In writing, we use form and content to make order out of chaotic life. The form I use is what I term the *known*, the *remembered*, and the *imagined*. My memory of my childhood appears to be nearly photographic. Remembered occasions, people, and places are intensely clear and precise. I smell smells, I see colors, I know voices and expressions from my past. What I don't know is whether these memories are true realities or are they somewhat false memories shaped and made orderly to protect some momentous feeling I have that is fragile. My brothers and sisters have different memories of the same events in which we all took part. (You know, sitting around the Thanksgiving table—I might tell a story in which something significant happened to me. And my sister might say, "No, Ginny, that's not the way it was. You weren't even there!") But that's what makes memory and imagination so interesting for the writer.

The *known* are the facts we put in order to write a story. I needed to know about horseback riding and Amerindian renewal and death rituals for my book *Arilla Sun Down*. I had to know about strip mining in order to write the book *M.C. Higgins, the Great*.

The *remembered* is that glimpse of memory or full memories that are the catalyst for the development of a story. My knowledge of woods, of farming, of trapping animals, also figured at this point in the development of *M.C. Higgins, the Great*. It was memory of certain African Americans from my past who had some amount of Cherokee or Shawnee ancestry that gave me the idea for *Arilla Sun Down*. So, too, did the remembered give me images from memory for *The Bells of Christmas*, *Cousins*, *Sweet Whispers*, and so on.

The *imagined*, the third element of the creative process, takes fact and memory, or the known and the remembered, into new dimensions of creativity. By means of invention and analysis, the imagined creates plot and action. It grows the story from the particles or seeds of the known and the remembered. So, finally, it is the work of the imagination that brings the known, the remembered, and the imagined together in plot formation.

It is thesis which is the subject, the author's starting point, and antithesis, which is the contrast or the opposition to the subject. Thesis and antithesis work at odds, fighting it out, to bring about the synthesis or unification of these separate energies. Thesis, antithesis, and synthesis turn the story inside out and bring it to fruition. Every position has its opposition; each positive, its negative. I write by using things (people) in opposition. M.C. at the top of the pole has his obstructive father at the foot of the pole. *Arilla Sun Down* has Jack Sun Run up on his horse, blinding her with his light. Cammy, in *Cousins* has the perfect and beautiful Patty Ann to live up to. Even with the people who could fly, there are those below who cannot. They are the ones left to tell the tale.

All of my books can be plused and minused in a similar fashion. As you read, look for positives and negatives, the opposing forces that figure so importantly in shaping and move the plot along. They aren't everything, of course, not the whole story. A book when it's finished has a life that should have grown through the process more than the sum of its parts. I write from an anonymous inside place and from the need to go out and know and be known by the community. I write as a member of a parallel culture of African Americans whose culture community was once wholly outside of the American mainstream and now weaves in and out of a larger group culture, of many cultures, really.

In my stories, there is nearly always present the protective structure of the family. Where it is not present, the structure is longed for by certain characters in varying degrees of intensity. Again and again, I return to adult and child relationships—mother-child, father-child, grandfather-child, grandmother-child—or the absence of any one of these combinations. The relationships among family members and the dynamics within households is my never-ending story. The need to be inside and safe with all the doors and windows shut tight has many possibilities for the writer. Raise a window, open a door, and there enters the real, disordered world of problems.

Writing is of course, problem solving. My writing takes on many kinds of structures, and I delight in adding to the kinds. I have worked at fiction, biography, and collections as well as original folktales in my Jahdu stories. Jahdu is my mythical creature who is born of no woman but in an old oven beside two loaves of baking bread. Ever after, Jahdu has the magic dust that covered him in the oven. He can be found now in a new collection entitled *The All Jahdu Storybook*. *Drylongso* is presented in the form of a story with pictures. It is wrongly thought of as a picture book. I loved doing a book of that length, and Jerry Pinkney's portraits were lovely for it.

My new book next fall is with Scholastic and is called *Plain City*. The only way I can describe it is to say that it is a novel about a strange, outside child. That's about all I'll say about it, although I did bring along a couple of Floyd Cooper's jacket sketches that I'll probably show in the next session. As of yesterday, I am still working on the copyediting of the book.

Always I try on new structures and ideas in writing. Collections are very significant to our literature. *In the Beginning*, *The Dark Way*, and *The People Could Fly* are deliberate, thought-out works to maintain the tradition of family and storytelling, of giving story, English language, to share in community. My new collection entitled *Many Thousand Gone* is a companion book to the evermore popular *The People Could Fly*, which will be coming out in paperback with *Many Thousand Gone*. Collections demonstrate the magnificence of human imagination from earliest times to the present and the courage of people. So many of us are unaware of the great body of oral narrative which has become literature, originally created in spoken language over periods of time. Children who will become adults, and some,

2 1 3

storytellers themselves, should be made aware of this wonderful tradition. They should look into these books, for it's a way to learn quickly the oral traditions of other cultures.

All of the stories in my collections were at one time told out loud. In the case of the slave escape narratives in *Many Thousand Gone*, they represent the body of the first expressions by African Americans in this country about their lives and themselves in their own words. In fact, the escape narratives that compose *Many Thousand Gone* tell us for the first time how human beings, who were considered property belonging to someone else, felt inside their suffering, inside themselves. Again, it is my way of presenting to you and children my concept of liberation literature, which is the literature that we read of others' struggles to free themselves. And through their triumphs we ourselves are made freer. Lest we forget what is freedom.

In the future, I will continue to do the kinds of books I've been doing. That is fiction, novels, stories with pictures, nonfiction, and fiction collections. Perhaps a biography or two. I do love doing the work of nonfiction. The research in the process is always fascinating. Next I will be working on a younger novel about two boys. And then, probably a collection.

My news from the front: My process never changes. But the most current news is that I've recently finished a weeklong book tour promoting *Many Thousand Gone*. I saw scores of young people in programs from Minneapolis–St. Paul to Richmond, Virginia. Young people were fascinated about where I got my ideas: How I could keep writing after so many years. "How do you fill yourself up," one student asked. Maybe the question really is "When will I empty?" Either way, there's no way of really knowing. But it's always a pleasure to go out to see you and talk to you. A great deal of what we do has to do with your response to it. As long as you encourage us, we will continue. Thank you.

HANS CHRISTIAN ANDERSEN AWARD ACCEPTANCE SPEECH

Given in Berlin, 1992; every other year the International Board on Books for Young People (IBBY) presents the Hans Christian Andersen Awards to a living author and a living illustrator whose complete works have made a lasting contribution to children's literature. The Hans Christian Andersen Award is the highest international recognition given to an author and an illustrator of children's books. The Author's Award has been given since 1956, and the Illustrator's Award has been given since 1966. The Award consists of a gold medal and a diploma, presented at a ceremony during the biennial IBBY Congress.

*I*T IS WITH GREAT pleasure and enormous pride that I accept this, the 1992 Hans Christian Andersen Award. I give thanks to the International Andersen Award jury, chaired by Eva Glistrup of Denmark, who has given so much of its time and effort in support of all the nominees and who bestowed this rare gift on me.

I give thanks to the United States Board of Books for Young People, Dorothy Briley, president, whose board and directors and members have shown high regard for my work over many years. They have demonstrated their unflagging interest by enthusiastically introducing my books to students, both children and adults, in their classrooms, in their articles and reviews in their journals and papers, and through word of mouth. Thanks to all, to IBBY for its concern for literature and children and its support of cultural diversity and to Ronald Jobe, IBBY's president, for being kind and gracious to me always.

To so many friends who are here, thank you for your kind counsel. Thanks to my American editor, Bonnie Verburg, who has an imagination to match my own, the editorial skill of a lancer, and the persuasion of a diplomat. She has come here with me and my husband, Arnold Adoff, a poet and prose writer who has published over forty books. He and I frequently travel together giving readings and lectures. Thanks go to him for taking such good care of our busy lives.

I thank the host country for its hospitality to me and for its generosity in getting me here. Although I have been to Germany, I am visiting Berlin for the very first time. I bring with me the multiple allegiances to sisterhood, motherhood, African American origins, and American citizenship. I am beginning to taste your culture and cuisine. However, I'm not a Berliner . . . nor a Hamburger! [Virginia's sly reference to President John F. Kennedy's famous remark at the Berlin wall was also delivered in German to great laughter and applause.] I appreciate your beautiful city, your museums, and your historic monuments. I congratulate you on the tumbling down of walls and on the preservation of democratic ideals.

I believe that Hans Christian Andersen himself would be most pleased by this gift to me. In no way do I mean to compare myself with him in what I am about to say. But I do believe that he in his time and I in mine hold certain aspects of our lives in common. That is, the experiences in my life and those in his were significant to what he has written and also to what I write. Having been born poor, Andersen had not only his family for support, but also had a devoted mentor. Above all, he had his talent to help him break out of the bonds of what I assume was then a somewhat rigid societal structure.

But of course, black people in America have had to break many bonds in their efforts to better themselves. I am no exception. I had a loving family; I had mentors all through my life. I still have them, they who seem to watch over me as interested, unselfish guardian angels. I think particularly of American educator Zena Sutherland, who hoped

2 1 6

to, but was unable to, come see me so honored. She is the former editor of the University of Chicago's *Bulletin of the Center for Children's Books*, a writer, and a critic. From the beginning of my career, she taught me by means of her fine eye for detail and constructive criticism how to sustain a level of writing that I considered would be my finest level. Throughout my career, Zena Sutherland has been a wise and trusted counselor.

And I think of Dr. Mary Lou White, president-elect of USBBY, who all of the years I have known her, as a professor and a scholar, has been attentive to my books and to presenting them and teaching about them to the widest audience possible. She is always there, a friendly sure hand, the best kind of educator. There have been so many mentors like these two; would that I could name them all.

Perhaps Hans Andersen felt some amount of empathy with those who were enslaved and ill-considered in his time, those stolen and chained African peoples. For in 1840 he wrote the play, *Mulatten* [*The Mulatto*] which portrayed the evils of slavery. At that time, my own great-grandfather may have toiled in the fields of the American South. For it *is* a fact that my grandfather was born a slave in Virginia—thus my first name. In the late 1850s, Grandfather Levi Perry escaped from bondage and ultimately became a free man living in Ohio.

Andersen's work, in the folklore and fairy tale genre, influenced me greatly in my youth by its beauty and integrity and by the regard with which he portrayed the less fortunate. Andersen's characters are not by nature villainous. In his tales, it is the human foibles of cowardice, selfishness, and indifference that diminish human beings. His work's strength is its moral realism. I try my best to imitate him in that.

At one time in his early years, Andersen wanted to sing opera. One of his stories, "The Nightingale," became the Stravinsky opera, *Le Rossignol*, and my daughter, Leigh, now an opera singer, sang the role of the Nightingale in a graduate school production at the Manhattan School of Music in New York. So you see, I consider Mr. Andersen of some personal influence in my life and in my family's life.

I hold in common with most authors of youth literature a high

217

degree of near-photographic memory from my own childhood. Indeed, it is often said that we authors write especially for children because our childhoods were so vital and heartfelt that we cannot let go of them, ever. We do not write about our child selves, necessarily. Indeed, I do not. But I do write about childhood awareness out of my rich, country experience. I truly loved being a child. I still keep inside me that curious six-year-old, that ten-year-old lover of pranks and jokes, and the defiant thirteen-to-fourteen-year-old.

My approach to creating narrative involves childhood memories that are the catalysts for a creative process. That process of imagination is then woven into the fabric of a fiction. The fabrication is my way of solving problems of experience and memory. It is how I retain the essence of my past, perhaps for future generations. My early childhood was of course not global. It was insular, rural, American, small Ohio village, and culturally African American.

I wanted to portray the essence of my ethnic group who are a parallel culture society in my country. Parallel culture rather than minority culture best describes the cultural diversity and equality of American ethnic communities. I've attempted to mark the history and traditions of African Americans, a parallel culture people, through my writing, while bringing readers strong stories and memorable characters living nearly the best they know how.

The imaginative use of language and ideas can illuminate a human condition and bring us mutual understanding. I want readers—children and adults—to care about who these black people, these characters of my books are. I want the books to create a world in which the characters relate directly to real people and move onward to universal emotions. At the same time, I want readers to evaluate through their own insights the worth and integrity of the created world.

My first book, *Zeely*, was published in the fall of 1967, almost exactly twenty-five years ago. And for a quarter of this century, my purpose as a novelist, biographer, and, lately, as a compiler of stories has not changed. It has been to entertain myself and others, to write well, to help reveal and define a people, to tell fine stories, and to introduce readers to the sheer joy of literate language.

Storytelling is my way of presenting to you and sharing with readers my specific American community. It is the way of my parents before me and theirs before them. I descend out of an age-old tradition of using story as a means for keeping my heritage safe, and to keep safe also the language usage in which that heritage is made symbolic through story. I use story as magic, as power. I transmit the magic and the power to those who read. What I gain from the transmission is a prolonged, nearly continuous sense of completeness and satisfaction.

The first generation of bond servants from Africa in the plantation era in the United States was able to save some of their various histories and cultures by adding their African languages, which they were forbidden to speak, to their newly acquired American English. Black folktales out of that era are replete with Mother Africa images and longings. African words were used in the Afro-American stories to empower the teller and to safeguard the aspects of the mother language.

Sitting around the fire and telling stories, African Americans of the plantation times felt powerful as they retained through story some of the pride of African peoples. One of the few pleasures they had was telling tales about themselves and others, tales about animals, and also embellishing stories of escapes to freedom from so-called masters. The truth of the telling was in the radical experience of bondage and in the strengthening, vibrant voice of the teller.

What I do today is much in the same tradition of Africans. Instead of oral telling, I write down my stories in order to preserve something of my present-day life and longings, using much of the regional, colloquial American and African American speech, the ethnicity, and the mores of my parallel culture.

I learn new ways of storytelling all the time as a means for keeping my culture and heritage safe, to keep safe the very language in which that heritage is made symbolic in story. I sometimes re-create some of my own experiences in books through memory and imagination

2 1 9

formed into a creative writing process. My thoughts and ideas are translated at once into characters. Characters redefine the artistic self and re-create it. Created characters are my way of reaching out from inside myself to readers. That is how we meet, I and they, in understanding and community. Indeed my stories reach an ever-widening range, touching young people at home and abroad.

Unfortunately, those young people who might need most to read books like mine may never read them. These would-be children of the world languish in poverty and are enfeebled by hunger. Ours is not a pretty world, where we allow our children to starve or experience the ravages of war. In America, too many children, also, are never still enough, focused enough, or have a calm environment in which to read. In my country, where there are thousands of children's books published each year, thousands of children are unable to read. Reading and writing are often seen as leisure, elite activities pursued for pleasure and relaxation, not meant for every child. What a shame and a tragedy. But we continue forward with our work and our attempt to capture those young people who can be brought to the joys of reading.

I take to heart the U.S. member of the Andersen jury, Jeff Garrett's, suggestion that the two hundred and fifty books submitted for this year's competition be offered to a library or other institution. And then monies from the sale might allow African countries to submit nominations for 1994. It is a generous thought he's had.

I've perhaps spoken too long. It is a long way from home to here and a large transition. Moreover, my books have spoken to you, but I never have. Now I have. From writer to reader. Ours are polycentric, pluralistic nations of the "world village" where we must enter into the bond of learning and understanding together in community. May there always be room for one more teller, listener, and the call and response around the fire. And may the circle of our humanity, the foundation of our literature, go round and round. Let the circle be unbroken from America and from here, from there, from everywhere, to the children of the world. Thanks to all. Good evening.

EVERYTHING OF VALUE:
MORAL REALISM IN
THE LITERATURE
FOR CHILDREN

*This is the 1993 May Hill Arbuthnot Honor Lecture, presented on April 4
in Richmond, Virginia. The 1993 Arbuthnot Lecture was sponsored by
Scott Foresman in cooperation with the Association for Library Service
to Children, the American Library Association, and the Virginia
Center for the Book. The lecturer, announced annually at the ALA
midwinter meeting, may be an author, critic, librarian, historian,
or teacher of children's literature, of any country, who
then prepares a paper considered to be a significant
contribution to the field of children's literature.*

I AM SO PLEASED to have been designated the 1993 May Hill
Arbuthnot Honor Lecturer by the committee of the American
Library Association's Association for Library Service to Children,
Marilyn Iarusso, chair. I am grateful to the committee and Ms. Iarusso
for the invitation. The Virginia Center for the Book, Beverly Bagan,
executive director, selected to host this lecture, honors me by this special attention given over to my work. Many thanks for your enthusiasm and superb preparations for this event. Warm thanks also to Scott
Foresman and all of the sponsoring groups who've made my presence
here possible.

It is my great pleasure to be here today in Richmond. Virginia is, as many of you know, my namesake state. It is the state from which my grandfather Levi Perry fled from bondage. I have little more knowledge than this of Levi's origins. And yet, as a student of history, I find that his beginnings as well as my own are of more than personal interest to me. That early period was a deeply troubled time and a tragedy for a people. It was another world, really, but one from which there is much still to be learned. Today, the great tragedy of many peoples makes one ponder the circumfluent nature of history.

I was given the name Virginia by my mother. I am the late Etta Belle Perry Hamilton's youngest daughter and last-born child. I was in league with her longer than most daughters are with a parent. She died at the age of ninety-seven in 1990. But for many, many years, we talked together every day. I don't remember ever having an argument with her. That doesn't mean I didn't sulk or get angry with her. But she was my sapient companion, my mother-sister, for more than half a century, who is irreplaceable in my life. She named me Virginia lest I, or any one of us who were Perrys, forget the past. She and I spoke little more than "where from" about my name, but she knew me well and knew that one day I would need respond more deeply to it, thus fulfilling whatever questions and promise the name might hold.

My presence here today completes a circle of history in which my own family is profoundly centered. Being here carries me back to Virginia, where my mother's father and his mother labored. I come of my own volition as Levi Perry's mother left under hers, leading him. And it is reasonable that I concentrate these few remarks on him rather than her. She remains nameless throughout oral accounts, as does her husband, sold away from his wife and son. [In later years, Virginia would state with some certainty that Levi's mother's name was Mary Cloud.] She delivered Levi to friends in a town nearby my hometown, revealing to any historical sleuth that she well knew where she was going, after which she promptly disappeared. The boy, Levi, never knew her name more than Mother. Or at least, he never spoke it. We suppose that Great-grandmother Perry worked on the Underground.

Something happened to her, likely, and she was forever gone. This last is a story I tell myself, to finish her life in my mind. Novelists always have to know the ending. If they do not know it, they make it up.

Presently, I feel no deep antagonism caused by this historical past circumstance. Perhaps I would have, I know I would have, if I'd lived in that time and place of Levi. But I believe our human existence represents our struggle to consciousness. Now what I do have is a sense of compassion and enormous curiosity about the rest of my family history, which is tantalizingly, forever out of reach. Unlike the late tennis great, the extraordinary Arthur Ashe, a Virginian, who could trace his ancestry to the 1700s, mine begins and ends in the late 1850s. In a sense, I create a past through writing. I create beginnings as well as endings. My mother, toward the end of her life, had an imagination in full throttle. Aware of an effect of something, say smoke coming in from somewhere outside, she would make up the cause: "Virginia there is someone living in the cellar under the house. Go down and see. Make him stop smoking!"

Having learned much from history, I regard knowledge of past events as one of the best teaching schools, and a systemic narrative in relation to periods of time and social upheavals. My family time line would seem now to have formed a circle. This is a momentous occasion for me in a very personal, highly imaginative way, and not any less real for all that. My grandfather Levi would have been astonished to see me stand here. My own father, K. J. Hamilton, a great teller of stories out of history, would have been most proud. My mother, bless her kind heart, would have said, "I knew you would go far, Virginia; I always told you so." And she did. She and my aunt said I was different, and whatever that meant to them, they certainly relished it.

223

Twenty-six years have passed since the first clock ticking of my professional career. *Zeely* was published in 1967. It has been in print in foreign and domestic editions, and hard- and softcover, without interruption; it still lives on. Considered now an American classic—I am not certain what that means or how one comes to that term for a book—*Zeely* is also used as a supplemental text by school systems and is printed as such. I am told that the young people who read it in its first edition a quarter century ago now present it to their children. Nothing can give a writer more satisfaction than to have a book of hers stay alive.

My thirtieth, most recent offering of literature is published this spring. Titled *Many Thousand Gone: African Americans from Slavery to Freedom*, it is a gathering of true accounts, historical narratives, which I have recast for children. The stories are confessional, originally related by fugitives like Grandfather Levi Perry, who attempted escape on the secret Underground.

Levi's disclosure is not in the book. However, the record of it began as his admonition to his ten children, of whom my mother was the oldest daughter. According to Mother, once a year Levi sat his children down around him and began: "Listen, children, I am going to tell you about slavery and how I ran away from it so it will never ever happen to you."

This type of confessional, Levi's and the narratives in *Many Thousand Gone*, reveals the first instance when African Americans realized they were persons. They knew all along they had selves, but they were told they did not, that they were more like cattle or sheep. And I suppose if those with power over one tell one something long enough, one will come to believe it.

But the Underground former slaves through an act of will were able to know themselves and others and to talk about themselves. With freedom, they could confess all that they felt. They were no longer mute, as were cows and horses. They were not property.

One fugitive, Isabella Baumfree, became famous in her lifetime. After escaping, she confessed,

> I felt so tall within. I felt as if the power of a nation was with me! . . . I went to the Lord an' asked Him to give me a new name. And the Lord gave me Sojourner, because I was to travel

up an' down the land, showin' the people their sins, and bein' a sign unto them. Afterwards I told the Lord I wanted another name, 'cause everybody else had two names; and the Lord gave me Truth, because I was to declare the truth to the people. (Truth, *Narrative of Sojourner Truth*, 1850; *Sojourner Truth: Slave, Prophet, Legend*, 1993)

The time period of *Many Thousand Gone* is from 1619, and the landing of the first *negars* as the Dutch called black Africans whom they brought to the North American shore — one year before the coming of the *Mayflower* to Plymouth in 1620. It was a most terrible time for blacks. And, as the Quaker poet John Greenleaf Whittier wrote in his "Farewell of a Virginia Slave Mother": "Gone, gone, — sold and gone / to the rice-swamp dank and lone, / From Virginia's hills and waters; — / Woe is me, my stolen daughters!" (Whittier, "Farewell of a Virginia Slave Mother to Her Daughters Sold into Southern Bondage," 1838)

Not only a most terrible time for the state of Virginia, but for all Americans on whichever side and an especially frightening time for the slaves. Incidentally, in 1772 certain Virginians, alarmed at the growing number of slaves, petitioned the British king to stop the slave trade. They said that bringing slaves to the colonies "hath long been considered as a trade of great inhumanity . . ." Nothing much came of the petition.

The period would end with the ratification of the Thirteenth Amendment to the Constitution on December 18, 1865. Then there was finally freedom for all of the four million African Americans who had known bondage for almost three centuries. Never before or since has freedom been delivered all at once to so many.

I mention both the first and my most recent published work of literature for the young because again I see the symbolism of a circle. The slim volume *Zeely* looked toward Africa in the very height and darkness and dignity of its protagonist, Zeely, who appeared to be a

Watusi queen to the younger heroine, Geeder. *Many Thousand Gone* carries its strength out of Africa to America. The aphorism is true: What goes around, comes around.

That, in turn, brings to mind the poem "Africa" by dramatist and poet Maya Angelou, and I quote:

> Thus she had lain
> sugarcane sweet
> deserts her hair
> golden her feet
> mountains her breasts
> two Niles her tears.
> Thus she has lain
> Black through the years. . . .
>
> Now she is rising
> remember her pain
> remember the losses
> her screams loud and vain
> remember her riches
> her history slain
> now she is striding
> although she had lain.
> (Angelou, "Africa," 1987)

The poem is not aphoristic. It has a quality of dream; there is the longing for progress and the wish for historical truth. In her prose writings, Ms. Angelou extended the slave confessional and enriched it as a contemporary biographical art form, through which she vividly defines and identifies herself.

I don't mean to belabor the importance of past times. I'm told that when I discuss certain aspects of the plantation era, audiences are made uncomfortable. I'm sure that's so for some, on occasion. I sometimes feel uncomfortable by being compelled to talk about slavery and the slavery system. But I didn't come here to assuage or allay. As Americans, we share the discomfort as we do the history. And we all certainly are aware of how history can dreadfully repeat itself. Many feel ashamed of slavery and its consequences. Some African Americans feel shamed that their ancestors were slaves. I do not. Some whites feel remorse that their ancestors were enslavers. Well, we are all emotional beings. Indeed, there is shame and there is regret. Yet, there is room for our pride — pride in the unsung heroes of different races. Pride in my running-away grandfather Levi and pride in abolitionist John Rankin, who was a white transplanted Southern minister who gave Levi shelter in the North. Feelings are never wrong as an expression of moral outrage, whether they be of contrition, anger, or compassion. It's my belief that history can and must inform our lives in the present.

After a quarter century of creating books, fiction and nonfiction, for the young, I want to talk about "Everything of Value" and the creative impulse as it affects the literature. A writer looks inside herself, creating fictional time, place, and characters. I would say that she has indeed absorbed her personal history as well as African American history within the broad plain of American history and that she has, to quote critic Paul Heins, "transformed them into literature."

I wasn't certain then, in 1975, when Paul Heins wrote his article about me in *Horn Book Magazine* during my Newbery year, whether I was a realist writer. Knowing seemed important at the time. As Mr. Heins mentioned, I had thought of myself as something of a symbolic writer, a symbolist. Thus, just as symbolist painters sought to reveal ideas and emotions by the colors they used and the objects they represented, so I sought to express subjective visions by the dramatic use of language and style in the expression of unusual images of nonobjective reality, in order to evoke feelings.

We see six-and-a-half-foot-tall Zeely, thin as a pole of ebony, transposed by darkness into the Night Traveller. There is M.C. Higgins atop his forty-foot pole, envisioning himself M.C., the Great. And from the same novel, poor Sarah, struggling up her mountain, escaping, hiding, a babe nestled in her weary arms. And more images — the Underground, hidden paths, the hidden treasure in *The House of Dies Drear.* Certainly there are large amounts of realism in my writing. But realism does tend to weave into subjectivity and symbolism. Junior Brown, playing a piano that has no metal strings in *The Planet of Junior Brown.* Miss Peebs, Junior's piano teacher, powdering her feet so her footsteps will trace where she has been. Arilla's father in *Arilla Sun Down,* howling at the moon, saying he is the gray wolf grown weak, wounded too many times.

Mr. Heins said that I am perhaps an inventor, one who takes her experiences and intuitively molds material from them into a pattern and structure. If we need a definition, I rather like his. There have been times, I believe, when I have been inventive, something of an originator. It's not easy talking about myself this way. Yet, who but I can explain my process better?

There's an interesting true story about the inventor, Robert Kearns, who on his wedding night was opening a bottle of champagne when the cork flew up and hit him in the left eye, causing a bloody mess right there in front of his startled bride. His vision was permanently impaired. The freak accident led him to think about the eye's function. Later on, he invented a wiper that worked like an eyelid, and he is credited with inventing the electronic intermittent windshield wiper, which I thoroughly enjoy on my minivan.

But the anecdote about the champagne bottle and its cork is a classic invention story, the invention depending upon this "flash of genius" for its creation. I found this gist of a long story fascinating. Mr. Kearns, who might be described as somewhat odd in the first instance, was said to have been driven crazy by the automobile companies, who refused to acknowledge his patent on the intermittent blade. But after many years in court, at last Kearns was awarded ten million dollars from a single company. And now, he has won millions from the whole industry. Buried somewhere in all that money is the question, Who owns a concept?

Kearns won his case against the automobile industry because of the Principle of Un- or Nonobviousness, which became law in the Patent Act of 1952. The rule appeals to my sense of hilarity, obviously. Before the law's existence in the Patent Act, it was felt that all inventions must reveal a flash of creative genius and not just the skill of the inventor's art. To receive a patent, which is a monopoly, and monopolies are unsuitable in a democracy, an invention need be nonobvious to a person of ordinary skill in the field at the time the invention was made. Therefore, the Kearns patent was valid and the automobile companies had infringed on it.

Yet, Mr. Kearns had the ability to express in court the "flash of genius" concept, which had prevailed since the beginning of patents. This flash, revealed in the incident of the champagne bottle and the cork, is what impressed the jury.

An amusing tale which I can relate to, being aware of in myself, not a flash, but perhaps a streak—a run, a mark—of discernment every now and again in my writings and which feels rather inventive. I hope that I don't write the obvious, that my concepts remain subtle or unobvious to others. I hope my individual experiences have stamped my concepts as my own.

The creative process for me involves a sudden cognizance of image or language, of place, which I uncover all of a moment, as though they had come out of nowhere. I wonder if it was like that in the first time of myth for all those creators of "in the beginning" ideas. An instance of faint feeling, as if all had been emptied, or else, had always been empty. Then in a flash, nothing filled with—something. Mysteriously, ideas for books come to me out of extremely thin air.

In addition, there is, on my part, an understanding of the developmental line, the historical stream of children's literature. I build on what has gone before, just as do inventors like Mr. Kearns, always attempting to stay out of the way of obviousness. My patented inventions, as it were, follow long-established orthodoxy. My fictional plots are based on established conventions for form and content. That I give the story lines my own twist and style and my characters certain distinguishing qualities is perhaps an important feature of my writing creativity.

However, I began my literature from the omission and not from a flash concept. I took what had been neglected or absent from the canon, which would be the black child, and ran with it. I soon became aware of historical literary prototypes of white children — that of the diminutive adult, the mirror-image child with its incomplete reflection. As types, there came the puritan child, the moral child, the learned child, the good child, the bad child, the angel, the brat, the athletic one, the manly one, the weak sister or brother. I have been aware of those shifting ideas and early and late visions of childhood, while searching the heart of the child within myself.

My thinking leans toward the moral sense of the Danish author Hans Christian Andersen and to the classic literary and ideological sensibility of the African American scholar W. E. B. Du Bois. Dr. Du Bois fashioned a "children's number," as he called his children's periodical, that grew out of his work as editor of *Crisis* magazine, the official publication of the NAACP. In January 1920, Du Bois began publishing *The Brownies' Book*, a monthly magazine devoted to "the children of the sun." Jessie Redmond Fauset, a teacher in the New York City schools and a novelist, was the feature editor, bringing poems, stories, and biographies for black children to read. Dr. Du Bois became "the Crow" in his column "As the Crow Flies":

> The crow is black and O so beautiful. . . . He flies far above
> the Earth, looking downward with his sharp eyes. What a lot
> of things he must see and hear and if he could only talk — and
> lo! *The Brownies' Book* has made him talk for you.

The Crow always said how wonderful it was to be black. Above all, *The Brownies' Book* gave the children a magazine published and written by leading members of their African American literary community. The time was two years after the end of World War I. Dr.

Du Bois and his *Brownies' Book* taught me that there were no concerns of adults that when written properly couldn't be of interest to children. Of course, it was possible to introduce the moral sense of things to the young and ideas such as fairness and equality. It is important that I continue to bring what I call the black American hopescape into the literary canon and to present images of black children front and center of the story lines and not as background or politically correct secondary characters.

The fact is that such writing by African American authors was begun in the forties with authors such as Lorenz Graham and Jesse Jackson from Columbus, Ohio. And in 1967, when I started, there was ample room in the youth literature field for new perspectives on the black experience. There was every reason and opportunity for me to make stories of my very own kind. After all, if multiculturalism means anything, it means that a particular ethnic group has a strong and growing sense of itself in the world.

My affinity with Hans Christian Andersen is less obvious than my empathy with Dr. Du Bois. I discussed what I felt was my spiritual connection to him in Berlin, in my Andersen Award acceptance. Hans Andersen decided to leave home at the age of fourteen to seek his fortune; and he told his mother, "It is quite simple. One suffers greatly for a while and then one becomes famous."

Somewhere in my child's heart, that romantic thought lives. The course of action toward the desired career is like that and it is not like that. But the writer is inspired by romantic notions of struggle for one's art, which turn out to be entirely different from the real toil and toll of actual writing.

Andersen's work is inspiring for its integrity and beauty. His portrayal of the less fortunate seems true. Noteworthy is his respect for his characters, even when one is a tiny, powerless toy soldier. Children are quick to respond to the idea that they themselves are persons, even though they are small and powerless. I relate to the fact that Andersen used the classic fairy tale form to create stories of his own, which are

231

so precisely attuned to the style of fairy tale that they are mistaken for these older classics. In fact, reading Andersen's tales, one has the feeling that they have forever been told in the world and that it's not possible that an artist had conceived them. In Andersen's stories, it is human weakness that makes human beings less than what they might be. Clearly, much of his work is autobiographical. An indication of his personal suffering can be found in disguise in the tale of the ugly duckling.

I grew up on the outer edge of the Great Depression. More accurately, I was a child of World War II. I don't remember the Depression, although my ideals were shaped by my parents' response to it. My mother baked and sold cakes. My father was a waiter in a college tearoom. They worked hard on our farm as well—Mother had her six hundred leghorn chickens. I often fed them and pulled morning glories out of the corn for my dad. I received a penny a row for my labor. For Mother, I worked for free. Dad saw to it that the fields were plowed and planted in season. He and my brothers took care of our wallow of hogs, about thirty razorbacks. The aroma of farm life is indelible in my brain.

What I remember clearly were those great ponderous B-17s that flew directly over our house from Patterson Field air force base on their way to the European theater, wave upon wave of them, pulling down the sky. Had I been able to describe the feeling I had on seeing them above, I would have made a story about them.

The time was one of really frightening "isms"—Nazism, Fascism, great threats to democracy, my dad said. He was an FDR New Dealer, and later, a Wendell Wilkie One Worlder. Wartime was a period of economic development also and migrations of peoples, especially black people, as populations shifted in line with expanding opportunities. It was a time also that exploited class and ethnic attitudes. There were large themes to ponder, such as war and peace, a woman's place, and a man's job. All through the forties there were also racial incidents of all kinds that found blacks defending themselves. At the same time, there was much advancement in race relations, both through government intervention and private initiative.

All of these ideas had been a part of adult literature for some time. There was genius and imagination as well as war, in which our country revealed its power, its inventiveness, in bringing its people together to win against totalitarianism and keep safe the ideals our country held dear.

I grew up then, after this great war, at a time when imagination and morality came together in new expressions of equality for all, ethnic self-expression and the like, and attitudes of equal opportunity and a fair share. This was in large part lip service. There were good, caring people out there and their lips were moving. However, the service to progress was infinitely slow. In 1942, black and white advocates of nonviolent action organized the Congress of Racial Equality, CORE, in Chicago. In 1946, President Truman created a Committee on Civil Rights. Yet, African Americans were disillusioned by the forgotten promises of postwar democracy.

In children's literature, there was a growing trend toward more realistic fictional characters in several categories, as in adventure stories for both boys and girls, animal stories, career stories, holiday stories, historical and series stories, and so on. Writer Jesse Jackson's *Call Me Charley*, published in 1945, began his Charley realistic adventure series depicting the life of a young African American in his black neighborhood and in school. Jackson would go on to write vivid stories that seemed true about black youth. He had been writing youth literature more than twenty years when I began.

I think we can say that my work falls into a general story type, which I would call *moral realism*, that has evolved from the old moral tale. I write rural or what I call "town" novels (with the exception of *The Planet of Junior Brown*, which I consider my one city book). Characters are supported by complexities of plot and structure. Morality and values are expressed in themes encompassing ideas of ethnic, cultural, generational, environmental, and egalitarian concerns. I rarely

2 3 3

write single-idea books, unless they are nonfiction. *In the Beginning* comes to mind, but as a one-subject book offering many ideas of creation.

I believe with Andersen that our humanity as it is portrayed in the literature is revealed in the inner strengths or weaknesses of the characters and not by outside agencies, such as social conditions or class structures, although these are certainly elements of contemporary, socially conscious writing. I do not write about discriminatory practices or prejudices as a central theme. Rather, having grown up within the American historical assumption of equality and equal worth, and having been taught that I could strive as hard as I wished and accomplish whatever I was clever enough to, my characters rise or fall on their strengths or weaknesses and what they learn by living. We are of course aware that in former generations my progress would not have been possible because of unenlightened yet powerful social forces against black progress.

Yet, societal pressures of my generation are reflected in the type of books I have produced for children and young adults over the last twenty-five years. It was my opinion that real children, including children of parallel cultures, were having stronger, more varied and realistic experiences than the existing literature would suggest. Let me pause a moment to explain that I use the term *parallel culture* to describe groups formerly called *minority*, to suggest to you that so-called minorities—those blacks, browns, and yellows—make up a vast contingent in the world view. It seems fitting to acknowledge that all peoples stand as equals side by side. Thus parallel culture is a more apt term than minority, which imposes a barrier and a mighty majority behind it.

The strengths of the American adult literature which I respected highly in my collegiate days can be uncovered in some of my novels. I think specifically of *The Magical Adventures of Pretty Pearl*; *M.C. Higgins, the Great*; and *Sweet Whispers, Brother Rush*. They may have greater complexity in plot and writing style than some of the earlier books. There is and was a stream of Carson McCullers, Eudora

Welty, Ralph Ellison, and William Faulkner in my work. Later, when I continued my education in New York, I greatly admired the stately eloquence of Dr. Du Bois's writing. There is sometimes a taste of Robert Louis Stevenson, whose adventuresome style I enjoyed as well as the situations I found of moral conflict.

The works of Mr. Faulkner taught me exceedingly well about the techniques of writing prose. Many mornings before I begin my work, even now, I may leaf through a Faulkner story and read a passage aloud. Reading Faulkner out loud steadies me and allows me to focus myself inside where the writing that is truly mine begins. Faulkner writes in the initiation story "The Old People" about Sam Fathers, the half-Indian, half-black great hunter who takes the white McCaslin boy out hunting to teach him this ancient skill so that the boy can be formally admitted into the exacting hunter's club, into the man's world, by killing his first deer.

These are the Faulkner words that follow the sound of the gun going off:

> The boy did not remember that shot at all. He would live to be eighty, . . . but he would never hear that shot nor remember even the shock of the gun-butt. . . . He was running. Then he was standing over the buck where it lay on the wet earth still in the attitude of speed and not looking at all dead, standing over it shaking and jerking. . . . "Don't walk up to him in front," Sam said. "If he ain't dead, he will cut you all to pieces with his feet. Walk up to him from behind and take him by the horn first, so you can hold his head down until you can jump away. Then slip your other hand down and hook your fingers in his nostrils."
>
> The boy did that—drew the head back and the throat taut and drew Sam Fathers' knife across the throat and Sam stooped and dipped his hands in the hot smoking blood and wiped them back and forth across the boy's face. (Faulkner, "The Old People" from *Go Down, Moses*, 1942)

This is realistic writing combined with fierce romanticism. The romantic hunger for manhood, the romance of the Indian great hunter. The black man, part of both—the romance *and* the Indian; the boy and man both involved in a rite of passage within a very Southern social order.

I wanted to read that passage because it is shocking in its wild beauty of language and action. The picture of the deer lying on the wet earth as if it were still alive and running is a still shot. And then, the "hook your fingers in his nostrils" is totally unexpected.

Social commentary runs through the passage. Sam Fathers never oversteps his place, nor does the boy, in this story. They both know where they belong. The social order of an earlier South is present in that Sam Fathers orders the boy in a manner that would be an unacceptable approach to a white adult male. Yet, reading the whole story, we find out that any command given to Sam Fathers by the adult white male goes unanswered or undone or done within the time that Sam Fathers deems proper. No one tells him what to do. No one can make him do anything he doesn't want to do. Such is the power of this great hunter. He is, for Faulkner, a prototype leading back to Africa and the ancient Amerindian nation. Moreover, it was as if Faulkner would not allow himself the romance of the hunt completely, and he hooked the fingers in the nostrils and had blood spill to remain true not only to the hunt, but to honest writing.

All of Faulkner is full of ideas and learning for anyone who wants to discover. I learned from him and others, like Dr. Du Bois, that good writing for any age can reflect the society in which the author lives. There was a time when the patrician Faulkner lacked respect for black people, although some of his black characters are extraordinarily drawn. He came to learn more and revised his opinion. Many of his stories are about children, and men who are children. Like black Luster, the caretaker of the white man with the mind of a child, Benjy, who loved firelight, in *The Sound and the Fury*.

My romantic notion is that I write fiction and nonfiction, and whatever I may decide to do that falls in between, such as the historical reconstruction *Anthony Burns: The Defeat and Triumph of a Fugitive Slave*, because I am impatient to uncover the spirit of individuality and originality in people real and imagined. And the best way I know how to do that is by writing something all the time, something new that I had not thought of before. There is another reason for writing *Anthony Burns*. He came from Virginia, as did Levi Perry. They were two ordinary men. Burns's story and my grandfather's are classic escape stories.

Always I must test what are my own limitations. I want to believe that the wall of limits moves back before my advancing perception. I truly think that when I see something, I am changed as the something I see is changed. I believe that readers are changed, as I am, by what I write. I hope to change what is real for them and what is really there for them as they read.

Change is what we learn is real. And the real is always changing. I want to change the perception about young people, that generally they are not capable of enjoying complex stories. And I think I have, because young people tell me how much they enjoy the complexities they find in my books. I want young people to know, reading my books, that what they thought should be there was in their minds when they came to read, else how could they know and understand what was in my mind when I wrote? And when they have read and found my mind there, they find something different waiting inside themselves, something of value that may have always been there but that they had only just then perceived.

Reading, perhaps they find they have things in common with an ordinary pole-sitter (M.C. Higgins). They understand the fraught emotions of the leader Bambnua, the huge and ugly winged Slaker of an earth a million years hence in *The Gathering*, book two of the Justice Trilogy. They feel for a retarded young man in shuffling light shoes (*Sweet Whispers, Brother Rush*). They find they can know a small child a-wander in the night snow to find her father sledding a dangerous hill

(*Arilla Sun Down*). Reading, the reader is inside the child, living its childish point of view. Perhaps the youth reader learns that the young person within will always be there, will always be the measure of the would-be man or woman.

So it is that I believe creating fiction and reading fiction relate to the reader and the writer directly. I believe that at the point where I am most excited in writing a passage, so, too, will the reader find excitement in reading the passage. Some of the excitement in writing is figuring out what will open the readers to feel and think and see themselves while reading. That is a wonderful part of the writing process. What will the reader think about at a certain passionate juncture? Will he or she relate the reading experience to a personal experience and, thus, perceive greater meaning?

I am not too concerned about whether the reader knows the theme of the story or a generalization about the story. I am more interested in the reader being in the story. I leave room for readers there inside, if they want to partake. I want to have them live with the landscape, the time of the book, and the characters of the book's world. I am not really sure if the reader will understand all of it. I care deeply that the story move him, the reader, change her, the reader, and overwhelm readers with a new sense of knowing.

Books of mine such as *Many Thousand Gone*, *Anthony Burns*, and *The People Could Fly*, I term *liberation literature*. In this literature, the reader travels with the character in the imagined world of the book and bears witness to the character's trials and suffering and triumphs. To the extent that the protagonist finds liberty, so, too, does the witness, the reader, recognize the struggle as a personal one and perceive a spiritual sense of freedom within.

Life for me has the most meaning in its valuable movement through time. Writing for me means "Everything of Value" that I can put into it that is real according to my lights. Place and voice are of utmost importance to the writing. Before I can complete an idea, I must ground it in its proper place of hopescape and use the proper voice to establish it. Place establishes the multicultural and generational aspects of my work. Place seems nearly to have a life of its own when I write, as when a child, place had vivid life for me.

Children are unique survivors in the real world, where they are powerless to change whatever circumstance. I write about children who struggle to define their own selves. There is an overall plot in the books and in the fictions. But beyond the main plot, there may be story after story. Characters tell stories to themselves and to one another. The narrator, me, tells stories about this or that character. Self-stories that characters tell to themselves are not always the objective truth. And because they are not, the characters falsify reality to make it fit their limited understanding, causing the false reality to eventually come in conflict with the real or objective truth. I will tell story after story to such a degree the reader may be unaware that stories are being told, not only as a method of teaching, but as a technique to expand or contract the narrative in the time of the book.

I think I continue to do what tribal people have in their communities the world over. I weave the history of my tribe into my art, into the fabric of my fiction and nonfiction. I work now in the next year or two in turning ideas into fictions. Inventiveness comes over me at odd moments. I read something or see something, and with the aptitude I have for coming upon what I need by accident—serendipity!—I'm off and running.

Everything I do in writing and will continue to do is based on simplicity of design, the life equation. I am your basic storyteller person, helpless to not tell. There is one large story in my head. I have been trying to tell it on paper the way I see it in my head, all this time, all these many years. Each of us has a story we tell ourselves. It is the story not of what we have and where we are but of what we think is the best for us. It is what we want for ourselves in our secret heart. It is the story of our living right, true, in the world. It is telling ourselves about something of value that we respect.

My new novel to be published next fall is about a girl, Buhlaire, who lives in the town of Plain City, which is the title of the book. It will be published by Blue Sky Press, Scholastic's new hardcover imprint, where you'll find me and my books from now on.

In the novel, *Plain City*, people have made up their minds about Buhlaire Sims simply by looking at her. "Some leftover sixties flower child, took a wrong turn down the highway to Plain City," one of the characters says about her.

It puzzles Buhlaire why people makes things up about her:

"They think they know me," she tells her almost friend, Sandy Brown.

"Buhlaire," says Sandy, "if you'd just not act like you think you're better'n everybody, just to act normal, and like you cared about something half the time, people'ld forget what you look like." Sandy sucked in her breath. She blurted out the last part before she'd thought. She hurried off with her friends.

Buhlaire rushed to the restroom the first chance she got. Peered in the mirror again to see what she must look like to everybody. She had no idea what she looked like outside herself, to people. She knew all the parts but she couldn't place them in any kind of order that was Buhlaire. Each time she looked in a mirror, it was as if she saw this person she didn't know and never expected to see.

While uncovering this remarkable, twelve-year-old Buhlaire, I realized that I see young people, particularly young females, as seeking strength, much the same way I viewed fugitives from that earlier period. Runaways from the slave system ran symbolically in search of self, which is, of course, the ultimate freedom. For when they found freedom, they found their selves. Young girls, developing toward womanhood, are on a quest for self and maturity, as is my protagonist, Buhlaire. In one sense, there is no one quite so free as the one who is oppressed. For that one has developed such liberty of mind and imagination through suffering as to make all things possible by an act of will.

I feel that I have come full circle in this talk, from my past, to meander in the grove of language and ideas, to the present of my work. And my tree in the grove is evergreen, I am pleased to say.

I began writing books with the idea that, being a shy country woman, I would be able to stay at home and thrust my books out into the world. I would be safe under cover of my ancient Osage hedgerow that shields my study and my house from public view. Then my publisher informed me, "Virginia, if you refuse to travel and talk, you might as well start up the tractor and go plow the fields." Or words to that effect. When I talk like this, the sound of my voice speaking seems not quite right. It reminds me of the time my mother was interviewed on the local radio station. When they played the tape back she commented, "That's not me."

When I hear myself speaking I feel that way. I try to make it me. But really, the silence and comfort of written rather than spoken language is who I am. I am every one of those scenes and all of the characters in some part in all of my books. I am indeed of the democratic tradition.

By this forum, the Virginia Center for the Book has given this reluctant speaker a special, suitable environment to feature the ideas and language of her work. Writing has for me meant making language magic. And to present the written word to readers is to make writing glow with incandescent light.

I feel privileged to be here. Thank you again.

A STORYTELLER'S STORY

Keynote speech, given at the Fourth Pacific Rim Conference on Children's Literature, Kyoto, Japan, August 24–28, 1993

A VERY GOOD day to everyone. It is a pleasure to be here in Kyoto for this, the Fourth Pacific Rim Conference on Children's Literature. The Japanese language is not easy for me to say. But I have been listening to tapes and studying. And so, *Ohayoo gozaimasu! Konnichi wa. Ogenki desu ka. Konban wa!* Please forgive me, I am still studying!

I would like to begin this lecture by saying that I write from an anonymous place within myself and from the need to go out and know and be known by the world community. I write as a member of a parallel American culture of African Americans. In past centuries, the African American culture community was once wholly outside of the American mainstream. Now it weaves in and out of many parallel cultures in America, of Asian, Hispanic, Eastern European, Caucasian American, and so on.

With a population of near 250 million, the United States of America is likely the most multicultural nation in the world. There are six or seven important ethnic groups in the country, including those of African, Hispanic, Asian, and ethnic European descents, in relation to the larger Protestant group of white Anglo-Saxon ancestry. To understand America's parallel cultures' imperatives is to know that each of these parallel cultures considers itself a very important and equal part of the fabric of America. In other words, the weave of this fabric represents multiculturalism. New immigrants who are not yet citizens have certain human rights also.

Parallel cultures rather than the term *minorities* best describes the polyethnic, culturally diverse, sometimes integrated and often segregated communities of the present-day United States. You might say that many of us of parallel cultures are still searching for America, looking for what our imaginations tell us is the American heart and dream, and yes, its possibility—the egalitarian democracy it must stand for.

Educator Mabel Segun from Ibadan, Nigeria, who is president of the Children's Literature Association of Nigeria and director of the Children's Literature Documentation and Research Centre, Ibadan, writes, and I quote:

> Multicultural societies are complex in nature. Children who grow up in them are caught up between cultures, sometimes with disastrous results . . . Children of African Americans who have been treated as second-class citizens for a long time have lost their self-esteem. Lack of understanding of other people's cultures often creates a rift between children from different ethnic groups. Children need to be equipped to live in multicultural societies, and a minority of librarians, teachers, parents, and intellectuals and community groups have advocated the use of children's books with positive orientation to combat racism, restore to children their self-esteem by giving them a place and a good image in children's literature, and providing them with information about their countries of origin so that they can become balanced and well-adjusted children.

I and my husband, Arnold Adoff, have attempted to do this through our books over the last twenty-six years.

Ms. Segun goes on to say that "An added 'bonus' is the enrichment value of books which introduce children to the wealth of cultural diversity existing in their societies, as well as in other societies" (Mabel Segun, "At Home Abroad? Multicultural Life in Children's Literature," 1992).

I create and re-create my own experiences, who I am, through memory and imagination formed into a creative writing process. My thoughts and ideas are translated into characters. Created characters are my way of reaching out from inside myself to the reader and what we hold in common among us. That must be our sensibility and our humanity.

There is an important reason why I write. Telling stories allows me to connect with the past generations of my cultural group while writing about the present. I connect my writing with the future by inference of both past and present. In order to do that, I use knowledge of history and present events as well as my own experience.

The first generation of bond servants from Africa in the plantation era in the United States—from 1619–1865—was able to save something of its history and cultures by adding their African languages to their newly acquired English. Black folktales out of that era are replete with Mother Africa images and longings. To northern American ears, Afro-English words of that period, best exemplified in the Gullah language, might seem quite foreign sounding. Gullah, thought to be a corruption of the word *Angola*, the country from which many Africans came to America, is a combination of African languages, American English, and Caribbean colloquial speech. It was at one time one of the most widely known African American languages (black English) in America and was spoken by slave owners as well as slaves.

There are examples of Gullah speech in my *The People Could Fly* collection, as in the tale, "Bruh Alligator Meets Trouble." *Bruh*, in the title, is colloquial speech for the word *brother*. Here is a Gullah sentence from this tale: "He yeddy but he ain't shum," which means in standard English, "He hears him, but he doesn't see him." *Yeddy* is the Gullah word for *hear*; and *shum* is the Gullah word for *see*.

In the plantation era in America, African words were almost always meant to empower the teller while saving some aspect of the mother language. Often the words meant magic, as in the tale, "A Wolf and Little Daughter," from the same collection and these sung words: "*Tray-bla, tray-bla, cum qua, kimo.*" The last three words in Gullah are quite African sounding. The wolf in the story asks his would-be victim, Little Daughter, to sing that "sweetest, goodest song again." And to escape from the bad wolf, she does. "*Tray-bla, tray-bla, cum qua, kimo,*" she sings and is saved. It is a tribute to the power of African folk custom and culture that these stories and words still survive in English and now in Japanese. *The People Could Fly* collection is available here in Japan.

One of my books is called *Drylongso*, published in America in 1992. Its title is taken from the Gullah and from the very earliest black generations in America. The word *drylongso* is the Gullah word for *drought*. The word has never lost its power nor its magic, even in today's African American community. Wherever I go today in the United States, I come upon people who have recently heard the word used. Its meaning has changed somewhat over time. Added are other meanings, such as "ordinary" and "plain." A plain-looking person is known as drylongso. An ordinary condition of weather or having nothing to do — boredom — is drylongso. Also, the word came to mean a human condition. Drylongso has also come to mean destiny and fate.

For the first time, I gave the word *drylongso* a personification, a character. In the book *Drylongso*, a stranger comes to the home of little Lindy and her mother and father in the year 1975, in a period of drought. The character's name is Drylongso. He has with him his talisman, the dowser or divining rod, with which he can find water in the ground. Lindy's family no longer has water, since their well has dried up. Drylongso is a modern folk hero. With his dowser, he finds the water and thus saves the lives of Lindy and her family.

The book *Drylongso* is one story with pictures. It is rather long and part storybook, part novel, and part picture book. It is graced with lovely paintings executed by a master watercolorist, the renowned African American artist Jerry Pinkney.

So then, we can say that I connect the present time to past times

245

through storytelling. How wonderful it must have been the first time a story was told about daring and danger, adventure. How extraordinary to create all of the excitement of the real thing with just words while sitting inside in safety. The teller could tell whatever she wanted while safe and sound, rather than having to be outside, afraid, living an actual experience. Writing one word down after another in narration, making an account of events, brings actual events to life and also marks the passage of time.

I write from the aforementioned parallel culture of African Americans. In past centuries of the plantation era, that culture was completely outside the American mainstream. Presently, it weaves strongly and much more democratically in and out of other group cultures.

In the creative writing process, we use form and content to make order out of chaotic life. The form I use is what I term *the creative triad*, or the combination of fact, memory, and fictive inventiveness.

Facts in the creative triad can be thought of as the objective truths that I need in order to write a story. I needed to know what was in fact the geological formation known in the local lore as the "blue hole" — a bottomless whirlpool in a river — in order to write scientifically about it in my novel entitled *Cousins*. I had to study strip mining and the giant mining machines, coal and steel mills, in order to write the Newbery Award-winning novel *M.C. Higgins, the Great*.

I take from my memory certain associations from my past and heighten those memories through fictive inventiveness toward new dimensions of creativity. By means of intuition and analysis, fictive inventiveness evolves in plot and action. It grows a story from seeds of fact and memory. Finally, it is the work of the imagination, so hard to define, that brings fact and memory together in plot formation. The process involves the subject and its contrasts, or the opposition to the subject. We can call this *thesis* and *antithesis*. These two opposing elements work at odds to bring about a synthesis or unification of story. In the collection *The People Could Fly*, we find the opposite — those who cannot fly. But the ones who cannot fly are also the ones left behind to tell the tale.

The character Teresa, called Tree, in *Sweet Whispers, Brother Rush*, published here as *My Ghost Uncle*, is opposed to her brother, Dabney, and her mother, M'vy.

In my stories, nearly always there is present the protective structure of the family. Where it is absent, the structure is longed for by certain characters, in varying degrees of intensity, as in *My Ghost Uncle* (*Sweet Whispers, Brother Rush*). Again and again, I return to adult and child relationships. The relationships among family members and the dynamics within households, within community, is my personal, never-ending story.

My storytelling combines all of the elements of fact and memory, feeling and imagination, to evolve finally into something somehow greater than the sum of these parts. The prime tool of my writing is narration. By placing events before us, narration tells the story. The movement of an event within narration is by means of time, going from one point to its end. We start a story or even a unit of a story when something is ready to begin. A condition is set, but it is alterable; therefore, it is unstable. We end when something has happened and the condition is now stable and unalterable.

The books I write fall into a category I term *moral realism*, which has evolved from the old moral tale. I write rural or what I call *town novels*. The atmosphere of country, space, environment are important settings of the stories. Characters are supported by complexities of plot and structure. Morality and values are expressed in themes encompassing ideas of ethnic, cultural, generational, environmental, and egalitarian concerns. Rarely do you find single ideas in my books. My plots have many strands. Humanity is shown in my writings by the inner strengths, or by weaknesses, of the characters and not necessarily by outside agencies, such as social conditions or class structures.

247

I do not write about discriminatory practices or prejudice toward African Americans in our society as a central theme. Rather, having grown up within the American historical assumption of equality and equal worth for all, and having been taught that I could strive as hard as I wished and accomplish whatever I was clever enough to, my characters rise or fall on their strengths or weaknesses and by what they learn through living. Yet, you are aware, of course, that if I had lived in earlier generations, my progress would not have been possible because of unenlightened, yet powerful social forces set against black progress. These forces still exist in America. We ethnic Americans still fight the good fight for equal justice and rights. The difference now is that we have political power and government empathy. We also have progressed in huge numbers. There are some thirty million African Americans alone in America.

However, societal pressures of my generation are reflected in the type of books I've produced for children and for young adults over the last twenty-five years. It was my opinion that real children, including children of parallel cultures, were having stronger and far more varied and realistic experiences than the existing literature would suggest.

I write books of strong plots and opinions. They are books for survival. They teach youngsters how best to live in their worlds of limits. Always in writing, I must test those limits through the story lines. I believe that the wall of limits moves back before my readers' advancing perception. I believe that when the reader reads something, she is changed by what she reads. I know that I am changed by what I write. And when I write, I hope to change what is real for readers and what is there before them as they read.

Change is what we learn is real. And the real is always changing. I want to change the perception about young people as well. In America, it is thought by some adults that the young are not capable of enjoying very complex stories. But I know differently. They see complexities of the world and horrors on the nightly news. They know the realism of life. I believe that both positive and negative aspects of television can be a powerful teaching resource on the education of children. Young people write and tell me how much they find pleasure in the complicated text, such as *My Ghost Uncle*.

It is my desire to have young people know, as they read my books, that what they thought should be there was already in their minds when they came to read. Else, how could they know and understand what was in my mind as I wrote? And when they read my words and found my mind there, they found something different waiting inside themselves, something of value that may have always been there but that they had only just then perceived. My words acted as a catalyst.

Reading, perhaps they find they have things in common with an ordinary country lad who sits on a high pole (in my book *M.C. Higgins, the Great*). Or they feel for a retarded young man shuffling around in shoes that shine with lights in my novel *My Ghost Uncle* (*Sweet Whispers, Brother Rush*).

So it is that I believe creating fiction and reading stories relates to the reader and the writer directly. I believe that at the point where I am most excited in writing a passage, so, too, will the reader find excitement in reading the passage. Some of the excitement in writing is figuring out what will open the reader to feel and think anew. That is a wonderful part of the writing process. What will the reader think about a certain stirring moment? Will he or she relate the reading experience to a personal experience and thus perceive greater meaning?

I attempt to reveal through the story lines, both in my fiction and nonfiction work, the voices of young women, particularly those girls who have difficulty expressing themselves in words. Girls like the fictional Teresa Pratt, called Tree in the book *My Ghost Uncle*. And the girl in my new novel, *Plain City*, called Buhlaire Marie Sims. If one can teach young women the words to be used, they might better work through the emotions that cause frustration and anger. Young women are looking for new ways to self-expression. Words are often far down the list in their search. But words are always true, and young women need them more than they may know.

But I often make concessions in my stories. My main characters are always hopeful that there will be solutions to the situations in which they find themselves. My periphery or minor characters are very strong because often they must carry the burden of societal truths in the story lines. In my novel *Plain City*, it is the father of my female protagonist,

Buhlaire, who suffers greatly. Buhlaire experiences her father's suffering through her caring and love for him.

The book *Plain City* ends on a peaceful note. I hope you all will be able to read it someday. There are choices that the young woman, Buhlaire, has made and more to be made. Thus, these acts of selection are her empowerment and are meant to be seen as a part of her gender identity. It is my belief that females in our society are reluctant to make their own decisions because they are not used to being called upon to do so. In my work, I'm interested in pursuing that certain sense of being female, which of course, crosses all racial, cultural, and economic barriers.

Plain City marks the thirtieth title of the books I have had published. I am only sorry that so few of my books have been translated into Japanese and other languages. Twenty-six years have passed since my first book, *Zeely*, was published in 1967. It is about the child, Geeder, who thinks an older girl, the pig herder, six-and-a-half-foot tall Zeely, is an African queen. I believe at one time there was a Japanese edition of the book. In the story, Geeder finds out who Zeely really is. *Zeely* has been in print in foreign and domestic editions for this quarter of a century and it still lives on.

My other most recent offering of literature is published just this past spring. It is titled *Many Thousand Gone*, and it is a companion book to *The People Could Fly* collection. *Many Thousand Gone* is a gathering of true accounts, historical fugitive slave narratives, which I have recast for children. It has wonderful black-and-white drawings and a gorgeous full-color jacket by the premier American artists Leo and Diane Dillon. They also composed the jacket art and illustrations for *The People Could Fly*.

The stories are confessional, originally related by fugitives from slavery like my own grandfather, Levi Perry, who made his escape as a child with his mother on the secret Underground Railroad. Before the end of the American Civil War, they fled from the state of Virginia to the state of Ohio.

That is why my name is Virginia. My mother, Etta Belle Perry Hamilton, named me Virginia so that I could always remember my origins. Grandfather Levi told my mother about his escape and she passed it on to me.

Levi's disclosure is not in the book *Many Thousand Gone.* However, the record of it began as his admonition to his ten children, of whom my mother was the oldest daughter. According to my mother, once a year Levi sat his children down around him and began: "Listen, children, I am going to tell you about slavery and how I ran away from it, to let you know, so slavery will never, ever happen to you."

This type of confessional, Levi's and the narratives in *Many Thousand Gone,* reveal the first instances when African Americans realized they were free persons. They always knew they had selves, but they were told they did not, that they were more like cattle or sheep. And I suppose if those with power over one tell one something long enough, one will come to believe it.

But the fugitives on the Underground Railroad, those fleeing former slaves, through the act of will in escaping, were able to know themselves and others and to talk about themselves. They could confess all that they felt. They were no longer mute, as were cows and horses. They were not any longer property, owned by others.

One fugitive, Isabella Baumfree, after escaping, confessed this way:

> I felt so tall within. I felt as if the power of a nation was with me! . . . I went to the Lord an' asked Him to give me a new name. And the Lord gave me Sojourner, because I was to travel up an' down the land, showin' the people their sins, and bein' a sign unto them. Afterwards I told the Lord I wanted another name, 'cause everybody else had two names; and the Lord gave me Truth, because I was to declare the truth to the people. (Truth, *Narrative of Sojourner Truth,* 1850; *Sojourner Truth: Slave, Prophet, Legend,* 1993)

Sojourner was a famous slave out of the history of that period.

There is not much more I can say to you to express the feelings I have about writing and literature. I am very happy that I am here in Kyoto, this beauteous place! I am so pleased to have so many friends here. I have known Noriko Shima and her family for many, many years. Years ago, she and her then little daughter came to my house in Ohio and stayed there with us for a short time. She met my family and she knew my mother, now deceased. Noriko and I are what we say in America are "soul sisters." Our spirits, our life forces are very much alike. She admires good literature, good writing, as I do. She loves things of beauty, as I do. I struggle with Japanese as she struggles with English, but she is much better at my language than I am with hers! Noriko, my lovely friend, thank you for all you kindnesses!

So then, everyone, thank you all for this wonderful occasion. I hope I have left you with some idea of who Virginia Hamilton is and how her stories sound.

Always I come back to this as I finish — that we all tell part of a story that is the story of our lives, our common ground. There is an essential agreement between us, the writer, the reader, publisher, educator, and parent. We are not without the other. All of us must gather in community, in the common bond that is reading and literature. And last, but never least, let us enter as one into the humanism of our children learning.

Thank you.

VIRGINIA HAMILTON: CONTINUING THE CONVERSATION

Transcribed conversations in the New Advocate, *Vol. 8, No. 2 (Spring 1995), pp. 67–82; Nina Mikkelsen is the author of the biography* Virginia Hamilton *(New York: Twayne/Macmillan, 1994).*

BY NINA MIKKELSEN

*I*N THE SPRING of 1992, Virginia Hamilton and I met in Kent, Ohio, to discuss her books. She was giving an annual address at the Conference on Multicultural Literary Experiences for Youth, which had been established in her name at Kent State University. She was also waiting anxiously to learn who the winner of the Hans Christian Andersen Award would be, since she was the American nominee for writing. I was preparing a critical biography of her work and bursting with questions on every aspect of this prolific and gifted writer's work—themes, narrative strategies, storytelling process, and multicultural concerns. For the next three years, our conversation continued with phone calls, letters, and postcards, as I completed the book and she began to balance the fame and duties of her newly acquired Andersen Award with a busy writing schedule.

The recipient of numerous awards, Hamilton was the first African American writer to win the prestigious John Newbery Medal for *M.C.*

253

Higgins, the Great (1974), a novel about a rural, Midwestern African American family. An earlier book, *The House of Dies Drear* (1968) received the Edgar Allan Poe Award for Best Juvenile Mystery. Two later books were awarded Newbery Honor status: *Sweet Whispers, Brother Rush* (1982), an intricate novel of magical realism, which has garnered more awards than any of her books, and *In the Beginning* (1988), a collection of worldwide creation tales. [*The Planet of Junior Brown* was also a Newbery Honor Book.] Nearly all of Hamilton's books have been named ALA Notable Books, including the intriguing and timely novels of The Justice Cycle (1978–81), a science fantasy trilogy that remains popular with early adolescent readers.

During the last five years, Hamilton has published five more books. *Cousins* (1990) is a strong contemporary novel for younger readers about the friendship—and rivalries—of three female relatives. *Drylongso* (1992) is a long picture book, illustrated with exceptional artistry by Jerry Pinkney, which focuses on an African American family besieged with drought. *Many Thousand Gone: African Americans from Slavery to Freedom* (1993) is a companion volume to *The People Could Fly* (1985), Hamilton's famous collection of black folktales, each book accompanied by the striking illustrations of Leo and Diane Dillon. *Plain City* (1993) is the story of a young girl's search for heritage and cultural identity that echoes one of Hamilton's earliest and best books, *Arilla Sun Down* (1976). And most recently there is *Jaguarundi* (1995), a picture book illustrated by Floyd Cooper and a totally new venture for Hamilton. "This one," she told me just before the book made its debut last October, "is my rain forest book. It's a fantasy about rare and elusive animals. And in the African American tradition, the animals talk."

A farmer's daughter who has a special knowledge of the land and an intense concern for keeping the land safe and green, Hamilton was born in Yellow Springs, Ohio, in 1936. After living in New York City during the turbulent 1960s, where she launched a writing career and a family, she returned, in 1969, with husband Arnold Adoff and their two young children, to her hometown—and the green land of Ohio. There she has remained for the past twenty-six years, producing more than thirty books for children and adolescents.

Frequently praised for her unique blending of artistic integrity and cultural learning, Virginia Hamilton is also recognized for introducing the term *parallel cultures* into the ongoing dialogue about multicultural literature and for her tireless research regarding African and Native American history and folklore. Bringing black heritage, experience, and history together in so many of her books, Hamilton has created her own special version of the theme growing up African American. And all of these subjects—ethnicity and identity, environmental issues, the creative process, and the way heritage, history, and family storytelling affect a writer's work—were what we talked about as the conversation continued.

NM: *It's been a hectic time for you lately—speeches in Germany, Denmark, Canada, Japan, as well as all the talks in this country. How do you manage to do it all? I somehow imagine that you just send in a manuscript and it is published with very few changes. Is it that simple?*

VH: It depends on the book. With *M.C. Higgins, the Great*, the whole book was taken apart and put back together again after I heard from the editors. With *Drylongso*, very few words were changed. *Sweet Whispers* had some editorial suggestions. And there are always scenes you think are great but they are too long, too much description for the movement of the story, and you don't see that.

NM: *Do you revise a great deal before you send off a book?*

VH: That also depends on the book. If I get it right from the beginning, there may not be much difference in the earliest drafts and the final book. Anything that's stream of consciousness, like *Arilla Sun Down* or *A White Romance* is very easy for me. Once I know the material, it's not that difficult. *Cousins* was easy. *Plain City* was the ultimate in difficulty because it was a mental "mind-type" book—interior monologue—action, too, but a lot of gesture-meaning and sign-meaning which is very difficult to execute. The sequel to *Dies Drear* was immensely difficult to do. And a lot of times it depends on whether books are mood pieces, like that one [*The Mystery of Drear House*], more psychology than action-oriented, since they are more difficult.

NM: *And you have to redraft a great deal then?*

VH: I never completely redraft. There may be sections that are harder than other sections, when the concept is abstract and you can't turn it into an action easily. Look at *Willie Bea*. It's all action, very easy to keep moving. The action moves the plot and the characters. I have some scenes of lots of people in tight spaces, in grandparents' houses, and I know what it's like to have a room full of relatives and to see the interactions. I know; I've seen it; so that's very easy. And usually if you notice in my books, I play on threes. There are three characters and they revolve. The threes will work one against the other in opposition. That contrast I use a lot (the opposing forces).

NM: *Was this use of three characters something you noticed that you did naturally (or unconsciously)? Or was it something you consciously developed as a strategy?*

VH: I think the triangle is something you can work easily. I think maybe it has to do with your family orientation. I had two sisters and two brothers. In the Justice books there were two brothers and a girl.

NM: *So three characters move the action more easily?*

VH: Well, there were situations, when I was growing up (and I think for most kids), where, if you have three friends, two will always get together and one will be apart at some point, and sometimes that single person will shift in the group. But it's always two together — and one. And I play on that in a lot of books.

NM: *It sets up a tension, increases the drama?*

VH: That's right, and you notice in *Cousins*, there are three girls, Cammy, Patty Ann, and Elodie.

NM: *Were they based on you and your sisters or cousins?*

VH: The thing is, two things are working here. It really comes out of a true experience I had as a child, and it has a lot to do with where I grew up — the physical location — and where I went to day camp. The terror of the blue hole was so frightening that we never went in. But I always imagined what it would be like. The same way with the book *Zeely*; there was never a Zeely, but I imagined what it would have been like if there had been. A lot of times I do that; I finish a childhood insecurity, curiosity, anxiety.

NM: *With* Cousins, *did you feel you were more Patty Ann — or Cammy? Or did you enter into it at all? Did you ever think of yourself as the girl who was so perfect and did everything so well, since you must have been very gifted in everything yourself? Or were you more Cammy, the rebel?*

VH: There was a little girl in our town who had a little white fur coat when we were in the second grade. She had long, long hair that she could sit on, beautiful, beautiful hair, and once a week we'd all line up to touch her hair. And only the kids who were "in" were allowed to touch her hair, and I was one of them. Now we hated her for that, but we loved her because she had this beautiful hair. (And nobody had hair like this. It was extraordinary — thick and long.) The funny thing is it started out that I had written a story called "Remembering _____," a short story in college about three children — like in the short story in the mini revolution where the populace or the masses turned on the little princess. That was our story; that was our dream. But we never did it. And the same thing about the drowning; there was never a drowning. So when I came to do Cammy and Patty Ann (and Elodie), Patty Ann started out as the little girl who had everything, but as it turned out, she developed her own character. (The girl, in reality, never got good grades [like Patty Ann]. She was a C student.) The story just took off on its own. And there wasn't an Elodie, either, although there was a girl in school whose name was similar to Elodie.

NM: *You're "in" it, but it's not necessarily you as one of these cousins.*

VH: Not unless you say I'm all three of them, which is true because I'm all the characters in a sense; I created them all. If I were

257

a split personality, Cammy would be the integrated personality. And the other part of that story was that at the time I wrote the book, my mother was in a Quaker nursing home, a wonderful facility, and I spent a great deal of time there the last two years of her life.

NM: *I have read that your mother had Indian ancestry. Was it the same for your father? And I always thought as I read* Arilla Sun Down *that it was probably "your" story as a child in a biracial family (that you were Arilla).*

VH: My mother's mother was part Cherokee. My father was not the inspiration for the cross-cultural conflict. He was black, of fairly light complexion and of Creole ancestry. As far as I know there was no Indian. The father in *Arilla* does have the job my father actually had for years at Antioch College, as service manager of the dining halls. But Arilla is not about me; I have always known my identity. I thought it would be interesting to take a case where the Indian influences in a black family were as strong as the black. I remember clearly wondering, what would happen to the siblings, the whole family?

In the book, Arilla is having a problem with identity because her brother has such a strong identity, and my premise was what would happen in a strong black identity family if the Indian identity became *very* strong? The father kept himself separate because he was Native American; the mother was more in the community. Arilla can't identify with the mother, and she isn't sure about identifying with her father because of her brother and his strong feelings of heritage. So there was a kind of problem that I wanted to set up and solve. My Amerindian ancestry has little meaning for me, other than the fact that my mother often talked about it. As far as I know, none of my grandmother's heritage survived to my generation. (There was no cultural imperative to have it survive.) And yet, I seem to have some sensitivity to Amerindian life. At least, my Amerindian friends seem to think so.

NM: *Was Susanne Shy Woman in that book based on someone you knew?*

VH: I created her. I did a lot of research into that aspect of *Arilla*, the black Indians on Cheyenne, Sioux, and Shawnee reservations. The

Cherokee were also quite helpful to blacks, took many into their tribes, after they decided that slavery was wrong.

NM: *So the experiences of the characters are not those of your family or you.*

VH: The whole scene of the Fourth of July is right out of my own Fourth of July experience as a child in Yellow Springs, but the horse riding is not real. My brother's children rode horses, his second wife was a horsewoman, and my children rode horses. But that really is all I know about horses. I had to study in order to write that, and I had my sister-in-law read it. She said everything was technically correct. You'd have to be a very good horsewoman to know I didn't ride horses.

NM: *They tease the mother at the end of the book about whether she will get on a horse.*

VH: Yeah, that's me! And my daughter was always on the small side, although she's now five feet six inches. I wanted her not to be afraid of horses, and she didn't want to be afraid, so she took horseback riding and she was terrified of horses — but she did it. She was determined she was going to control this big horse. She could barely hold its foot up when she was cleaning the hoof, but she rode. I know the smell of the stable and my kids riding and the contests. But she didn't really like it, and I didn't like it.

NM: *The mother is also a dancer or a dancing teacher. Were you a dancer, or was someone in your family a dancer?*

VH: I went to a very artsy school. I knew dancers there, and dancers are so wonderfully funny when they develop their duck walk. It was just a wonderful literary kind of existence and artistic, and maybe that's where I got the idea. But other things were actual [like] the little shrouds of birds in those fast coming storms. I've seen that. And the sun thaws them and they fall, just as Sun falls. Sun falls off a horse because a bird comes down and hits him, and the birds fall because their wings get covered with ice and they fall, too. Another true story is the part when Sun opens the door and says, "Come on in, flies." My brother would get mad at my mother and open the door and say that.

259

NM: *Sun is such a wonderful character. He never does anything to hurt Arilla. All the time he is helping her, even though she's saying he's trying to kill her.*

VH: I love him. That's the sleight of hand that I love to do. What appears to one of the characters (usually the main character) [regarding another character] is not the way the other character is. It's the same with Thomas in the Justice books. What he at first appears to be is not finally the way he is. And Jack Sun Run is not at all as he appears to be, either.

NM: *Arilla and Justice both are the youngest and both feel—*

VH: Vulnerable.

NM: *Is that how you felt, having older brothers?*

VH: Billy, who is four years older, was my tormentor, also my playmate, and he was the one who had all the imagination. He drove me crazy because he played drums. But what I did [in the Justice books] was switch my real brothers' personalities because Billy and I were tight friends by the time he was the age of Levi [Thomas's twin brother]. He was no longer that little bully from when we were younger, and Buster [two years older than Billy] was the smart-alecky one, with the "Thomas" kind of thing. But neither of them was that kid [Thomas]; that's an exaggeration.

NM: *Why did you make Thomas and Levi twins in those books? And there are twins in the Drear books, too [Buster and Billy].*

VH: In the Justice books, I wanted mirror images—light and dark. That's a recurring theme in my books. In the Drear books I wanted to give an indication of mystery. They [Buster and Billy] are just the height of the quatrefoil, when they feel the air, when they stand in front of the door of the Drear house.

NM: *I've always imagined that the Drear house was a real house of the Underground Railroad that you or someone in your family had once lived in. It seems so real.*

VH: It is based on the "idea" of such houses in that part of Ohio and not on any specific house. I knew these houses from osmosis, because in Yellow Springs there were houses with secret rooms and secret passages. I hadn't been in the passages, but I knew that my grandfather came there on the Underground Railroad, so it seemed like I'd always known about them because I've been in them. The orphans in the underground passage of the second Drear book, that's a true account. There were many such orphans at the time.

NM: *I find the second book the richer of the two, for ideas and crafting. But you have said that the first one is the most popular of all your books. Which one do you like best?*

VH: I like them both for different reasons, the first for its action and the second for its psychology and drama. It's a different kind of book [the second one]. It was enormously difficult because I wrote it eighteen years after the first, and everything had changed. Once kids read Stephen King, all bets were off. There wasn't that innocence, and I had to do things a little differently. I had to suggest more but not do any more. I had to make it *seem* more dangerous, but not *be* more dangerous (I can't go into blood and gore). Those books have a classic feel to them because they relate to the past and because I try to create in them a world outside of time, a world that lives on its own.

NM: *You have said that crafting fiction is your way of solving a problem. But you created a sequel to the first Drear book. Was there something else to solve?*

VH: Yes, the problem was the trunk that was never opened in the first book—the trunk hanging from the ceiling in Pluto's cave. Thomas says, "We forgot about the trunk. We never opened it." Then he says, "Let's leave it a mystery." The artistic integrity was allowed to remain in that you leave something for posterity. But psychologically for me, the book wasn't finished. So I opened the trunk in *Arilla Sun Down* and did not discover until years later that there was something missing in the first book. And it bothered and bothered me. There was something wrong with the book. What was it? The mother! There was no Darrow mother in the first book. We don't ever see the mother.

NM: *So you write sequels then—*

VH: If I don't think a book is finished.

NM: *And in the beginning you write the book to solve or resolve some problem.*

VH: Well, I don't know if anybody really knows why they do an artistic thing. But it is some kind of momentum or energy and a certain way of channeling it. I think it has to do with problem solving and with what I call the *known*, the *remembered*, and the *imagined*. I don't know how you write novels. The only way I know is to write them. Whatever that story is that I have to tell, I don't know how to do it except to write it. Each story has a different way that it presents itself, and the problem has to be solved in order to tell the story.

NM: *Do you write to uncover a problem or do you know what the problem is in the beginning?*

VH: I think I'm very story oriented. I think I create characters and the characters create the society in which they live. Once the characters are defined, they have brought their world with them, and so I have uncovered that world. We don't live in a vacuum; we live in a community. And every character is [created] like that. In a sense it's like a painting. You fill in all this around the person — the history, the time, and the place. It's an amazing process. If you start out and you have this picture, then the problem is finding words to describe what you see. And I take everything step-by-step. In some books I describe what I see by the way somebody moves or what they say or how they act. It depends on what story I'm telling. *Sweet Whispers* is probably a classic problem-solving example. When I was a child I saw a ghost. Well, as an adult I know that ghosts don't exist. So there's the conflict: the childhood memory, which is absolutely pure and I know it to this day, and the adult knowing that it didn't happen.

NM: *It sounds like* Zeely. *Zeely says the very same thing about the turtle and the snake.*

VH: That's right. In the real happening for me [in *Sweet Whispers*], I was in my bedroom, which I shared with two sisters (they're both older than me). I was five or six at this time, and I was in a little white slip that I used to wear, and they were talking or singing and the ghost ran across the room into the closet and disappeared. And I said, "Oh! A ghost ran in the closet." My sister ran into the closet and beat up the clothes, and she said, "There, he's gone!" And I knew it wasn't gone, but I went along with it. And I've never forgotten that. When I went to do this book, there was a separation in my psyche; two things were existing together that were diametrically opposed. So the only way to make it work psychologically was to make everybody believe in the ghost. That was the problem, making readers believe that Brother Rush was *there* in the middle of the table (as Tree said, "'Be a damned ghost'"), because you can't resolve something like that. And I have almost a photographic memory of important things. But the problem is whether the memories are *true*. I don't know what you do in the process of growing up, in terms of memory, but I have a feeling that a lot of times you change memory to fit what happens to you as you grow. I have a very strong memory that I saw the ghost. So I was convincing the reader to believe in my original childhood belief.

NM: *You were resolving something for you.*

VH: That's right.

NM: *And do you think you were aware at the time that you were resolving something from the past (it was a conscious rather than an unconscious way of working)?*

VH: Yes, and I think a lot of my books resolve things in my life. And although they come sometimes out of a dark feeling, they're positive, since I'm basically very positive. I have the idea that books for kids have to have some kind of meaning that is not going to bring them down although this is a very bad time.

NM: *When you say "a very bad time," I think of ecology and the environment and the story you tell in the book* Drylongso. *How did it come to you? Why* that *story at this time?*

VH: I had the word *drylongso* in my mind for years before I wrote the book. I think it's a wonderful word. It comes from the early plantation era of the Georgia Sea Islands and is the early black American word, or Gullah word, for *drought*. In this book, a boy is portrayed as a folk hero who uses a divining rod to find water. He represents fortune or destiny, rain, and drought, since it was dry long so [dry for so long]. I wanted to do something with the word for a long, long time, but it was something I never talked about because I didn't know what it was going to be.

When I started researching, I found that there have been very severe droughts every twenty years somewhere in this country. And not too long ago (1975 or 1978), there was what they call a black dust storm in Colorado, and cars and the highway — everything — had to stop. Nobody could see. After the Depression and the dust bowl of the 1930s, conservative measures were taken and certain areas were not to be farmed. A certain way of farming was outlawed and it has been forgotten. All the grasslands are being planted again. But you cannot plant those lands and keep the soil. We're losing tons, thousands of tons a year of topsoil, and this was very interesting.

So I did this story of a family on a drought-stricken farm, a black family [mother, father, little girl] living anywhere west of the Mississippi, and the land is turning to dust. As they plant, the dust sits over everything. And this can happen very quickly, particularly in places like the Midwest where we've had drought for several years but not like they've had in California. So what happens, she looks up and she sees a wall and that's the way the dust storms come. There's no warning, except there's a strange feeling and the ground begins to move. (I've seen pictures, I've read about it, I've seen a little bit of it, and my brother who lives in San Diego and goes to Las Vegas a lot has told me about it — dust devils that rise up and get bigger and bigger.)

NM: *Were you problem solving with this one or was it more of a social concern?*

VH: Well, it's hard for me to separate that. Drylongso comes before the storm. You know the Woody Guthrie song, "Pastures of Plenty." He's talking about all of the people who were uprooted during the Depression and in the dust bowl and they come into a town with the dust and they go with the wind. It's just a beautiful image. So

Drylongso comes with the dust and he goes of course, and Lindy [the young girl in the story] says, "He'll come back." This is the hope. He is another hope-bringer. I just thought it was a wonderful, mythical kind of thing, and yet it's grounded in a reality.

NM: *What's so eerie about the book is that it's the 1990s now and we know that all the things you're talking about in this book, in so many of your books, are coming to pass. Children must be "starters" now that adults have destroyed the earth, you seem to be saying in the Justice books. They are the survivors—or at least these particular children are because of their genetic giftedness.*

VH: Yes, the children in those books are like spaceships in the fact that they carry the genetic information on through society. That giftedness, that clairvoyance, it stays. It is their protection. Justice as Watcher. So in a sense the human body is simply a carrier for the knowledge they have. It's another generational kind of thing. They are able to go to the future and give their information, because they have been given this gift of survival. (The fit will survive.) Why is it some people survive and others don't, I was asking. Why is it some people survive plane crashes?

If you think about the black actor, [Richard] Lawson, in the New York plane accident a few years ago. Why did he survive? A couple of things happened. Somebody gave him another seat. In the row he had been in, the people died. He was put in first class and he survived. But when he crashed he found himself upside down in the water, and a part of him said, "Just go peacefully. You're going to die." Another part of him said, "No, you don't have to die." And I like to think that that part is the part that is passed on. That is the genetics of his ancestors having survived the Middle Passage [the journey, in bondage, across the ocean from Africa to America]. The black people who survived the Middle Passage are the strong people that survive, and they survive for a reason. There is something in them that makes them survive. That's the idea I was perpetuating.

NM: *In terms of historical associations and speech patterns in the*

265

Justice books, race is very subtle, yet as you are revealing here, it has crucial underlying meaning for the story. In the Drear books, the cross-cultural aspects are also especially intriguing. The Darrow mother of the second book is somehow imprinted in my mind as Indian, probably because she tells the story of the Indian Maiden. Or is she black?

VH: She's black. There may be some Indian ancestry. But that's the whole thing with trying to put race onto identity, onto people who have more than one ethnic influence. I grew up in Ohio and, in southern Ohio, black people are black and Indian, black and other things, and they don't talk like anyone else and they don't look like anyone else and they don't act like anyone else. The influences I grew up with were farm, populace, black church.

NM: *The very influences seen in the Drear books.*

VH: Yet there are books like *Cousins* when I deliberately don't mention race because I've written thirty books where I've had to care about what color people are because my society says I have to. I said, this time I'm going to write a book that doesn't say anything about color. The only way you know anything about color is maybe the way they talk and the book jacket.

NM: *By "the way they talk" you mean—*

VH: Town or country black people, rather than city. You see I'm a rural writer, definitely, because that's my experience. Walter Dean Myers said he didn't know there were black people like Virginia Hamilton. He didn't know there was a rural black American because he grew up in the city—in Harlem.

NM: *The Darrow mother [in* The Mystery of Drear House*] was an interesting rural character, and her mental condition [catatonia] was left very open—or timeless, although we could find it in the medical books.*

VH: Yes, sometimes my books go into a kind of time warp, since I don't like to allow certain things in them like electronics or TV.

NM: *The characters are storytellers or characters who often tell stories to one another. It seems to be a structural device to bring the story world to life for us, as well as a psychic necessity at times for the characters themselves, especially characters like Mattie Darrow.*

VH: I think how I use stories is the way I was taught what the world was like, what my family was like, what was expected of me, what values were. My family and my extended family were storytellers. And I learned about my social order through the way they told family tales. I learned about how people lived and what was expected of them. So I think story means to me that everybody has a story, that our lives are stories. And that's how we relate to one another. I realize now that a lot of people don't know anything about telling stories. They don't know that it is a way of carrying on traditions. My family storytelling meant continuing a family history and continuing a family.

NM: *Being the youngest, you must have heard stories from everyone about what happened before you could remember.*

VH: Often I would put a tape recorder on the table at Christmas and everybody would sit and joke about what percentage of the book they would get from the stories they told me. Then they would forget about the recorder. My brother Buster would talk; he always wanted to give me stories for books. He would say, "Did I ever tell you about the Great Snake Race?" And I'd say no. And he would proceed to tell me about how they raced snakes and what they would do, these boys. And I, like Justice, completely misunderstood. I though he meant that you raced them, although it was how many you caught. So I added that to the story. And he told about going to the river and when they came out, they had all these leeches on them. They didn't know there were leeches in the water and so that all became the Justice Cycle—from that one story.

NM: *So the storytelling experience entered you by osmosis.*

VH: Yes, I think I learned about beginnings, middles, and endings and that storytelling was a way to diffuse scary things [and a way] to show you how to live.

NM: *I think your books continue to teach us a great deal about living, especially living in a multicultural, multifaceted world. As I read* Plain City, *I thought of ideas you were exploring in* The Planet of Junior Brown. *Each book has a homeless person and each book has a musically gifted child who is searching for an identity.* Plain City *also reminds me of* Arilla Sun Down *since each book has a character who, because of her mixed heritage, is also very much the outsider in her town and her peer group. Maybe we even feel drawn to these characters because of this "outsider" status.*

VH: I think books like *Plain City* mean as much as you can see through them. I created a world, a social order. And I do that in my books in "feeling" terms, rather than "thinking" terms. By that, I mean I think story but write feelings. Hard to explain. I take thinking apart and make it express emotion somehow through words.

NM: *What stories, what books are "happening" for you at this moment? More novels? More collections? More illustrated books? Anything ready for publication that you can talk about?*

VH: Another collection [illustrated by Leo and Diane Dillon] is complete and to the publisher for fall of this year. I'm doing about a book a year now — easier on the head. I keep up my daily pace of writing, but thank goodness I've gotten rid of some of the pressure. Female members of my family have a Cousins Club that meets once a week on computer. The engineer in LA, the lawyer cousin in New Jersey, my sister in Columbus [Ohio], my niece who has moved back here from California, my niece in Columbus, my sister's daughter, and me. I am disappearing inside the information highway cyberspace. Some fun!

LAURA INGALLS WILDER
AWARD ACCEPTANCE
SPEECH

Given at the American Library Association annual meeting, 1995;
the Laura Ingalls Wilder Medal is awarded by the Association for
Library Service to Children, part of the American Library Association.
The award was first given to its namesake in 1954. The prize, a bronze
medal, honors an author or illustrator whose books, published in the
United States, have made, over a period of years, a substantial and
lasting contribution to literature for children. The award was
given every five years between 1960 and 1980; from 1980
to 2001 it was awarded every three years; beginning
in 2001, it has been awarded every two years.

*I*T IS MY PLEASURE to be here and I thank the Laura Ingalls
Wilder Award Committee of the Association for Library Service
to Children, a Division of the American Library Association, for this
medal. That early morning phone call certainly took me by surprise!

I stood at a podium similar to this at a Newbery/Caldecott occasion in San Francisco, exactly twenty years ago this year. Sometime before the ceremonies, I remember having my eight-year-old son, Jaime, with me and our peeking in at the vast ballroom, where, I explained, I would give my Newbery acceptance. Clutching my hand, Jaime pulled me inside. He stared openmouthed at the seemingly endless rows of brightly dressed tables, as waiters busied themselves, setting places.

"Wow, Mom," he said, "you never told me *this* is what you'd been doing!"

Jaime called me after hearing about this award. He's now twenty-eight and living in New York. He said, "Congratulations, Mom. I see you are still doing it."

Well, yes, I am. I don't know how else to *do*. I simply write. It is my pleasure and my reward to be able to write novels and biographies, and the art form of collections of stories, both fiction and nonfiction—books such as *The People Could Fly* and the new one coming out in the fall with Scholastic, *Her Stories: African American Folktales, Fairy Tales, and True Tales.* I find that I get tremendous satisfaction from connecting my own sensibilities to storytellers long since gone. I definitely feel that I am in contact with those tellers through their spiritual selves, that they've passed to me their personal expressions in the tales they've told. My call is to bring to light again what it was inside those individuals that made them want to inform us of their lives and to confess to us their hopes and dreams.

Perhaps my hardest work is novel writing. Through such fictions, I attempt to capture the perfect pictures and perfect scenes and ideas in my mind. I never do. But my challenge is to come as close as possible through words to what I see. It is the heart of the child, the young person that I am in search of in these books. And it is the goal of my imagination to make the perfect book; but of course, I never have, never can. And yet, the wish, the dream stays with me and sees me through difficult books such as *Plain City* or *M.C. Higgins, the Great.* My Plain City is a fictional town, but the real Plain City, Ohio, which I've never seen, is not far up northeast on the interstate. Recently I received a letter from a fourth grade class and their teacher, at a Plain City elementary school. Every student had signed the letter. The letter writer wrote that they wanted me to come visit the real Plain City: "Oh, its not like your wonderful book," said the writer. "We just have this super-duper supermarket on our main street. And we have this humongous restaurant that seats three hundred people all at once." I

had a vision of that many people rushing in and simultaneously grabbing chairs.

"Oh, won't you come?" the child wrote. "We'll show you all around.
Everybody wants you to come to our school and to see the real Plain
City. It's not grand but we like it a lot." So I wrote back and told them
that one day when it was warm and the sun was full over the real Plain
City, I was going to try to walk in and have lunch with them. It would
be a surprise. After all, I did borrow the name of their town and made
up my own Plain City. And I'm telling all of you, as a kind of pledge
or warranty, to make sure that I do go visit someday.

You know, I don't mind saying it: I do like the books I write. They
come out of the real in my life, I believe. I love the book, *Anthony
Burns: The Defeat and Triumph of a Fugitive Slave*. It is not quite a
novel and not a biography. It is best described as a historical reconstruction. And I found that through the life of this unfortunate black
man, there was a true spirit, a gentle human being whose bravery and
persistence to be free gave courage and impetus to others of his time. I
come from a different time than Anthony Burns, but I am of the same
African American parallel culture as he. The same urge and need for
freedom and equality is where I stand by him.

I call work such as the *Burns* book and the *Her Stories* collection, *liberation literature*, because the writer as well as the reader bears
witness to and experiences vicariously the tribulations of others who
triumph finally over hostile forces. Their triumph is ours; we live
through their experience through our understanding of and empathy
with the words, the very language which re-creates their all-too-human
condition.

Most of the time I write close to my own original source — my
hometown, my Perry/Hamilton family and ancestry. I draw as near
as I can to that deep well of fact and memory. One finds my autobiographical signature in books such as *Cousins* and, of course, *Plain City*.
Some of the cleanest scenes in those books actually took place, with
new settings and a new cast of people, mainly children. Those scenes

271

often grow from hearsay, as well. They may not come out of my own life, but from incidents in the lives of people close to me, from my sisters and brothers, friends, and elder relatives. I pull out the incidents, true or good tall tale, from the lives of family generations and the ghosty memories of times gone by. One finds such essence as well in the mythmaking of a book like *The Magical Adventures of Pretty Pearl*, which is the longest book I've ever written.

With *Her Stories*, stories of the female kind, I go farther back than my own family generations to bring into the light long past times and the collective imagination of African American women. So many different kinds of *her*-stories in one gathering reveal who we women were and are in all our shades of difference, our separate passions, in what we hold in common, and in our most secret imaginings.

In these twenty-eight years, from where I began as a professional writer with *Zeely* in 1967, there is no way that I've reached this point in time and place without the help of many friends and sisters and fellow librarians and other professionals.

This award is for the body of my work and I need also to acknowledge my debt to my editors, who taught me, encouraged me, fought with me over syntax, sentences, ideas. And gave me the last word—whether a woman or man—the final word was always, "It's your book, Virginia." They remain my friends, and I am fond of all of them. Editors make writers feel that each one of us is the only one. And writers are so insecure that they believe for a time, in the presence of their editor, that they are the only importance, the only significance. It's a marvelous subterfuge very necessary for the ego. I admire the editors—you who cared so deeply about my words—for that. And over the years, for that great association. I believe the past prophesies the future. And I'd like to thank, in order of service, Richard Jackson, now of Orchard Books, who was my first editor when I started out, who said—and I've never forgotten—"Virginia, there is only one way to write a book." I've pondered that for years. What did he mean by that?

Susan Hirschman, head of Greenwillow, who taught me how to think about my writing; she and her colleague Libby Shub certainly taught me how to think about M.C. Higgins! Ann Beneduce, Patricia Gauch, of Philomel; Virginia Buckley at T. Y. Crowell; Stephanie Spinner, Frances Foster, then of Knopf/Random House. All are splendid appraisers of the written word. Janet Schulman, of Knopf/Random, my college chum and oldest friend, guided my books over the years through Macmillan, Greenwillow, and Knopf. She was unable to attend on the occasion of my Newbery Award, but is here tonight. And Robert Warren of HarperCollins, who didn't mind at all that *The Magical Adventures* ran to more than three hundred pages. He just let it fly.

And to my present editor, the editorial director of Scholastic Hardcover, and editor in chief of Blue Sky Press, Bonnie Verburg, I give thanks for her always wanting to do things right. We've been in association for about ten years now. It seems like only yesterday we started on *In the Beginning*. I remember her with me in Ohio. It was four in the morning, and we were, to say it politely, "discussing" a somewhat obscure philosophical point in an ancient story. What we were doing actually was taking each other's measure. And since then, we've had some pretty good, long, hard battles over words. There's nothing like a great editor and the first streaks of dawn to make an author see the light. We both became winners by making the best books we know how. Bonnie Verburg takes the kind of care that is needed on a work. She will go that extra hundred miles for a project and she will see it through. She will enter deeply into the racial and cultural milieu of my literary vision and not only into the literary style of my writing. Bonnie Verburg and the other editors I have known all have had a commitment to a true American literature for the young that is inclusive.

Which brings me to my present publisher. To Scholastic's Richard Robinson, Barbara Marcus, Jean Feiwel, Judy Newman, John Mason, and so many others at the company: I salute all of you for finding the

273

many wonderful ways you have for presenting all kinds of books to all kinds of kids—not just my books. You have found a method to include practically every wish and dream of children. Whether it is guidance for the millions of readers of certain titles, or the thousands of readers of other titles, you do wonderful work with regard to all readers, and I am proud to be associated with you.

I thank all my friends at ALA and all my professional friends concerned with children's books. Twenty-eight years ago, if I may wax nostalgic for a moment, some of us were pretty young together. Ethel Ambrose; Bette Peltola, who was on my awards committee twenty years ago; Amy Kellman, also on that committee; Augusta Baker, oh, so many of you, I can't name you all, I am terrible with names, but bear with me while I name some of you—and all the new ones I keep adding to the list of my friends, those of you who invite me to your area for a lecture in the library or to meet students in a local bookstore or school or who simply love to read a Hamilton book: I thank you. You have never failed to be interested in my work and to take it seriously—sometimes, you take it too seriously! But gamely, you followed the books as far out as they might go, always looking, trying to understand. What is she up to now, you wonder. A trilogy? A book about planets? What is this animal, Jaguarundi? You come along. You have presented my material many times to students who might otherwise have been too cautious to enter into a Virginia Hamilton book. Binnie Tate, Betsy Hearne, Ginny Moore Kruse, Trish Wilson, Mary Lou White, Gertrude Herman, Effie Lee Morris. Henrietta Smith, Carolyn Field, K. T. Horning, Anne Izard, Jane Botham, Mary Liz Ledlie, Connie Harris, Mary Somerville, G. T. Johnson, Maggie Kimmel, Helen Mullen, Peggy Coughlan, Floyd Dickman, Kathy East, Marilyn Iarusso, Carolyn Brodie, Rudine Sims Bishop, Zena Sutherland, Jeff Garrett, Hazel Rochman, Spencer Shaw. I could go on over practically the whole room. So please, everybody else, wave!

It follows that storytelling is my way of sharing in community. When I was a child, the story lady at the library read stories to us children as we sat around her on what seemed to me to be a magic carpet. I have ridden that carpet all this way. And I have been making multicultural literature for everyone for over a quarter century.

I see my books and the language I use in them as empowering me to give utterance to my dreams and wishes and those of other African Americans like myself. I see the imaginative use of language and ideas as a way to illuminate a human condition, lest we forget where we came from. All of us came from somewhere else.

My work, as a novelist, biographer, and a creator and compiler of stories, has been to portray the essence of a people who are a parallel culture community in America. Through my writing I have meant to portray the traditions, the history of African Americans, a parallel culture people, as I see them, while attempting to give readers strong stories and memorable characters. Young readers have the right not only to read, but also to read about themselves, about who they are and what they want. My books entertain and they also express my feelings about the equal worth of us all.

My assumption is that all parallel cultures are equal, that there really is no minority or majority people. The experiences of us all are vital to the American fabric. And through writing I attempt to recognize the unquenchable spirit of us all.

I need to thank my husband, Arnold Adoff. We celebrated our thirty-fifth wedding anniversary this year. My goodness gracious. And they said it wouldn't last! In all those years, Arnold has been my most faithful friend and stalwart supporter. He is wise and insane and never, ever boring. Thank you for everything, my dear heart. Thank you, Leigh and Jaime Adoff, our children, for being yourselves such an inspiration.

Finally, I would like to say once more, thank you for this. I will cherish this medal and what it stands for. I will keep it safe in my "little house," which is almost on the prairie.

Good evening to you all.

WITTENBERG UNIVERSITY DISTINGUISHED AUTHOR LECTURE SERIES

Speech given in Springfield, Ohio, on September 6, 1995, in conjunction with Wittenberg's "common learning" course, "Darwin and His Legacy," required of all new students during their first term. The course began with a consideration of creation accounts based on the book In the Beginning: Creation Stories from Around the World.

I T IS MY PLEASURE to be here in the light of myths. I want to talk about how a book such as *In the Beginning: Creation Stories from Around the World* came into existence, among other things. And why I made this book, which in original hardcover is considered fine bookmaking. All elements—typeface, layout, content, story, illustration and bookbinding—are of the highest quality. It is a book I am very proud of. When it was published it was the only one of its kind in print. Still it is considered a model collection. We like to say it fits well in the palms of those from ages eight to eighty.

I'll try to read a few of my favorite myths—and I do have favorites.

To begin. The Swiss psychiatrist Carl Jung called myths the memories of the human race that represent in each of us the conflicts between the rational mind and the subconscious. No doubt you've heard of the high school teacher who announced to her students that "we will now read about orgies, diabolical plots, child eating, and bloodbaths—in other words, students, we're going to read the Greek myths." Myths are supposed to show us how the human race thought and felt untold ages ago. And yet, on rare, extraordinary occasions, they are being made today. The Aborigines, Australia's native inhabitants, believe their earliest ancestors created themselves from clay. Then they began to wander over Australia, singing out the names of everything they encountered: animals, plants, hills, rocks, streams. In this way, the ancestors sang the world into being. Present-day Aborigines believe that their country is crisscrossed with their ancestors' invisible pathways — known as *songlines*. And they say they can follow the trails of the songs left along their ancestors' footprints. A song is like a map, they say. If they know the song, they can sing-find their way across the country. Thus, songlines make all of Australia sacred to the Aborigines; they feel the land should remain untouched, just as it was when their ancestors sang it into existence.

There's a story that took place in Australia's bare scrub country, the Burt Plain. A railway company decided to make a cut through a small hill to save miles of track. Well, the Aborigines of the region became extremely upset. They warned that there would be a disaster if the hillside were cut: "Blackfella die!" they said. "Whitefella die! All people die! End of Australia. End of world!"

It turned out that the songline along the hill told of an ancestor who had failed to perform the correct ritual for controlling the breeding cycle of the bush fly. As a result, hordes of maggots had overrun the Burt Plain, stripping it bare of vegetation, just the way it appears today. This ancestor rounded up the maggots and crammed them back under the rock, where they've been breeding underground ever since. So the present-day Aborigines said that if the railroad cut into the hillside, there would be a gigantic explosion. A cloud of flies would spew up, covering the whole earth and killing every living creature. How did it originate in the present day? Perhaps this is the answer: During the 1950s and early 1960s, England tested a series of atomic bombs on tribal lands in Maralinga and Emu Field, South Australia. They attempted to inform the Aborigines of the test area and posted KEEP OUT signs, but many Aborigines didn't see the signs or couldn't read English. Later, Aborigines throughout the region reported hearing tre-

277

mendous explosions and feeling the ground shake. They saw strange, dark clouds, trickling streams of sticky dust. They called it the Black Mist. We know it was radioactive fallout. The Black Mist drifted across the outback and the whole area was contaminated with radioactive debris. Many Aborigines were stricken with deadly illnesses. Their tragic encounter with test bombs and the Black Mist fit perfectly with their ancestor myth. And also when the railroad company cut into the hillside and there was an explosion, a Black Mist came, and Blackfella did die. Thus, the modern historical event became grafted onto the ancient story. And a new, remarkable myth-tale came into being. The story can be found in the book *The Songlines*, by the late Bruce Chatwin.

My *In the Beginning* book got started in early 1986 when an editor in chief of a large publishing house asked my husband to do a book about beginnings or creation stories. Overhearing the conversation, I interjected, "No, it's mine. Give that idea to me. I want to do it." Arnold is a poet and only very reluctantly a prose writer so he didn't really mind if I took over the editor's offer. She was happy to have me do it. All the time, I had no idea if there were even enough stories about beginnings to make a book. But some instinct made me speak out. It's curious, the way a writer knows when something belongs to her, when a moment before, she had not even considered it. Yet, I was absolutely enthusiastic about it. I explained that first I would have to do a cursory investigation to determine what type of American myths existed. The editor said, "No. I mean I want it to be worldwide, if possible." "Aha!" I said. "All right, I will investigate." We were then living in New York for a couple of years, teaching at Queens College at the time. Although the New York Public Library is a wonderful place to make a study, researching in the main library in Manhattan can be extremely frustrating. Most of the time, half the library seems to be on carts overloaded with books being put back where they belong. Other obscure volumes necessary for my research, the kind that are readily available in most libraries, in the New York Public had been checked out by scores of scholars, other authors, and students all doing research in that one place.

But finally, I was able to get an overview and felt confident that I would be able to research enough material to choose from. I am only satisfied with overkill. I will gather a great amount of material. The editor, who was based on the West Coast, had contacts at Berkeley and was able to make material available to me, which was unavailable or missing in New York.

So that is how I began. Long, long hours spent in the library. We taught in the afternoon, so every morning I was there at the main library as soon as it opened, along with a small cadre of other researchers, maybe thirty or forty people ready to begin their own work. I tracked down sources all across the disciplines. Various language and ethnic groups, time periods. Fragments of thoughts.

I spent three months gathering raw material, until I had stacks of it. Most of the early gathering was done in New York. I think the final discarding, putting together, recasting, and writing was done here in Ohio. A great many stories began with "In the beginning . . ." so that became the obvious title. I'll tell you more about that later. After that I searched for the center story, the story that I depend on to hold the whole book. It is the story for me around which the rest of the book revolves. Maybe you will have another center story. For me, in a book like this, it reveals the point and substance of creation stories. It is the watermark, the highpoint, perhaps the book's most difficult, complex story. It holds the belief system of a people who were at once, and at one long time ago, great and powerful, yet, warlike and cruel. The longest myth in the book, it demonstrates a people's inspiring, imaginative side and the overwhelming beauty and meaning of its myth. I'm talking about the creation myth of the Quiché Mayans of highland Quatamala. (There are four creations in the Quiché myth. And as I talk, I will read each creation, and I think that way the tedium, if any, of listening to a rather longish tale might well be diminished and its power and my reasons for it in this book are more clearly revealed.)

[Read "The First Creation" from "Four Creations to Make Man"]

This ancient tale reflects what we know myths are. They are society's earliest stories. Myth depends upon belief. There is an awesome

279

religious aspect to it. Its central figures are gods and goddesses, heroes and heroines who have some direct connection to the gods. The myth stories explain spiritual and physical mysteries. The moon, the stars, the very earth and sea. The Quiché Mayan myth of creation explains the impossibly complex idea of creation itself.

[Read "The Second Creation" from "Four Creations to Make Man"]

Other myths have other aspects. I've shown all the main categories of myths in the "More About These Myths" section of the book at the end.

The Quiché myth is of course like the Western creation text from the Holy Bible, creation by the word. In the Holy Bible, God utters, "Let there be light." And there was light.

As for myths, mythology, one hopes for a response to them that has feeling, that is emotional. They are said to be prescientific explanations of natural phenomena. They are supposedly the description primal societies made up to explain why the seasons change, why there is a sun, why it rises and sets, and so on. Through metaphor and analogy the descriptions of the unknown give humankind a sense of control over its destiny.

I believe we enjoy myths, and reading them or reciting them, because of their varied levels of symbolic meaning. They are compelling, wondrous stories, and they give expression to humanity's most thrilling aspect: its endless creative ability.

[Read "The Third Creation" from "Four Creations to Make Man"]

Remember that all of the myths in this book and all of the myths everywhere were devised by human minds. Some people believe the creative ability is of God, the supreme creator.

280

I do not read the Mayan language of the Quiché Maya. I had to depend on English translations. The Mayan document from which this creation text was originally taken was called the Popol Vuh, the Book of Counsel, or Wisdom. It is invaluable as a source of knowledge of the oldest Mayan mythology and culture. It is the most widely known Native American composition of pre-Columbian tradition and history. A sixteenth-century manuscript was discovered in the eighteenth century by Fra Francisco Ximenes, parish priest of a small town, Chichicastenango. Copies derived from the one prepared by Ximenes have survived. The original text in the Quiché Mayan language was a compilation made by one or more descendants of the Quiché race, according to the tradition of their forefathers. The Quiché were conquered in the sixteenth century and their religious books were destroyed. The Ximenes translation chronicles the creation of man, actions of the gods, and the origin and history of the Quiché people. I uncovered English translations that had wide variations in language and place names and style.

Let me read a small bit from one of the translations. Then I will read my recast story, the last creation part of the Mayan myth.

I tried always to stick to clarity, simplicity of language and style. The translation goes on for some thirty-five pages. My rendering is nine, not counting my commentary at the end and Barry Moser's illustrations.

[Read from the source.]

Now I will read the entirety of my recasting. [Read mine.]

Other translations gave me what I felt was a simpler translation of the Place of the Corn, rather than Cleft in Bitter Water. Broken Place is how some translate this. I felt that was simpler. Feathered Serpent is also known as Quetzal Serpent. "Quetzal" being one of those words people don't know how to pronounce by sight. I translated it to "feathered."

There are always choices to be made. And I had to make them first. Then editors come along and say you can't do this. Editors felt this story was too hard, that maybe, Virginia, you should save it for another project. But I insisted. Right or wrong, a book of mine has to be mine. To me, the Mayan myth from the Popol Vuh is a stupendous accomplishment of a people. I think it's brilliant in that people made it up. People cherished it with religious belief and zeal. We cherish our Holy Bible, another book of belief and accomplishment to say nothing of its scholarship and sacred depth.

I took the title *In the Beginning* from the Jewish name for Genesis,

Bereshith, which means "in the beginning." Genesis is also the first book of the Hebrew Pentateuch known as the Five Books of Moses. And "in the beginning" is the first Hebrew word in its opening sentence.

Barry Moser, who illustrated my *In the Beginning,* is a master watercolorist. His rendering of the God Ra, which graces the book jacket, makes you feel that that well-known statue with the hawk's head has just come off the playing field of the gods' world. It has come alive. I'm happy to say I am fortunate to be able to own the watercolor, which isn't very large, but it is so perfect to my mind. And I wanted it very much.

I think the God Ra creation myth is also pretty spectacular. From the book: "Ra was the first to be. 'When I came into being,' he said, 'then being itself came into being.' He spoke these words so they would not be forgotten." Again we have creation by the word. It ends with, "These are the words that shall be spoken and never forgotten: Now and Forever, Ra, the Sun-God, rises in triumph, and he sets the same."

Other kinds of myth show the earth complete with God and man in place but with the need of a bit of correcting as in "Spider Ananse Finds *Something*: Wulbari the Creator." It is a myth of the Krachi people in Togo, in West Africa.

[Read]

Here's a myth from the Greeks. The gods commanded Prometheus, whose name means "forethought," and his brother Epimetheus, which means "afterthought," to create man and all the animals, which they did in their making shop. But man was cold on earth, so Prometheus stole some of Zeus's fire to warm them. Zeus, who sees all, saw and devised a punishment for both Prometheus and Epimetheus. I am going to read that myth of punishment. It is called "Pandora: Zeus the Creator."

[Read]

I had a great time making up specific suffering to come out of Pandora's box.

By the way, the illustration which graces the back jacket of the book is of Barry Moser's daughter. Barry has placed himself in the book, as he will, and he is rendered as Prometheus on page 132, holding his stomach, looking like he just swallowed a hot chili pepper.

This was a very timely book in that it was at the forefront of multicultural presentations. I think it's fascinating that all peoples have creation stories. And interesting, in the light of Darwinism, that the Mayan creation myth from the Popol Vuh, the Book of Wisdom, has survived. Why do myths survive? What is the dynamic that has kept this one and so many others alive for centuries? What is the need of human beings to perpetuate belief systems, religious or otherwise? Today, the Guatemalan people of the highlands still speak a Mayan language. They still say prayers to Mayan ancestors, tell time according to the Mayan calendar. The force of the creative mentality has an overwhelming need to survive and may well be part of Darwin's explanation of organic change. Every day, archeologists dig and uncover new elements of the Mayan culture, the mystery of Mayan thought and life. We need to know what made them tick, how their knowledge and they evolved.

With this introduction to *In the Beginning*, one is able to realize how very creative all peoples are. And that all, wherever they are and whenever they lived, need to find someone, something greater than their human selves, to define who they are, to direct them toward what they must do and become, to show them what is good and right. They are impelled to pass this creative process of discovery along through time and generations. It is the direction and the way of all peoples. It is, I think, compelling evidence of our equal worth and our humanity.

Thank you.

283

REFLECTIONS

The Marygrove College Contemporary American
Authors Lecture, given April 1997,
in Detroit, Michigan

GOOD EVENING. We can call this lecture "Reflections," a fixing of thoughts on something, casting back, too, and careful consideration of all aspects of a subject. My subject is books for children and all that encompasses. I'm going to read from sections of books as I talk.

I write books exclusively for the young from about age seven or eight, and for their older allies, up to eighty and on to ageless. My books are read in elementary, middle, and high school, and in college, in paperback and hardcover, in textbooks, and in such foreign countries as Japan, mainland China, Taiwan, Africa, Spain, France, Scandinavia, Germany, and so on. First and foremost, I write for myself because if it were not difficult, fun, hard work, and a pleasure, I don't suppose I would do it. Writing engages the total of myself. And I write for strangers who become my readers and occasionally my friends. I have many invisible friends on the Internet who write me e-mail as they make reports or just because they want to tell me they like a particular book or to tell me a frog joke. I collect frogs—the animatronic type. I have an extensive website and kids love visiting. I put letters from them on it from time to time and, of course, the frog jokes. Here's one: What happens when frogs park illegally? They get toad away. I also receive lots of snail mail at the post office from students and adults as well.

Many different types of books are in my basket. Novels, such as *Plain City* and *M.C. Higgins, the Great*; biographies of W. E. B. Du Bois, the great black scholar; one of the formidable baritone Paul Robeson; and an historical reconstruction of the fugitive slave Anthony Burns: I make collections, which are not anthologies, but groups of certain genre stories, mostly from the plantation era in America—that is, from approximately the latter eighteenth century to the mid-nineteenth century. Most of the black collections I create result from forgotten archival materials that I have uncovered, recast, and rewritten in an accessible colloquial speech, which I will talk more about later. But most of the collections fall into a category I created for myself called *liberation literature*. In books such as *The People Could Fly*, *Many Thousand Gone*, and *Anthony Burns: The Defeat and Triumph of a Fugitive Slave*, the reader travels with the character in the imagined world of the book and bears witness to the character's trials and suffering and triumphs. To the extent the protagonists find liberty, so, too, does the reader, as the witness who understands the struggle as a personal one and responds within with a spiritual sense of freedom. All of my work can be considered to have the same subtext, no matter what the category, and we'll talk about that more as we go along.

I also have devised a writing form, which now some people—other writers who want to borrow it—call the Hamilton. I made it for the long-story-with-pictures, which doesn't fit within the picture book format very well, nor the storybook category. I used that longer structure form for the texts of *The Bells of Christmas*, *Drylongso*, and *Jaguarundi*. It's an interesting form. It works for the novelist like myself who tends to write a rather long single story that she wants to have illustrated. Forms and structures of my own creation are useful for the kinds of stories I write. In my work there are many genres or influences—mystery, magic, realism, time-travel, science fantasy and what I call folk "telling," and liberation literature. In the novels there is that bridge between children's and young adult and adult literature, which helps the young cross boundaries more easily. Older novels, such as *A White Romance*, *The Planet of Junior Brown*, *Arilla Sun Down*, *Sweet Whispers*, *M.C.*, and *Plain City*, give clues on how to survive and how not to live. Younger novels like *Cousins* and *The House of Dies Drear* are full of cultural learning. I've written seventeen novels since 1967. I don't remember doing that many. Well, there are thirty-four books of mine in print and one for fall being printed. So there are thirty-five titles since 1967 and my first book, *Zeely*. This is the thirtieth anniversary of *Zeely*. It has never been out of print in hardcover and paperback. All of my books are in print and new editions come out all the time. That makes me extremely happy, and I thank you for considering my work when you read and study.

Reflecting is the usual start in my thinking about writing something. Reflection is an integral part of my writing process of the known, the remembered, and the imagined—the elements I call the writing or *literary triad*. In my work, the *known* is my personal history, my memory, and I am absolutely a product of African American extended families of my generation. We were Depression and coming-out-of-the-Great-Depression families. During the Depression, Mother made cakes and sold them at church bazaars and moonlight picnics. My father waited tables in dining halls. And they ran practically single-handedly, with sporadic help from their five wild children, a twelve-acre truck farm on which they produced all the food we ate and sold to grocers. What they didn't produce we didn't eat. In this paragraph are many ideas for novels.

My parents met in Canada where Dad had been working as a steward on the Canadian Pacific Railway. Mother, being bold in the late twenties, went to Canada to visit a sister and met my father at a ball. Ballroom dancing was all the rage. Mother says that Dad came waltzing into the room to the orchestra rendition of "Bye Bye Blackbird." She said she knew he was the man for her. He really was a fine ballroom dancer. A year later, they married, and came back to America to my mother's hometown of Yellow Springs, Ohio, a year after my sister Nina was born. That's when they bought the truck farm (or, to be more precise, they bought a mortgage) and had over the years four more children. Nina was born in Calgary, Alberta, Canada. I was the last of Kenneth Hamilton's and Etta Belle Perry Hamilton's five children.

We brothers and sisters thought Nina thought she was better because she was born in Canada. She certainly was smarter. We didn't know for sure if that was because she was born in Calgary, Alberta. But the fact of the matter is, and I won't make any more of this, she was and is the brightest in the family. She should have been the writer. She was a journalist for a time for the *Cleveland Call & Post*. But she had no desire, no heart for it, which is great. I tell you this because family history has a way of evolving to the *remembered* in the literary triad, which gives rise to the creative process in my imagination, from which I create an entirely new set of circumstances out of what was truly the known and remembered.

In my parents married time and when I was a youngster, learning life skills meant being made aware early on of much of our society's skewed and distorted image of the African American parallel culture. The idea in extended families like mine was that the more a child knew about life and the world, and quickly, the more opportunity that young person would have to grow up prepared for what might come. Keen perception helped one live productively. You learn a lot in the AME [African Methodist Episcopal] church. One learned most things at home. My father never stopped talking to us and telling—about W. E. B. Du Bois (a Du Bois cousin had married a relative of Dad's), and the blues singer Blind Lemon Jefferson, and Mr. Robeson, and muckraking journalist Ida Wells. He told of the last great Indian pow-wows on the high plains in the late 1800s. Smoke curling up from a thousand teepees. Dad told and I could see it. He told of Chinese men dying building the Canadian railroad; how the trainmen stacked the bodies of the deceased in empty train compartments. And I shuddered and could see it.

Everyone in my family told stories. I could see them all. They talked on and on. Nothing today pleases my adult children and their cousins more than being at a reunion of relatives, some two or three hundred of them, who descend on the Perry places (we call it simply Overhome, in southern Ohio). Everybody talks, on and on.

And my niece, my brother's daughter, the corporate lawyer now for Condé Nast, hauls out her computerized family tree and checks us all in our places on the tree and adds new branches. A reunion is held about once every two or three years. It is a physically taxing enterprise. So many stories, cross-referenced family relationships. My house is full of visiting kin. My own adult children expect elaborate holiday meals, cookouts, too, and gourmet breakfasts "like we had as kids," they say. And I say, "You never had it—you never had time." But they want me to prepare them food practically every day. They completely revert to kiddy mode. Until I say, finally, "Do it yourselves or go home."

Five generations of my extended family have lived in southern Ohio. Grandfather Levi was the fugitive from slavery. It was his mother who brought him to Ohio from Virginia. I was named Virginia by my mother lest I ever forget where I came from. Great-grandmother Mary Cloud, Levi's mother, delivered Levi by Underground Railroad conveyance, by foot, to friends in a nearby town. Mary Cloud was black and part Patawatomi Indian. We believe she was forced back into bondage. That was the deal, that she would go back if Levi could go free. What a story. And like all strong narratives of the folk, it may be at least part folktale. But it has lasted down the generations to me. It allows me room to create fictions out of a past question, the answer to which remains ever tantalizingly out of my reach.

The fiercest and strongest concepts in my writing are home, place, time, family, and generations. I'm going to read at this point from *The Magical Adventures of Pretty Pearl*, published in 1983, almost fifteen years ago. It is my longest novel and perhaps my best. It is a historical folk-fantasy fiction. It takes place at the time of Reconstruction in America. A time when former slaves, now freed, are being subjugated again. It is about gods and men. About Pretty Pearl and Mother Pearl and John Henry and John de Conquer. Heroes and *her*-roes, spirits and gods. And the hundred and fifty inside folks, black people hiding out in the great Georgia forest. They are on their way North, in this section. They are helped by their friends, the Cherokees, Aniyunwiya, who call themselves The Real People. Their leader is Old Canoe. But the inside folks have lived in the forest for many years, hiding. The Real People take the ginseng crop the inside folks grow to the port sources so it can be shipped to China, where there is a large market for it. Actually, ginseng was grown in bulk at Chardon, Ohio, and there was quite a market for it in the Far East during the 1800s.

[Read]

My personal concept is that, as I live my daily life, I attempt to create books that will give insights and cultural learning to young people, but not only to young people but also to adults and significantly women. I'm as concerned with female empowerment as I am with cultural learning. And I am concerned with young black men who feel lost, many of whom are immensely talented and bright. Not much room is given them in our America.

[Read from *Junior Brown*]

The creative instinct was handed down to me. And the story I know best, and which caused my imagination to leap, is the tale I was born into. My cultural learning, as I've said, came from true tales and tales of speculation from the mouths of loved ones. What wonderment of memory there is in the tellings out of history as well as the present, from ways of being, from made-up jokes and sayings and language from long-gone days; and in ideas for living with one another, getting along in the present.

[Read from *A White Romance*]

289

The female children in my extended family were raised by good talkers, who mainly were females, too. Women who were our mothers and elder aunts and grandmothers loved to get together and to talk "true," as my mother would say. We girl children rather circled these womenfolk. They made me and my cousins feel safe, having them always around, always the same good folks. All of them had a way with words that was, in a traditional sense, female. And on an evening, they would get together while the men listened to the radio or finished up chores, varnished wood and things. They'd tell stories about women's concerns, such as the safety of the children, dealing with illness, birthing, their missionary work in the AME, food supplies, caring for home and hearth. In my life, women talkers worked with their hands, stayed close to home, and were fiercely independent. What they had to say they said firmly, yet gently. They told comical and serious household tales with great skill. Farm women all, they had strong ways and kind voices. Their rather odd, Midwestern sensibilities, feelings, and tastes were passed on to their children as were their keen perceptions and sensitivity to others' needs.

I had my mother near me for a very long time. She died at the age of ninety-seven in 1990. I deeply missed her and began thinking about her stories, all those tales she told me over her long lifespan. Gram Tut in *Cousins* symbolized my mother and the last years of her life in a care center run by Friends—Quakers. I spent every afternoon and some evenings for two years there, watching my mother's life slow down and finally stop. Hers was a profoundly natural life and death. Let me read from *Cousins*. The book is actually about Cammy, Gram Tut's granddaughter. Cammy sneaks into the care center to see her grandmother.

[Read from *Cousins*]

And thinking about my mother and her stories, suddenly those two words, her stories, leaped in my mind. I missed the way she spoke. Even at ninety, her voice was as young as springtime.

Angry at me when I was a child and teen, she'd snap, "Don't you abuse my word." It was worse than a slap. From that warning, I grew. "God won't love ugly," she told me. And I believed He wouldn't. "Here comes falling weather." I felt it touch my bones. "Don't care won't ever have a home." I knew it was true. I would always have a home, she and Dad struggled to make that so. And I wondered whether there were other her stories by other women like her and I wondered, if there were, would there be enough of them to gather into a book of all female her stories. From my research I discovered there were. Here's one of them.

[Read "Miz Hattie" from *Her Stories*]

Her Stories connects women—elder, young, female children—together in one place of story. It's a lovely book, an example of fine bookmaking in every way. I have a publisher who cares about that.

Well, we're coming down to an end before I read from all thirty-four of my books. I'm going to read one last story from my new book, which is a collection of tales entitled *A Ring of Tricksters: Animal Tales from America, the West Indies, and Africa.* It will be out in the fall. Here's the jacket art. It is glorious. Here's the story.

[Read "Bruh Wolf and Bruh Rabbit Join Together"]

I write about the amazing ways human beings have for prevailing over adversity. By dramatizing themes of individuals longing for connections and continuity in their lives, characters are shown involved in life that can be dangerous, unfair, lonely, exclusive, but also loving, caring, unselfish. It is marvelous that long-ago black tellers living under terrible conditions kept alive their tellings of animal tales and their creating of human story. They did so because they knew they were passing and saving their culture and parts of it. This is what liberation literature is all about. And that's why I'm here, to talk and read to you. Often, stories have African words embedded in them. People who were denied their native language found ways to save a bit of it and to make that bit magic. You will find many tales in *The People Could Fly* that have words that make magic. In the title story, for instance, "Kum . . . yali, kum baba tambe," and the people step upon the air, like stepping upon a gate and they would fly away. Over the fences, over the houses and fields, and on to freedom.

I am essentially a rural writer, for that is my experience. The colorful southern Ohio farm region where I come from is full of shades of gold and ochre light, deeply dark soil, white farmhouses, and gray silos against hues of blue and black skies.

All of it, throughout the day, moderates into somnambulant dark green in summer before the night hangs down. My books encompass concerns about ecology and the life of rural communities. There, in the country towns and villages, we find households, women, children, elders, cousins, husbands, aunts, and uncles surrounded by nature. It is this natural rural experience that you find mostly in my collections and many of my other books. Its wind, rain, violent storms, floods, great snows, and long droughts are for me powerful metaphors and conduits to my imagination and the process of evolving story through and over time.

The language of expression is not so hard and not so easy. We learn words and how to use them, writing and reading, because of the complexity of our thoughts, which in turn grow and change as our needs develop and we mature. My way with language is through a glass window of story through which I project who I am and what I've learned about America as it relates to myself and others over generations. I write from the African American perspective. I use the term *parallel cultures* rather than *minority* to identify my ethnic group. Parallel cultures best describes the culturally diverse communities of present-day America. Parallel cultures is a worldview. We are not minorities in the world. We are parallel culture peoples, who are searching for what our imaginations tell us is in the American heart and dream and its possibility—that equality for all we hear so much about and a caring community and nation. Parallel cultures best describes the polyethnic, culturally diverse, sometimes integrated and ofttimes deliberately separated communities of present-day America. If we intend to ever make it better, we must admit to what this nation is and what we are dealing with.

I will not lie to children. There is a great deal I won't write about. I don't want to depress children, and some things are too depressing. Other people can write about that scene. I cannot. I have to have hope.

I believe there is a world narrative that we are all a part of. We all know one another through our words and actions. I tell my own grown children to listen to the story inside them. Their mind and heart story. That if they'll stop to listen, the story will expand in them and define who they are when they make sure it is true. I'm interested in that, and in the fact that we grow more whole by communicating with one another. That's really the main reason I am here. Speaking isn't my forte, although I do it all the time. I didn't dream of being a speaker as I did of becoming a writer.

But all of us together, especially women, gathered together in community, have much to learn from one another. What we have to say makes for a very good story. It delivers us in a common bond of understanding and cooperation through which we can accomplish much together. We can remember this occasion. Memory is so important to the story of us.

So tell the tale. Tell about one time and about wanderers and givers. Once, a wanderer came upon a house in the woods. In the house lived a father and his beautiful daughter. The moment the wanderer saw the daughter, he fell in love with her. And he asked the father for her hand in marriage.

The father thought about it a moment, looked over at the daughter, but she gave him no clue. Finally, the father said, "You may marry my daughter if you can build her a castle on the air."

The daughter giggled and covered her mouth with her hand. The wanderer thought about it. Finally, he nodded at the father. "I'll build her a castle on the air," he said, "as soon as you lay the foundation." And old African tale. It's lasted us all this time. So it must mean something.

Thank you.

REFLECTIONS ON
THE ILLUSTRATOR'S ROLE:
AN INTERVIEW WITH
VIRGINIA HAMILTON

Transcribed conversations in Art & Story: The Role of Illustration
in Multicultural Literature for Youth, the Virginia Hamilton
Conference, *edited by Anthony L. Manna and Carolyn S. Brodie,
Highsmith Press, Fort Atkinson, Wisconsin, 1997*

BY ANTHONY L. MANNA AND
CAROLYN S. BRODIE

SOME OF THE most distinguished illustrators of our time have
graced Virginia Hamilton's texts with their art. As a writer in
search of illustrators who share her deep respect for the struggles
and triumphs of African Americans, Virginia Hamilton—for over
thirty years now—enlisted the extraordinary talents and passionate
attention of a highly respected and prized company of artists: Floyd
Cooper, Leo and Diane Dillon, Nonny Hogrogian, Barry Moser,
Jerry Pinkney, and others. Their collaborations have offered up an
elaborate cultural duet on the page, with the pictures and other visual
elements providing stunning interpretive images that work in tandem
with the writer's invigorating and poetic style. These images enrich
and illuminate her vibrant portraits of the soul of black America.

In her many discussions about her work, Virginia Hamilton has rarely focused exclusively on her partnership with her illustrators. In this interview, then, we invited her to address the illustrator's role in her books and her feelings about the vision of culture her illustrators have brought to her texts. We spoke with Virginia Hamilton in early March 1996, in her home in Yellow Springs, Ohio, a former station of the Underground Railroad, where five generations of her family have resided.

M/B: *What do you think the illustrator's responsibility is when working with a text which you've written?*

VH: To begin with, illustrators should be true to their art. But, given the form they're working in, they also need to respond in kind to the particular textures of the text they're presented with. The illustrators I work with are so extraordinary that their response is always appropriate. This is the reason why I leave them to their own devices most of the time. I believe in their art, and I know what they're capable of, and they rise to the occasion of my texts. I seem to get some of the finest work out of illustrators. In fact, reviewers and critics of my books often say that this is the best artwork so-and-so has done, the most accessible, and so forth.

M/B: *Do you collaborate with the illustrator once a book is underway?*

VH: The process of fitting the artwork to the text begins as soon as I have a firm concept for a book. Now with *Her Stories,* for example, the process was really hurried. As it turned out, I put together a manuscript larger than was economically feasible to publish, and all of us were working under a very tight deadline. The Dillons had to have the stories while I was still working on them and my editor and I were still choosing which ones to include in the book. So I would complete a few stories and rush them off to my editor. The Dillons may well have illustrated several stories that weren't included in the book because of space constraints. You've no doubt noticed that the illustrations in the

295

latter part of the book are different from the others. The ones near the end are like little portraits. There just wasn't enough time for them to do the detailed pictures that are found throughout most of the book. Actually, those little portraits work beautifully, though they're set in a different format than the others.

M/B: *Once you send off a manuscript to your editor, are you usually given an opportunity to give your opinion about the illustrator's renderings? How involved are you in the process of putting a book together?*

VH: The editor is always in the middle of any negotiating once a book is underway. She knows us all very well, and all of us have enormous trust in her, just as we trust one another. But there are occasions when it's necessary to talk about the fit between the illustrations and the text I've written. With *Her Stories,* for example, Leo Dillon asked if I would be willing to change a small part of the text because he and Diane had completed the illustration that accompanied the text prior to a change I had made in the writing. I altered the section in question because it was just a matter of a few words. In another case with *Her Stories,* the Dillons gave the fairy story "Mom Bett and the Little Ones A-Glowing" an interpretation I questioned at first. They cast the fairies in an Egyptian mode. I was a little put off by this at first sight, because in my mind I saw Western-type fairies with wings and such. But the more I looked at the Dillons' concept, the more I could see that it made perfect visual sense. Although situations like these do arise from time to time, most of the time illustrators discover their own sense of my books without any input from me. Whenever I do research for a book, though, as I did with *Her Stories,* I'm in the habit of sharing at least some of the research with my illustrators, knowing that they'll do more research if they see a need.

M/B: *Have you ever rejected the artwork for one of your books?*

VH: Yes, I have.

M/B: *Do you ever have a say in choosing an illustrator?*

VH: I work that out with the editor as soon as the project is conceived. For example, when I first came up with the idea for the *Her*

Stories book, Bonnie Verburg, my editor at Scholastic, asked me if I had an illustrator in mind. She named several illustrators who might work well, but she agreed to approach the Dillons once I told her they would be perfect for the book.

M/B: *And that was before a word was written?*

VH: That's right.

M/B: *So you're pretty much in control from the beginning.*

VH: Yes, I do have the option to say what illustrator I would very much like. I knew from the very start that I wanted Barry Moser to illustrate *When Birds Could Talk & Bats Could Sing.*

M/B: *Why is that?*

VH: Because I believe he is the greatest watercolorist working in children's books today. You see, I think of the book as a whole, which means that I know which illustrator can make the book come alive visually. First of all, Barry was raised in the South, and the stories in *When Birds Could Talk & Bats Could Sing* are based on African American folktales told in the South during the plantation era. I knew he'd adore those stories, and he did. He started painting almost from the moment he read them and kept painting until he had completed nearly forty watercolors. I understand from Bonnie Verburg that only a small number were ever changed from the original renderings. His first thought for the design of the book was to make the whole book about four inches high, a small pocketbook to fit in the hand of a small child, which is a sweet idea. The book, of course, is quite a lot bigger than that. We laugh a lot about how it kept growing. All the birds are anatomically and scientifically correct, except that they wear hats, which is a marvelous touch. And their expressions are hysterical. There's an interesting story behind the development of Barry's wonderful painting of the boy Alcee holding the pumpkin in the opening tale, "How Bruh Sparrow and Sis Wren Lost Out." The text reads, ". . . Alcee tore the pumpkin from the vine. He held it in his arms and strolled off across the field. Sadly, Sis Wren and Bruh Sparrow watched him go." Originally, I wrote it so that he put the pumpkin under his

297

arm, but Barry responded by saying that he couldn't show Alcee carrying off such a large pumpkin that way and would I change the text to fit the action. As you see, that's what I did, because in this case it didn't hurt the text at all to make the change. In fact, it added to the drama of the story.

M/B: *When you have discussions like this, do you actually talk with the illustrator directly or do you work through your editor?*

VH: It depends. Sometimes, but not in that instance. I usually talk with Barry Moser directly because we know each other very well. And that's the way it's been from the very beginning, when he did the illustrations for *The All Jahdu Storybook*. He's an extraordinary human being. To give you an example of a big change he's made in his work, take a look at his full-page spread of the peacock in "Still and Ugly Bat" in *When Birds Could Talk & Bats Could Sing*. In the past, Barry didn't use to like to have an illustration cross the gutter of a book. In fact, he wouldn't do this at first. So, in a way, what you have when you don't move into the book's gutter are less vigorous portraits than you have when you do cross the gutter. There's much more movement to an illustration that uses the large space of the page that way. It's a risky thing to do, though, because it splits the image and could distort it. But as you can see in the picture of the peacock, Barry uses the entire page brilliantly. No distortion whatsoever.

M/B: *Mr. Moser seems to have had a lot of fun with these stories. There's such a sense of playfulness about the entire enterprise.*

VH: There's a lot to play with. For one thing, there are all sorts of verses and songs in these tales, because they're written in the *cante fable* tradition. What that means is that in addition to rhymes and songs, there's a moral at the end of each of the stories, which makes them much more interesting. The moral that concludes "How Bruh Sparrow and Sis Wren Lost Out" reads, "So, children, here's a leaf from the book of birds: *Pick on your own size. For it's no use squabbling over what's too big for you to handle.*" I made the morals stronger than the ones I found in the original tales I was working with for this book, and that strength is due partly to the way I position myself as a narrator who talks directly to children. The morals were great fun to work with.

M/B: *Where did you find these stories?*

VH: That's a story in itself. I was doing research for another project when a research helper happened upon these tales quite by accident. She didn't realize what she'd found, but I recognized their value at once. The stories I tell in the book are based on African American folktales told in the South during the plantation era. In the 1800s one Martha Young, a white journalist who sometimes wrote under a pseudonym, collected them and created many of her own, publishing them in newspapers and in several collections of folktales. She was three years old at the end of the Civil War, and her family's former slaves became the paid servants of her wealthy household. Martha Young was an extraordinary collector of black folktales, songs, and sayings, and she became a very popular "dialect interpreter." We have no way of knowing what she sounded like doing so-called black dialect at the turn of the century, but she became quite famous. She sold out Carnegie Hall and was reviewed very favorably by the *New York Times* and other newspapers. Then she completely disappeared. All of her books were out of print. They have been dead for over half a century.

M/B: *Do you know why that happened?*

VH: Joel Chandler Harris and the Uncle Remus stories is why. His work with animal stories was so powerful that he completely dwarfed her.

M/B: *And you respect her effort?*

VH: Of course I can't possibly know how she felt about black people, but from what I can tell from her treatment of the tales, I assume she respected the folks from whom she collected them. Still, there were times when she used the term *darkie*. She was, after all, a woman of her time. We are no longer able to know which were her own stories in the African American tradition and which she heard from black tellers. But having resurrected them, I felt I had a duty to take them back, even hers, because they are all beautiful and I hear the voices of black

299

tellers in them and even the imitative voice of Martha Young. I recast these stories for young people in a colloquial language that reads and sounds equally well. They were written down in a fractured English, part Gullah, part I don't know what.

M/B: *In the illustrations, each of the animals has a distinct personality.*

VH: As I said, Barry Moser fell in love with the stories. We differed, though, on clothing the animals. The animals in *The People Could Fly* have no clothes, as I requested they not have to Leo and Diane Dillon who illustrated it, and they agreed. Since Barry would have clothes and I would not, we compromised. Each bird and bat wears a hat, which really contributes to the animal's personality.

M/B: *When you're working on a book which will be illustrated, do you consider the visual images which eventually will enhance the writing? Are you a visual writer?*

VH: I am a visual writer, but it's not illustrations that I visualize. The characters and action are what I visualize. And, of course, I know my craft and form. With picture books I know there had to be something there for somebody to illustrate. Particularly in a book like *When Birds Could Talk & Bats Could Fly*, I make sure my language is full of description and detail so that the illustrator can take off on that. Not so specific that the writing will restrict the illustrator, but enough detail for an illustrator to play with. It's a matter of leaving enough room in the language and enough room between the people.

M/B: *You said that you know the craft of the picture book. How would you describe that craft, that form?*

VH: To answer that, I'd first have to say that with my books, the main thing is the writing. Illustrators come to my books and must fit into my work. If the main thing is the writing, then it's the writer's book. So I start out thinking only of the writing. When I began to conceptualize *Her Stories*, I was thinking about my mother, whom I missed, and the stories she told.

All of a sudden the book became an entity in my head. "Aha,"

I said, "I've never done a collection of traditional stories that looks exclusively at females." When I'm working with folk material like the tales I gathered for this book and for *The People Could Fly*, I'm actually recasting them, composing them anew in my own written-down style of telling. If you could compare my versions of these narratives with the raw material I work with, you'd see something of the process that goes into transforming the original sources into stories that read well both on the page and out loud. When I'm reshaping them, I'm also aware that they are going to be illustrated and how they are going to be illustrated. I want to be sure there are adequate visual details and visual action for the illustrator.

M/B: *You never call yourself a "reteller."*

VH: That's because I'm not a "reteller" of these tales, but a "teller." Sometimes reviewers will say "retold by Virginia Hamilton," but that's a misnomer. Look at the jackets of these collections and you see that "told by Virginia Hamilton" is the correct way to put it. After all, storytellers tell stories, and they tell them differently and uniquely each time they do. I believe that I've brought this kind of collection to a level it has never been brought to before. I actually recast the stories in a kind of colloquial speech that is also very literary and yet easy for anyone to read. I knew people would be reading these stories out loud to children, but that they would also be studied in college classrooms. I wanted them to have wide appeal, and to achieve that I had to spend a lot of time working on the language.

M/B: *All of your illustrated books are neither picture storybooks nor chapter books. They seem to fit somewhere in between these two traditional forms.*

VH: Well, my collections represent a traditional form—the anthology. *Jaguarundi* is a thirty-two-page picture book. But I get what you mean. The form in *Drylongso* and *The Bells of Christmas* is my own. We call it a "Hamilton." It's what novelists do when they try to write a picture book! I started wanting to do the illustrated books as standard thirty-two-page picture books, but I couldn't do that because

3 0 1

I found that I had too much to say. I had to come up with a picture book format that could integrate illustrations with a long story. And what emerged is the form you see in *Drylongso* and *The Bells of Christmas*. It suits perfectly a kind of writing I like to do occasionally, which is quite different from writing a novel.

M/B: *What functions do the illustrations serve in the form you're describing?*

VH: They open up the stories and invite you in. *Drylongso* is a good example of what I mean. When I wrote this story about a farming family, I had a locale like southern Texas in mind. Jerry Pinkney's illustrations for *Drylongso* so vividly portray the look and feel of that region of the country. He uses a white light and a sandy texture that capture the awful drought these people must endure. These visual elements greatly enhance the atmosphere of the story. Rarely does anyone write about black families in rural areas, so I hope the book broadens people's notions of the experiences of African Americans. It is only recently that half of the African American families haven't lived in rural areas, and many still do live on their own farms. It was this phenomenon I addressed in *Drylongso*, where I tell about a black family eking out an existence on an isolated farm during a terrible drought.

M/B: *Throughout the years, have you seen many changes in the way your books are illustrated?*

VH: I don't know if the changes are a matter of style or the increasing sophistication of children's books. Children's books in general have grown increasingly sophisticated to keep up with the sophistication of the readership. When you have three-year-olds working on computers, you have an obligation to live up to what they're learning. Kids are also reading voraciously, and good literature is getting into schools as it never has before. The more children see and the more they learn, the more sophisticated they become about artwork and text.

Now, in regard to the representation of African Americans in children's books, the changes have been very interesting. Since I started writing for young people, we've moved through a period when "black is beautiful" was the sentiment to a period in history when separation and black nationalism were a rallying cry. At this point in time, we are embracing the strong influence that American blacks have had in this country, and this attitude, it seems to me, is so much wiser than the back-to-Africa feeling that was so dominant in an earlier time. What I like best about young African American illustrators is their freedom that knows no boundaries. They now work in every conceivable style, and they illustrate books by writers from many different cultures. There was a time when that would not have been possible, just as there was a time when only a black illustrator would have done a black author's book. Of course, I defied that kind of pigeonholing early on when Symeon Shimin illustrated *Zeely*, my first book. If anybody knows ordinary people it's someone who knows the Russian peasantry, as Shimin did. He did a wonderful job with *Zeely*, which proves a point.

Today we're seeing many examples of good, sensitive illustrators doing a fine job of working in cultures that are not their own. So the world of the illustrated book has opened up more to a diversity of voices. Of course, if you didn't have adventurous publishers like Scholastic and adventurous editors like Bonnie Verburg, none of the changes would be possible. We're witnessing a period of very fine bookmaking and book design. And the content is forever broadening. While it is still true that many children's books are created through the prism of popular culture, which tends to avoid the broad cultural foundation of this country, things are changing. I think that my books have been responsible for many of these changes, because I have broadened the field and created a canon at the same time. Yes, there was a cultural children's literature before me, but there wasn't the diversity of genre and subject matter I've created in the more than thirty books I've published over the years. Nor has there been another writer for young people, black or white, who has done the amount of speaking and writing I've done about writing and my particular parallel culture. You can follow the history of my books through my published speeches.

When you trace my history, you see that my books have widened the cultural landscape and provided a bridge to the past and between the generations.

M/B: *Over the years, the Virginia Hamilton Conference has celebrated the work of many distinguished illustrators. What do you find most striking about their contribution?*

VH: The extraordinary diversity and range of their expression. What particularly stands out for me in this regard is the contrast between the styles of a Pat Cummings and a Sheila Hamanaka, for example. I find the differences in their styles and the responses to their work very enlivening and very exciting. Pat's art is open and outgoing, while Sheila's is more intensely political. In a way, Sheila's art is confrontational, but this in no way limits her own vision. Pat, on the other hand, presents us with symbols that immediately draw us in, because they are so familiar. They are so with us. The differences between Pat and Sheila stylistically are not unlike the differences between writers like Ernest Hemingway and William Faulkner. Both of these writers have amazing styles, as do Pat and Sheila, and like Pat and Sheila, both are remarkably different from each other. Hemingway's simplicity eases you into the work, whereas Faulkner's complexity makes the entry difficult. The illustrators who participate in the conference reveal a similar range of styles, temperaments, and subject matter. And given its cultural theme, the conference showcases the wide-ranging ethnicity that now characterizes the world of books for young people. This is particularly important for illustrators of parallel cultures who have to struggle to build a constituency.

M/B: *They have to do this even now when publishers are so much more willing than they were in the past to acknowledge the parallel cultures that make up this country?*

VH: Even now, because these artists are a minority in a huge country, and like all people of parallel culture, they have to work harder at proving themselves than do their colleagues from the dominant culture. This is a very good time for African American and ethnic illustrators. What they must do is to be consistent in their artistry and not get waylaid by commercialism. They need to remain true to their art and genuine about the cultural experiences they're depicting. That's the challenge for all of us working as artists in a multicultural world. If we do these things, we will draw people to work by the sheer force of our commitment.

VIRGINIA HAMILTON'S ILLUSTRATORS

Zeely. Illustrated by Symeon Shimin. New York: Macmillan, 1967.

The House of Dies Drear. Illustrated by Eros Keith. New York: Macmillan, 1968.

The Time-Ago Tales of Jahdu. Illustrated by Nonny Hogrogian. New York: Macmillan, 1969.

Time-Ago Lost: More Tales of Jahdu. Illustrated by Ray Prather. New York: Macmillan, 1973.

Jahdu. Illustrated by Jerry Pinkney. New York: Greenwillow, 1980.

The People Could Fly: American Black Folktales. Illustrated by Leo and Diane Dillon. New York: Knopf, 1985.

In the Beginning: Creation Stories from Around the World. Illustrated by Barry Moser. San Diego, CA: Harcourt, 1988.

The Bells of Christmas. Illustrated by Lambert Davis. San Diego, CA: Harcourt, 1989.

The Dark Way: Stories from the Spirit World. Illustrated by Lambert Davis. San Diego, CA: Harcourt, 1990.

The All Jahdu Storybook. Illustrated by Barry Moser. San Diego, CA: Harcourt, 1991.

Drylongso. Illustrated by Jerry Pinkney. San Diego, CA: Harcourt, 1992.

Many Thousand Gone: African Americans from Slavery to Freedom. Illustrated by Leo and Diane Dillon. New York: Knopf, 1993.

Her Stories: African American Folktales, Fairy Tales, and True Tales. Illustrated by Leo and Diane Dillon. New York: Blue Sky Press, 1995.

Jaguarundi. Illustrated by Floyd Cooper. New York: Blue Sky Press, 1995.

When Birds Could Talk & Bats Could Sing. Illustrated by Barry Moser. New York: Blue Sky Press, 1996.

About the authors: Anthony L. Manna and Carolyn S. Brodie are codirectors of the Virginia Hamilton Conference and coeditors of *Many Faces, Many Voices: Multicultural Literary Experiences for Youth* (Highsmith Press, 1992), a collection of proceedings from the Virginia Hamilton Conference.

Editor's note: The following illustrated books were published after this interview.

A Ring of Tricksters: Animal Tales from America, the West Indies, and Africa. Illustrated by Barry Moser. New York: Blue Sky Press, 1997.

The Girl Who Spun Gold. Illustrated by Leo and Diane Dillon. New York: Blue Sky Press, 2000.

Bruh Rabbit and the Tar Baby Girl. Illustrated by James Ransome. New York: Blue Sky Press, 2003.

Wee Winnie Witch's Skinny: An Original American Scare Tale. Illustrated by Barry Moser. New York: Blue Sky Press, 2004.

The People Could Fly: The Picture Book. Illustrated by Leo and Diane Dillon. New York: Knopf, 2004. Re-released in 2007 to include a CD narrated by James Earl Jones and Virginia Hamilton.

FRANCES CLARKE SAYERS LECTURE: LOOKING FOR AMERICA: A PROGENY'S PROGRESS

Given at UCLA, February 1999; this lecture series honors
Frances Clarke Sayers (1897–1989), distinguished children's
librarian, teacher, author, storyteller, and member of the
UCLA Department of Library and Information
Science faculty from 1960–1989.

THANK YOU so much. I am truly pleased to be here at UCLA, giving this, the 1999 Frances Clarke Sayers Lecture. It happens that I visit you here at the end of Black History Month. I must say, I am more popular this month than any other. But I compliment Virginia Walter and her committee for giving me dates to speak here in other months as well. It was this date that most suited my schedule.

This month holds the birthdays of two U.S. presidents—George Washington and Abraham Lincoln. It often has no full moon, being shorter than all other months. Curiously, February holds the birthdays of many blues singers—one wonders about that—William "Pa" Rainey, Josh White, Jimmy "Papa" Yancey, Birleanna Blanks, and Varetta Dillard. Last but not least, in February is the birthday of one Anna Madah Hyers, the black American classical singer, a soprano, born in 1856 in Sacramento who had a long, illustrious concert career in this country, accompanied by her sister, who was a contralto. Leontyne Price was born in this month, as was author Alice Walker and poet Langston Hughes. For some reason I'm fascinated by February, perhaps because Negro History Week, originated by Dr. Carter G. Woodson, was observed for the first time this month in 1926. I myself, a writer, formerly a singer, missed February by twelve days. I was born on March 12. But that's not bad because, for some years, we've designated March as Women's History Month. So I've taken you from the particular to the universally sublime.

I had engagements also in January to commemorate Dr. King's birthday and accomplishments. He, of course, was full of grace and generosity, and he inspired not only us but also the poorest and most powerless among us. I like to think that the belief in community, in equality, peace and understanding, ideals that not only Dr. King believed in, enter into the books I write. My parents believed in them as well. I knew Dr. King's wife, Coretta Scott King. She and her sister, Scottie, and my eldest sister Nina, all attended Antioch College in my hometown at the same time. I saw Coretta not too long ago at the Trumpet Awards in Atlanta. She and I had a nice talk. I'm happy to announce that I have been designated the honorary chairperson for the Coretta Scott King Award's awareness campaign for the next three years. And in that connection you will no doubt see my face and read my words in articles and in some amount of media.

So then, the months carry on and carry us to the very rim of the twenty-first century. I wonder, shall we topple over, clutching the letters and the number Y2K? Shall we teeter in, or with trepidation, anxiously make our way onward? Do we stroll along, do we contemplate, ponder, wonder, or imagine the worst? Or do we expect all good things for the future?

When I speak to young people, who are the main constituency for my books, I often ask them what they need to know in the twenty-first century. What will change for them and what will remain the same. I tell them I intend to share with them some of the coming millennium, as well as part of their reading lives. This is where they begin to stare at me. *Millennium*, big word. It gets very quiet and I know the young people are thinking. I am not sure exactly what they're thinking. For these are the children whose lifetimes have always included AIDS. They've never had a polio shot and probably don't know what it is. "You sound like a broken record" doesn't mean anything to them. They've always had cable. A remote control. There's always been MTV. And they've always had an answering machine.

I tell them the story about my mother, Etta Belle Perry, when she was a young person. Born in 1892; she died in 1990 at the age of ninety-seven. She saw great changes and extraordinary events over the span of her life. As a girl in school, there happened an occasion when classes were let out. All the children lined up outdoors in front of the school. Something outlandish was going to occur, she had been certain of it. "Perhaps a circus?" Mother said she thought. "Maybe a carnival?" The students stood waiting on the school grounds facing the road. It was a small rural school. As they waited there in the country day quiet, they heard something coming closer. And soon, they saw something. What it was frightened them. Some ran back inside the school. Others stood there, eyes tight closed, covering their ears. Mother said she clutched the teacher's hands. And what occurred seemed wonderful. Mother said that as soon as she saw it, she knew it was marvelous. She didn't know what it was, but it was moving. And it had no horses pulling it. It made noise, but not the sound of horse hooves. Yes, indeed, it was the Model T Ford, she found out. There were, of course, motorcars in the United States even before the Ford. But few people owned them, and rarely did you see one in rural communities. But the Model T was inexpensive and overnight it found its way smoothly into all American life.

I don't know if we can imagine what it was like for her and the other young people to see a horseless carriage for the very first time. Something that had never been for them was suddenly there for them. Such an event attests to the human ability to take in and accept profound change, the appearance of the new, in a matter of seconds. Change.

Years ago when I first started college, I bought myself a manual typewriter, an Olivetti. I never used an electric typewriter, even when out of college and working and I could afford to buy one. The light-weight Olivetti, weighing just twelve pounds, was the machine for me and traveled with me wherever I went. Until the day in the eighties when I began to type on a computer. And I never looked back. Intuitively, I gathered that the whole PC was good for me. Word processing. Writing.

I talk to children and young adults about that. They like the story about the horseless carriage, too. Many of them had never heard the term *horseless carriage*. It seems like ancient history to them. And yet, I can remember, as a child, sleighs at Christmastime, drawn by horses. Not a daily event, but an occasional one during the holidays. Horse-drawn sleighs and carriages were common events in my mother's and father's childhoods. I rather liked that connection of generations and made a story out of a Christmas event in 1890 in the book *The Bells of Christmas.*

In those early days, in the time of young Etta Belle Perry, ordinary folks referred to automobiles as horseless carriages. What I tell students is that, like my mother, like myself, they will see one day that which they could never have imagined. Their minds will take it all in in a moment and, forever after, their minds will have been changed. Who in this room could have imagined wormholes and black holes and charmed quarks? Change, discovery, is the key to all events and life. I love change.

I think and write for children who grow and change and face the unknown. I try to stimulate their imaginations by presenting them with new ideas, hoping to show them what they had not suspected, to teach them what they hadn't known they needed to learn. My fall 1998 novel, *Second Cousins*, tells them about Janina Madison, a computer whiz who has discovered a French mathematician's discovery called fractals and his Mandelbrot set. Janina nicknames herself Fractal. On the back of the book jacket is a fractal that I made using certain computer software. Well, the plot thickens, and you will need to read the book, of course, to understand what is going on. I don't think slightly complex ideas are too hard for young readers. They seem to thrive on my books. Nor do I feel that having a generational family community as you find in *Second Cousins* is difficult for young people to comprehend. They live in that kind of community themselves, whether it is family that dominates or friends, school with teachers.

I gave Cygnus Software's Fractal eXtreme credit on the book as the software I used to create the fractal I made. They were so pleased that the president of the company wrote me to say that they had linked their Internet site to my Web page showing the *Second Cousins* book. Also, they put a notice on their front page that Virginia Hamilton had created a character called Fractal Madison and that Fractal Madison in the book uses Cygnus software, and that I had put the fractal I'd created using Cygnus software on the back jacket of the book. That really is exciting to me. These software people don't play around, and they took the time to connect what I do with what they do. Incidentally, you are welcome to visit my website. I've had it for about three years now and it is quite extensive—having photos, events, speaking engagements, my books, and recorded books. The URL is www.virginiahamilton .com, for all you computer folks.

A writer always faces the unknown. First, the blank page. Next, what to put on it; how to put it. Having finished a new novel just a few weeks ago, called *Bluish*, I wondered how it happens that we face change with equanimity, though, too, with some amount of fear, and learn to take charge of it and power it by our force of will. I believe the new novel is my thirty-seventh or thirty-eighth book since the first one, *Zeely*, in 1967. Every pause, every exclamation point in the writing of a book has to be imagined. It's not easy because one can't see what's coming; one has no idea how it sounds and what it will do. How to think about it because it has never been thought of before by yourself. That's the writer's hope, at least, to create something new and original. But how is it done? Writing the new book, *Bluish*, I'm amazed that it got done. We'll get to how it's done in a moment. For when I

311

started I had no reason to believe I would find how to do it, nor how to end it. I knew nothing about it. Except this one idea of . . . *Bluish*. And I think that's all I want to say about it. Look for it in the fall.

All of my books are in print, in one form or another—as supplemental texts, as hardcovers, paperbacks, and foreign editions. Not all of the hardcovers or paperbacks will be found in the same bookstore. Some are currently more popular than others. You may find many of the new Scholastic paperbacks in their Point Signature edition. They include my Justice Trilogy, *The Mystery of Drear House*, *Plain City*, *Arilla Sun Down*, *Cousins*, *A White Romance*. A new large format paperback of my *When Birds Could Talk & Bats Could Sing* book just came out a month ago.

Recently, I looked back on the writing of *M.C. Higgins, the Great*, the Newbery Award book, published in 1974. And I'm amazed to discover that the book is a quarter of a century old. Reading it again one day recently, I felt I knew it, that I'd only just written it. Scholastic puts *M.C.* out in paperback in their school edition. The book was originally published by Macmillan. I know where I was when I wrote *M.C.*, and reading it again, I found my way back to the place I had been. By that I mean that, when the writer finishes a novel, she has progressed beyond where she was when she started. And never will she write that way or that progression again. At least, I don't—I hope I don't. She can experience the progression by going back and following the text from the beginning. Writing a book changes you; it makes new grooves, new signposts in your brain. *M.C.* was not an easy book to write, nor was *Plain City* or *Sweet Whispers, Brother Rush*—or *Second Cousins*, which is called a sequel. I call it a complex book full of ideas with many of the same characters as *Cousins*. But it felt to me as I read *M.C.* again that it was still a book full of light and shadow. Of verisimilitude, the sense of reality. And it moves, it grows in opposition to itself. It has positives and negatives, with characters who are juxtaposed. *M.C.* at the top of the pole slams into gritty Jones, his father at the bottom of the pole. His dependable, loving mother, a great swimmer, is in contrast to the elusive Lurhetta Outlaw, who nearly causes herself and M.C. to drown. I still feel that the landscape of that book teems with beauty, and its hopescape, the dreams of its characters as they envelop their inner lives, is drawn from my memories and the essential stuff of friends, relatives.

I am a social-conscious writer. There is no book of mine that does not give space and time to cultural learning and multiculturalism. I write about the ingenious ways people have of prevailing over adversity. By dramatizing themes of individuals longing for connections and continuity in their lives, characters are shown involved in life that can be dangerous, unfair, lonely, exclusive, but also can be loving, caring, unselfish, and inclusive. Children's books and adult books are not dissimilar. But in youth literature, the child almost always commands the center stage; the child changes, learns and grows, and is truly the shape-shifter.

I write about people of color, and my milieu is black America. I write my take on parallel American cultural experiences of African Americans. There are other parallel cultural experiences being written about that are also American—Asian, Hispanic, Indian, European—here in America. When we speak about cultural diversity, we are talking about parallel culture communities. As a member of one ethnic group, it's my artistic prerogative to give expression about that group. It is an expression of inclusion. We artists of parallel cultures want our . . . to be included in the canon of American children's literature. We do not want our work disregarded because we write about what we know. We are not less; therefore, we are not minorities in that sense. We have important, significant points of view to express. We who create books do so out of our own cultural sensibilities. The United States, as you know, is one of the more culturally diverse world nations and growing ever more so. It is multiethnic, multidirectional, multifaceted, and probably most importantly, multifactorial, having many different causes and influences historically.

To understand America's parallel culture imperatives is to know

313

that each culture is a significant part of the fabric of this country. The fabric's warp and weft is the texture of multiculturalism.

Parallel cultures, rather than the terms *minority*, *majority*, is a worldview and best reflects or describes ofttimes integrated but often deliberately separated communities of present-day America. As I write, I must take these ideas into consideration. I am not a propagandist or a nationalist. I am a multiculturalist. When creating characters, I take into consideration and define their imagined societies, their ethnic situations, their hopes and dreams, fears and sorrows.

Like most writers, I write because I love it, because I have to write, because I enjoy the challenge of solving problems. I write to entertain. All writers believe they have something original to share about the human condition, which we hope readers will understand, not necessarily to agree with, but listen to, comprehend, and respond to. The hope is that readers will collaborate in the literary and literacy experience with us. My wish is that older readers not depend on reviews for their knowledge of books and writing for children. The more one reads, the more knowledgeable and sophisticated one becomes about the process of story and reading.

I come from a tiered environment of the African American family. It is a clan environment in one sense. It is inclusive of a generational rural family community, six generations to be exact. All the kids I grew up with in my village of Yellow Springs, Ohio, white and black kids, came from similar tiered environment of families — grandmoms, great-grands, aunts, uncles, first-, second-, third-, and fourth-, even fifth-cousins. My tiered clan still has its hierarchies. Its black sheep, no pun intended. Its stars and wannabes. It is my mother's Perry clan of more than two hundred and fifty and still it thrives. Her father, Levi Perry, the fugitive from slavery, was a stern, strict man. When she was a young woman, she could date only divinity students, and then she had to be home by nine o'clock. It's probably the reason that one night she jumped out of her bedroom window and fled to Detroit, where she lived and worked until she found her way to Calgary, Alberta, Canada, where she met my dad. Several of my female relatives, my contemporaries, married ministers. These gentlemen within the clan are considered very high in the social order. But the clan has become somewhat less conservative. They no longer look on me as peculiar or odd because I write. They like how successful I've become at it. Some of my first cousins now feel comfortable enough to say, "I've always wanted to write one book and sometime I will." I comment rather dryly, "Better get started. No time like the present."

Here's something to contemplate. Not too long ago in this century, reading and writing were not separated but taught as one entity. Every child had a slate and piece of chalk so writing and reading happened simultaneously. There were no time slots for composition and reading. They were one piece of work. We've gone from there to blackboards, young author programs and conferences, to computers and the information superhighway. Now we are returning rather from where we started: You can take a stylus, write on a computer screen, and simultaneously read what you've written. Some computer monitors are touch sensitive, where a child's fingers will do the talking. Human hands as the entry point into a child's brain isn't a new concept. It's merely one that was for some time forgotten. Educators point out that children begin intuitively to write and that the child's hands are a powerful instrument for learning to read. Where there is the sound-word symbol connection, children learn quickly to put words on paper. When the child tells a story, writes one, hears one, she or he learns what words mean and what language is. I have always felt that I am a sculptor. Because I shape the words on the page and I care about how the page looks.

My books are designed for young people and their older allies, for their pleasure. I had no idea when I started that they would be read in college, in grad school. That they would be taught. My constituency has therefore broadened over the years. I write for the young from ages six or seven up to eighty and on to ageless. My desire is to make different kinds of books—novels, at one time biographies, collections, and picture books.

The late Paul Heins, editor in chief of the *Horn Book Magazine*, wrote that I am an originator. If I am, it's because when I started I really didn't know how to do what I was doing and, therefore, had to determine the depth and breadth of it and originate my own expression. A British critic once wrote that "the very furniture of my mind was different." I guess he meant that it differed from European writers in that their furniture was delivered from certain long-standing specifications that they arrange as they will. While my furniture never had any specs to speak of, and which began by my putting the pieces together from limbs, branches of a lush forest of discovery.

I do often fit personal form and structure to kinds of story. In some ways, I am a shape-shifter writer who shapes and shifts the novel structure to fit my story needs. I do that in the new book, *Bluish*. In *Bluish* there are sections of record before chapters. These records are separate from chapters and in the same time frame as the chapters, but they are rather closer to the first person point of view, while the chapters remain in the third person. The sections of record are more personal, intimate, and occur in the most private moments of a character's thinking.

One of my pleasures has been to make collections of stories. I presented the first one some fifteen years ago titled *The People Could Fly*. For the design of them is to reinvent or re-vision past African American folkloric materials that were somewhat long, rambling, and often denigrated by past collectors who had little respect for the individual black tellers whose tales they were recording. The more recent of my other collections are *A Ring of Tricksters: Animal Tales from America, the West Indies, and Africa*; *When Birds Could Talk & Bats Could Sing*; *Her Stories: African American Folktales, Fairy Tales, and True Tales*. All these stories originate from the plantation era in the American South. Some are quite old.

One other type of collection was *In the Beginning: Creation Stories from Around the World*. Different from folktales, creation stories or myths have a prophetic quality, an awesome voice or sound to them. We feel that they are inevitable and irrefutable. Another collection, titled *The Dark Way: Stories from the Spirit World*, reveals tales that come from a darker side of human experience. I find dark tales amusing, as well. Scary stories are a legitimate offering for children. I delighted in them as a child. What a wonder it was to experience fright in the cuddled safety next to a mom or dad.

Recasting plantation era tales was a way for me to express cultural learning and to introduce folktale collections as an art form. The short tale is very much easier than the novel for young readers to approach. With the folktales, I begin with existing stories that I like and I try to make better an established story line. It is like a collaboration between myself and many tellers who have gone before me. I hear their voices still. And I try to keep their sounds, their tellings, in the words I recast and write. The plantation era collections I term *liberation literature*, which reveals a people's suffering and growing awareness of self in the pursuit of freedom. In liberation literature the reader travels with the character in the imagined or factual world of the book and bears witness to the character's trials, suffering, and triumphs. To the extent that the protagonist finds liberty, so, too, does the witness, the reader, recognize the struggle as personal and perceives a spiritual sense of freedom within. It follows that in 1993 I would compose a factual biographical work entitled *Many Thousand Gone: African Americans from Slavery to Freedom*. It has been called a history or encyclopedia of slavery. And because it is nonfiction, with short entries, it illuminates the plantation era in an entirely different way from the folktale collections.

I believe in story and plot as the motivation for reading. I try to write younger novels, such as *Cousins*, published in 1990, and *Second Cousins*, published this past fall of 1998. In my 1999 fall novel, *Bluish*, the three main characters are all in fifth grade in a New York City public alternative school. Speaking a while ago about how a book like *Bluish*, or any of the novels for that matter, gets done from a blank, scary page, the question I get most often from students and adults alike — new writers — is how does one do it and keep doing it? What

317

is the secret? If there's a secret, I don't know it. I don't really know how I do it, either. What I know is that I work each day when I'm home. Now that I have a good laptop I can work away from home. With each new thought of a book, I must face the fact that I have no idea how to write it. I learn over and over again that I can't think a book. I have to write it. I always start by thinking it out. And then I stop. The only way to know how to write is to write, to begin, to know that you are completely vulnerable. You feel like an idiot. You know you are. And like a child, you get angry at your dumbness and that's when you begin to work. Every book is a new way, which one learns.

I do love writing but often complain bitterly when the going gets tough. I get very tired, I want to cry, be a child, and throw things. Or my brain goes dead; yet I push on. By pushing on, some years ago I made a discovery. I know that every book I write holds three elements. I call them my literary triad of the known, the remembered, and the imagined: fact, memory, and imagination. These combine to create something that has never been. I know about country life and rural communities. I know the people of my southern Ohio/northern Kentucky and Tennessee area. I know the black and Indian heritage of many of the people. I remembered that my great-grandmother was Mary Cloud and also part Patawatomi Indian. The idea came to me out of my imagination: What would happen if one created a black and Amerind family in which the mother was black, the father Amerind, the son, in a self-drama about himself as an Indian warrior, and a daughter who doesn't know what she is. Out of that known, remembered, and imagined came the book *Arilla Sun Down*. It was not an easy book. It holds the concept that we carry our pasts along with us in the present. We may not be aware of them, but they are there. And what I did was reveal the past in the *Arilla* book through different time frames. Not exactly flashbacks, but whole chapters that take place at another time in the characters' lives, that live, yet remain unknown, forgotten, invisible, inside those characters in the present. Thus, the lines between past and present are blurred, as they are in Amerindian societies, as they are in many African societies, and to some extent in African American societies. It is this space-time continuum between past and present that is most suited to my artistry and best expresses my own cultural learning. It is the reason I am a tier or generational writer.

I suppose I have many more stories to tell. I don't know what they are because they only come to me when I need them. That is, when I finish a book I have nothing to write. But then, suddenly, there's something there and it appears in my mind. And I must write it. The curious part is that I rarely remember the first idea. Suddenly I am working, but I don't know how it all started.

When my mother died, I put together the *Her Stories* book in memory of her and loving mothers like her. All of my books have their reasons for being. Memory is one of the reasons. Memory is my responsibility to all that I am. I remind myself to remember what has taken place before I was in place; that there are lives going on that I can talk to and know about. There are other lives that I recall seeing, which I must talk for through the experience of creating lives that reflect their lives in the writings I make. I think I remember large amounts of what my father told me when I was a growing child. Eventually, I understood he meant for me to leave our small town and go looking for America. He, a wanderer himself, went always looking for a place to be and become in the vastness of the American hopescape. It took years and years for me to understand my dad's meaning. But eventually I did. I found purpose in the entertainment of others and in writing well for myself.

I remember to pay homage through my literature to those who took care of me in my life, who "raised me up," as we used to say, who listened to me, swung me in the porch swing, soothed me, sang to me, and rocked me, and all the time taking the time to teach me.

Home, place, time, family, and generations are for me powerful concepts. As I live, I create books that I hope will bring something new to young people—something of value. And not only to the young, but to adults, and women, significantly. I am concerned with female empowerment as I am concerned with cultural learning. The story I know best and which causes my imagination to leap is the tale I was born into. My cultural learning came from true tales and tales of speculation from the mouths of loved ones, mostly women.

There is wonderment of memory in the transpositions out of history, from ways of being, from made-up jokes and sayings, and out of the true living of long-gone days.

For me, there is always something to care enough about to remember, something to figure out, and last, but not least, something to write about.

Thank you.

CHILDREN'S BOOK FESTIVAL

Speech given at Southern Mississippi University, March 22, 2001;
this was the last speech given by Virginia Hamilton.

GOOD MORNING, everyone. I'm delighted to be here this morning for the opening session of this thirty-fourth Annual Children's Book Festival. I am also looking forward to this evening's festivities. Our son, Jaime, is here with me. Arnold had an operation last month on the lumbar portion of his lower vertebrae. He's unable to be here, not quite able to stride through long airport corridors or await late planes, etc. However, Jaime Adoff, whose first book will be published in 2002, will be the luncheon speaker in Arnold's place. Not taking Adoff's place, of course, but he'll read you some of Arnold's poetry, and talk to you about his own life, and read you some of his own work. I think it will be fun. Arnold sends his regards and asks for your understanding. Believe me, he would be here if he could be. At the autographing time, Jaime has special dispensation to write in Arnold's books—Jaime Adoff, son of Arnold—if you wish. That way, you get two poets—and two Adoffs.

I knew Jaime had the writer's mind when as a small boy taking a bath, he yelled "Mom! Mom!" I came running. There he was, all wet, with the washcloth in his favorite place, atop his head. And he said, "Mom, but when do you grow down!" You can all meet him later.

When I accepted the invitation for this talk, I wanted to come up with a spiffy title that would give a point of view for the audience. And I wanted the view to be toward a theme that would deliver to you

321

something of value. I came up with various titles and discarded them. Writing is fun, but speech writing has its own problems, pitfalls, and hilarity. One title I thought of was "The Art of the Novel." I immediately had an image of this guy, Art, in a brown suit and striped yellow tie, holding a novel to his chest. And I was about to carry on with the deconstruction of the life of Art, or the Art of life, when I got hold of myself. My theme here is not the novel — I have many other kinds of books, and Art is not one of my characters, although as I think about it, he does have possibilities. But that sort of thing happens in my brain after having written so many novels. Twenty, to be exact. Every sight and sound is grist for the grinding mill of my noveling, so to speak. *Zeely* was my first book, published in the fall of 1967. The latest is *Bluish*, published in 1999, which is my twentieth novel. The year 2000's title is *The Girl Who Spun Gold*, which is a picture book illustrated by the master painters Leo and Diane Dillon.

So let's call my standing here and your sitting there a visit among enthusiastic admirers of books and literature for children. Reader and Writer have much in common.

When I was a child, I was a listener and watcher. I might as well have had rubber strings attached to certain grown-ups. The strings jumped and sprang back to me, entwining me and drawing me into the very warm and safe world of my close kin. My kinfolk talked, gestured, and I knew them through their particular physical traits long before I understood what they were talking about. It was enough that I would watch and know them before, and in spite of, the stories they told. There are sounds of voices that I remember quite clearly from an early age. Words and music and gestures from long ago are as clear as daylight today. Nothing enormous in themselves, but signposts of places even beyond story. Places of the heart.

I'm happy that the first book, *Zeely*, is still going strong, as are all the others, in one form or another — paperback, hardcover, school adaptations, foreign editions. That's what's wonderful about children's books. They can last and last. There are always children coming of age for one or another of the books. Young people read *M.C. Higgins* or

The House of Dies Drear as though they were written yesterday. I have thirty-seven or thirty-eight titles since the first book in 1967. Maybe more. I haven't counted lately. I lose track because there are several in production right now. I'm working on one that was supposed to be finished in January and I have one more to go, due in July, on my present contract. [*Time Pieces*, her final novel, was completed by Christmas of 2001 and was published after her death in 2002.]

Books get backed up in the pipeline, as illustrators and editors struggle to meet deadlines. It's not always easy, because writing and illustrating books is an art form. It's not like a nine-to-five job with work laid out in proper order and knowing exactly what amount is to be done at any given time. Often, I only know the extent of an idea for a book. I don't know how it's going to go day by day. Some days, I am able to write maybe three or four lines. Nothing more of it will come forth. Other times, I might write a chapter. I never know. And still other times, I announce to Arnold, "I quit! I can't do it anymore!" But I do do it. I go to work every day and do what I can to open, write, and close a story.

I've been working on that same book that is late for the last eight or nine months. Every sentence, every word isn't perfect the first time. I tend to write and rewrite until a paragraph, a scene, and the tone seem perfect. It's instinct and intuition that leads me in the right direction.

Young people ask me questions about writing. It is not so often "How do you write a book," but rather, "How do you keep writing book after book?" Depending on their ages, they say, "I get stuck after a page." Or, "I can't think of anything after about a half hour." I tell them that each day you live a little different than the day before, and so each day you can add something new to the writing. I tell them not to try too hard and get anxious about it. And then I tell them stories about myself, my family, and my life. Maybe to give them an idea as to how writing happens, that creative writing happens from living.

My approach to creating narratives has to do with memories out of childhood that fit within a creative process. This type of fabrication is my way of solving problems and presenting important aspects of

323

experience and memory. It's the way I retain some essence of my past to pass along, perhaps for future generations. My fictions and most of my nonfiction writing have some basis in the reality of a large or small experience, although they are only peripherally autobiographical. But the fact that my own grandfather Levi was a fugitive from the Civil War South gave me the impetus to research centuries of plantation era history and folklore in order to recast historical and folk narrative into modern day collections of stories and tales for the young.

Storytelling is certainly my way of sharing in community. It is the method my own parents used to define the boundaries of their living. They were fine storytellers; they drew me close by their stories, which taught me ways of living in the world—how to think about life and how to act toward others. I do the same while writing my stories down, and I learn new ways of storytelling all the time. Sitting around the fire or in a group with a teacher or family member telling stories is a familiar image. I told stories to my own children, true and half-true household tales, family, generational stories. They also heard them from their grandmother, Granny Etta Belle, my mother.

It is no wonder that Jaime is now a writer.

When I was a child, the story lady at the library read stories to us children as we sat around her on a hooked rug, which for me became a magic carpet. I was transported around the world, magically, by the sound of the story lady's voice and the wide range of tales she told.

Years later I realized that we use story as a means to keep our cultural heritages safe, in order to save the very language in which heritage is made symbolic through story.

The difference between myself and my parents' storytelling is that I was not gifted with their oral telling abilities. I had to write my stories down, just as did those authors whose storybooks my story lady read to us.

In my *The People Could Fly* collection, there is the story called "A Wolf and Little Daughter," a black variation on the "Big Bad Wolf and Little Red Riding Hood" tale. In my version, these words are sung by Little Daughter: "Tray-bla, tray, tray-bla tray, tray-bla cum qua, kimo."

Now that wily wolf asks his would-be victim to sing that "sweetest, goodest, song again." And to escape the wolf, Little Daughter does sing again, and she is saved. In the plantation era, African words in stories almost always were meant to empower the teller or singer, while preserving some aspect of the mother language. Thus, the sung words of Little Daughter are magic and have the power to save her (i.e., to save the African heritage).

My mother would sing to me songs of peddlers and vendors from her childhood. "Any rags, any bones, and any bottles today, the big black Rag Man is coming your way. Any rags . . . Any rags . . ." I found her singing magical, with a cadence of a faraway time and place. I've not forgotten the sound, as if, in it, time stands still within the long-ago melody. I think the song or, better, the street call is in the film version of *The House of Dies Drear*. I recall recording it for the producer.

Random/Knopf publishers put out a fifteenth anniversary edition reissue this fall of *The People Could Fly* with a CD of eleven of the stories being read by myself and James Earl Jones. Actually, he acts out the stories wonderfully. We both read the title story.

I see my writings and the language of them as a way to illuminate a human condition. All of my work—as a novelist, biographer, and as creator and compiler of stories—helps to portray the essence of a people who are a parallel culture community of America and, it is hoped, reveals the universality among peoples. I coined *parallel culture* to get away from the terms *minority* and *majority* and their connection to *less* and *more*. I didn't start out with any large concerns in my writing. Although *Zeely* was a sixties take on looking back to Africa, I started out writing what I had learned in college and still thought about. In fact, the book came from a twenty-page story I'd written in college.

Making up stories was so easy for someone like myself who had heard tales every day of her life, from parents, relatives, brothers, and sisters. My brother Bill often acted out what happened in school. He was my constant companion as a child. Older than me, he was the one who made up games for us to play. He was the one who wrote to his congressman to get more hours in a day because what he had from

325

morning to night wasn't nearly enough. He was the one who collected the great seals of the states. Living on a farm with hogs in rural Ohio when I was nine and he was thirteen, he was the one who taught me how to imagine and to dream. He was a great dreamer. He collected matchboxes. He counted makes of cars, setting up a table in the yard and writing down their colors, makes, shapes, tail fins, etc. Unfortunately, not many cars came by our house every hour—only about once a day. We called it "field traffic"—when workers at the air force base came home. We never heard them go to work in the early hours of the morning. Bill was the one who thought to dig a hole in the field to China. He and I watched soberly as, finally, the hole he dug slowly filled with groundwater.

My story writing has progressed to my present attempts to mark the history and traditions of African Americans, a parallel culture people, by bringing to all readers strong stories and memorable characters living the best way they know how. I want all readers, children as well as adults, to really care about the characters, to feel, to understand them, and to empathize with them. I want my books to make worlds in which characters become real to readers. And I want readers to see for themselves the worth, the integrity of the created worlds.

I think the writer and reader come to an agreement in reading. It's true that one of us is not very good without the other. Our bond is our common language and all the things we share in our lives—people, places and things, teachers, friends, school, games, you name it. I've tried to make books that bring new insights into the realm of youth literature, particularly for the young women and girls, significantly. *M.C. Higgins, the Great* and *The Planet of Junior Brown* come to mind as stories that seemed, when I wrote them, as natural to write as seeing the sun come up. Collections like *The People Could Fly* and *Her Stories*, and novels like *Cousins* and *Second Cousins* come to me as ideas that had been there all the time, just waiting for me to notice them. In a sense, I revise my past and create and envision stories that hold the essence of what I've seen and heard and learned in my life.

I speak a lot about re-visioning. That's what I do with the plantation tales that I, in a sense, reinvent in terms of today's world and the world's children. Many of the folktales I collect were recorded by people who were part of a time period in this society that did not recognize African Americans as equals. Consequently, many of the tales were recorded in a kind of quaint, so-called black English that is nearly unreadable today. And the texts were stereotypes of black speech. I attempted to bring the language used out of the morass of narrow-mindedness regarding a people. And I re-vision the language in terms of legitimate black cultural truths.

We are a multicultural society; we need many different kinds of books so that, when children read about parallel culture groups other than their own, they can better see how all cultures contribute and belong in the weave that is the American cultural fabric. They find characters like themselves in Beverly Cleary's *Ramona the Brave* or Laurence Yep's *Dragonwings*, or my *The House of Dies Drear*. There are books now about children who look like me and sound like me, whoever "me" may be. And there are always astounding books about tiny creatures with wings, imps and fairies and other kinds of creatures which can have human characteristics. I have one such title dealing with creatures, all set to be illustrated, in the pipeline to be published. [This book is forthcoming from Blue Sky Press/Scholastic.]

That's what we are all about, I believe. We who write, and we who take care that books are in libraries, schools, and in the hands of teachers who see that children are nourished with multicultural books and reading. For we believe that children are our treasure and that books are their pieces of eight. Tale collectors like myself delight in a discovery like the great New Orleans home story of Annie Christmas, three versions of which I uncovered in one day. In my version in the *Her Stories* collection, it begins: "Black folks tell about Annie Christmas, and so do white folks. Every kind of folk claim her as their own, and there are good reasons why. But let me tell you. Who am I? I am the kind of grandmaw that lives to spin a good yarn." This area of Louisiana and Southern Mississipi are gold mines of riverboat tales.

I do want to mention that I have a website on the Internet:

327

www.virginiahamilton.com. The website is quite extensive, more than sixty pages. I'm averaging over 200,000 hits a month, which isn't bad for a website that doesn't sell anything. I have a comments area where children and adults write comments to me and I answer back. It's a fun, running commentary about what kids are reading and what adults are doing with them. Many students do their reports from the site, as do educators, from undergraduate to graduate school. I also get email fan letters from children and adults. All send me frog jokes, which I try to eventually put on the site, a few of them, anyway. I collect inanimate frogs. I have over 300 now. It's fun, a pleasurable hobby for me — I need to keep in touch with the five, ten and twelve year old inside me, and outside myself.

[FROG JOKE]

When I speak to students, I tell them how important I think they are to their communities, and I say it's hard to imagine all the things they will need to know in this new millennium. I remind them that early Native peoples were astounded by the sight of the first trains. They called the trains the "iron horses," since horses were the only comparisons they could make to the giant machines chugging across the plains. My mother, who was born in 1892, recalled seeing an automobile for the first time. She said all the children were let out of school for a great event, and they were mightily astonished when this horseless carriage came down the road making this incredible racket. Some children ran back into the school, they were so frightened by the Model T Ford and its awful noise. There'd never been anything that loud in the countryside. Mother found the horseless carriage a great wonder, she said. And a grand learning experience. I believe today's children are going to be astonished by their future, too.

They and I have an important connection. For literacy is the ability to read and write. A book is forever changed by those who read it. Readers are changed by books they read, and they will have very different ideas about what they've read. Many times, what they think is not what the author had in mind at all. But once a book is out there, the author realizes the book is no longer hers.

Here I am, born in America, and yet I feel I write as if English were my second language. My first language happens when I sit down to compose a story. It is what I do with English when I look at the words that make the language mine. I know and keep English in rooms of my mind. Rooms of living that are full of furniture, fixtures, framed pictures, quiet and stillness of a kind that is only mine. Full of sound of curtains sucking against screens as the breeze tries to pull them outside. The rooms are my vision — mine alone. That is the first language that I write. The language of my sight and feeling. I see, feel, and write. The rooms and the furniture of my mind make a novel like *Bluish* or any one of my others different from anyone else's. It's what makes a character like Jahnina "Fractal" Madison from the novel *Second Cousins* different from any other character of my own or anyone else's. My first language of personal sensibility makes all the questions and gives all the answers in my books. I give to English all of my history, my time and my mother's and father's time, and my great-grandmother Mary Cloud's time, and my grandfather Levi's time, and the time now, in order to make my words. The way I see her, great-grandmother Mary Cloud, holding my grandfather Levi as she leads him north across the Ohio River in one harrowing time of words so secret and so powerful they were never spoken. No one ever said the Underground out loud. I imagine Great-grandmother Mary never looked back for fear of what she might see or of what she might've heard and had to reply.

I've had to find the language that I could write in order to tell some of the essence of my historical past, not my personal history, and the means to transform it into fiction. All that history of a people passed along through narratives, through memory of story and its truth and consequences. The significance is that I could put a new face to all those memories out of my own family and from a people to bring universality through fiction and nonfiction offerings. Like the true story my grandpa Levi told his children, my mother among them. Once a year he told of his escape, so they would never get stolen, so they would know — you run when you have to, always.

My books reflect how I was taught to see the world when I was very small and how I viewed my surroundings on my own. I think my mother and father were very special people. They knew what happened through story, and they told stories, lived stories all of their lives. I grew up in the forties on a small Ohio farm. In 1948, the train to Chicago stopped in my hometown. And one fine early morning, I boarded the train with my mom and dad to travel all the way to Los Angeles, where my father's mother and half sister lived. His father was no longer living, but my grandpa Hamilton had been an LA fireman at the time horses pulled wagons loaded with big tanks of water. The men on the wagons had to pump the water through the hoses by hand so the firemen could fight fires. My dad described to me the sight of his dad, my grandpa Hamilton, way up high on a ladder, holding on to the hose that shot hard streams of water into a burning building.

Well. These kinds of stories were told to me all of my life, so that by the time my parents were no longer living—my mother lived to be ninety-seven—I had a soul full of a certain belief system, a certain hopescape, and a great respect for privacy and freedom, respect for all that is living; a deep understanding of ecology systems, from having grown up on an Ohio truck farm. I passed it on to my own children and through books to children in general.

Mother raised five children and six hundred leghorn chickens. I collected the eggs. Dad raised forty razorback hogs—shades of the pig master Nat Tayber and the pig herder Zeely Tayber from the book *Zeely*. He planted fields of corn and vegetables. And slaughtered his own hogs and made ham and bacon and pork in the smokehouse.

I cleaned the corn rows of morning glories, a penny or two a row. Those were very long rows in the hot sun. But the morning glories climbing the cornstalks were spectacular. I've not forgotten them and now grow my own. I observed too little rain and too much drought and flood, cyclone, and blizzard. Tornadoes forever terrify me. Mom told stories at such dark times. Dad played stirring melodies on his Gibson mandolin. He was a classical mandolinist, and he had a New Orleans, Cajun, connection to names such as Oberchaun–noir. I can hear his voice even now, talking story as he played.

I was the child who grew up never being told she could not do something. If I made a mistake, I was advised how to correct it but never told that I couldn't make one. I write characters as if they were my children and adult characters as if they are my relatives. I build characters, watching them, discreetly advising and listening and suggesting. It's my great pleasure to create characters and landscape and story. Characters are symbolic human beings. Books are the symbols of whole communities and worlds. All of us have stories. Some of us write them as we live them. We change, we amend, create, revise. We continue telling our tales at least to ourselves. And story words are always on my mind. When I interrupt their flow to get involved with them, well then, I am talking back. When I'm talking back, I'm considering making up new stories for a book. Whether novels or collections, my books are full of stories. Characters tell stories to one another and to themselves. And all of them are expressions of my own cultural learning from living in households in which people cared about one another and showed that they did. A subtext of many of my works is the survival strategies that created characters suggest to me.

M.C. Higgins from *M.C. Higgins, the Great*, and Junior Brown and Buddy Clark from *The Planet of Junior Brown* all have survival schemes suggested by their own character building. I feel sometimes as if I'm simply an observer of their plans. The novel *Plain City* and the character Buhlaire were like a surprise. Buhlaire came to me suddenly, a complete being, with her strawberry Rasta hair and white snowsuit. I followed her as she grew and changed and created herself. I love the creation stories of the title *In The Beginning: Creation Stories from Around the World*. My editor and I had a huge argument about what stories would go in the book—and different ideas about what was a creation myth and what wasn't.

Much later, after writing *Cousins* about Cammy Coleman, Elodie, and Patty Ann, I wrote the sequel *Second Cousins*. It's a more contemporary story with a girl, Jahnina "Fractal" Madison, who has a computer and will travel, and who is related to the Cammy Coleman of the first book. There is a definite change in *Cousins* and *Second Cousins* from books like *Junior Brown* and *M.C.* The *Cousins* books are younger, with a kind of less complicated plot formation. And yet, I think *Cousins* is pretty perfect as a young novel. I really like it. I like *Sweet Whispers, Brother Rush* as well, an older, darker novel. Well, I like all of my books. I guess if I didn't, I wouldn't have written them. Would you write a book you hated? I'm not sure. That would be interesting to analyze.

My newest offering is the picture book *The Girl Who Spun Gold*, illustrated by the master painters Leo and Diane Dillon. *The Girl Who Spun Gold* is my take on the classic Rumpelstiltskin folktale. It is directly derived from a century old Caribbean version of Rumpelstiltskin. When I discovered the Afro-Caribbean version, I was really astounded. It never occurred to me there would be one. But why not? German folktales and folktales from India, which are probably the oldest tales, traveled the world. Similarly, the tale Catskinella, which I also stumbled upon, is a plantation era black version of Cinderella and can be found in my *Her Stories* collection.

Well, there's no way I can speak about every book that I have written, so I'd like to finish by reading you just a small part of *The Girl Who Spun Gold*.

[Passage unknown]

Most of the household tales I heard as a child were large or small lessons in living. My father's true tales of Canada, where he lived for many years, told about the last great gatherings of the high plains Amerindians. They were lessons in looking out, looking through, and looking for America. I go looking for story and find it. Tales such as the girl who spun gold are out there, waiting for someone like myself to rediscover them and re-vision them. They last the way Rumpelstiltskin has lasted, because they teach us words, language, and something of value. When you, the reader, open this book or any such book, the time of story begins; and you are there, just in time.

Thank you.

LETTER TO THE EDITOR OF
The Horn Book Magazine

MAY 24, 2001
FROM: VIRGINIA HAMILTON
TO: ATTN: ROGER SUTTON, EDITOR IN CHIEF
THE HORN BOOK, INC.

LETTER TO THE EDITOR:

RE: ARTICLE, "SLIPPERY SLOPES . . ."

*T*HAT OUTDATED argument is risen again. Who shall best tell the tales out of African American and Latino experience? Those who are African American and those who are Latino? And how should their excellence be rewarded? With the Coretta Scott King and Pura Belpré Awards, of course. Marc Aronson in his article, "Slippery Slopes and Proliferating Prizes," May/June 2001 *Horn Book*, would have us believe he has a better answer: ALA should rid itself of these two troublesome awards which, apparently, he is certain are based only on identity factors and not the selection committees' judgments of literary excellence in conferring their choices.

But no! By the end of the article we encounter the finish of a pseudo-intelligent "bait and switch" exercise. On the last page he states, after a long harangue as to why both awards would best be discontinued: "My suggestion is . . . keep the CSK, Belpré . . . awards, but honor content alone, not identity."

The American Library Association clearly understands that having "house" Newbery/Caldecott along with "house" CSK and "house" Belpré awards in the same community of excellence, shines the light on all three all the more brightly. It does not take away from Newbery/Caldecott if "house" CSK selects its own award books based on criteria of its own making. As happened when Christopher Paul Curtis's book, *Bud, Not Buddy*, won the John Newbery Medal, it was selected as winner of the CSK literature award as well. That both awards committees selected Curtis's book as the best of the year simply demonstrates the committees' comparable selection processes.

Certainly there will be people who will say, "We don't need to give this or that African American or Latino a Newbery (or) Caldecott; *they* have their own awards! Similar excuses have been voiced since the start of the CSK Award. It was more than fifty years of Newbery Awards before an African American was awarded the Newbery Medal, with my *M.C. Higgins, the Great* in 1975.

There is a difference in the way a member of a parallel culture community writes about the community through her own experience from the way one outside of that community might write about it. Race and culture and social consciousness give parallel culture artists and writers unique insights.

Both the Newbery and CSK awards committees responded to the universality in Curtis's rendering of a black experience. Contrary to Aronson's opinion, the CSK has always honored content. The integrated CSK awards committees have been responsible and reliable. The books they have chosen have been among the best. Occasionally, the committees have faltered, as has the Newbery committee, but on the side of literary judgment and social awareness, the latter being of deep concern to CSK committees. While my *M.C. Higgins, the Great* won a John Newbery Medal, it did not receive the CSK Award for text. But to suggest, as Marc Aronson does, that CSK awards committees are not as competent as Newbery and Caldecott, and the books, not as well deserving, is outrageous. The committees often have different opinions about a book. And I believe it is wrong to besmear the extraordinary writing and art that has been and continues to be produced by black artists and illustrators. It is unjust and the kind of biased thinking advocates, like Aronson, of cultural pluralism, pose as "the honest truth." Rather than verity, it reveals a fear of difference and of parallel cultures providing their own views and appropriating manifestations of their considerable power through parallel awards. Do they really not understand that, rather than balkanization of art and literature, multiculturalism thrives on the equal opportunity of all peoples of color to pursue their arts and awards on their own terms?

What is wrong with having an award based on African American experiences? It's not that we need it, particularly. We want it. Perhaps Marc Aronson should turn in his Robert F. Sibert Award. After all, it is a new award for informational books and likely contributes to stylistic balkanization of prose!

The fact of African Americans' singularity in being the only group, racial or otherwise, brought here against its will has everything to do with how we think and respond, and what we see, write about, and illustrate.

Our African American history and traditions entitle us to judge our own literary contributions, using an award system of our own making that is consistent with our parallel cultural views. To hold this belief in ourselves in no way takes away from our ability to judge the merits of our literature. Many times members of CSK have been members of Newbery Award committees. We should honor the tireless labor of both award committees.

Multiculturalism is the point of view of parallel cultures of which blacks and Latinos are a part. The multicultural view is one of equality of all cultures in a parallel or equal stance with one another. The view from here is other than that of cultural pluralism — Marc Aronson's view — which will recognize members of other cultures in the pluralistic literature as "minorities," remaining marginalized within a dominant culture, which culture is generally white.

The multiculture view is that a parallel culture people will create stories and make illustrations in which the central characters are of that very culture and express feelings and experiences, hopes and dreams of that culture. I see nothing wrong with that.

African Americans have learned from generations of experience with the white culture imperatives as well—because we've lived and prevailed within their structure. We are capable of writing from more than one perspective. But the time has long since passed when we will even consider giving up hard-fought gains in the continuing struggle.

VIRGINIA HAMILTON

Virginia Hamilton is the Honorary Chair of the three-year Coretta Scott King Awards Initiative. Her latest book is *The Girl Who Spun Gold*; Scholastic Inc., Blue Sky Press.

WORDS AFTER

BY KACY COOK

I NEVER MET Virginia Hamilton, never heard her speak, but I have long been drawn to her writing. It was my pleasure to "meet" the woman through the documents used to build this collection. I had the privilege of getting to know this extraordinary artist in the quiet of the office where most of her writing took place, amid the mementos and awards that represent her personal and professional achievements.

This book is part of a much larger project: the organization of an immense and exceptional legacy. It began in late 2006, about six months after I met Arnold Adoff, and it is an ongoing and evolving process. In the beginning, our task seemed almost overwhelming. The magnitude of the work Virginia and Arnold produced is, of course, staggering, in influence as well as sheer volume. Arnold tells me that they never had a secretary or personal assistant. Everything, literally everything, was saved in four rooms of their home, but the filing system was, shall we say, informal. Moreover, Arnold had found himself unable to enter Virginia's office in the years after her death. He had taken to opening the door a crack and tossing things on the floor inside.

So the process began by making stacks. The first order of business was to gather five large boxes of Virginia's manuscripts and editorial correspondence to send to their important destination: the Library of

Congress, where they are housed with the papers of other great American writers of the twentieth century.

I began filling a shelf with speeches as a purely organizational aid. Other nonfiction writing was gradually added to the stack, which quickly spread to a second shelf. Our appreciation of their significance also grew. We decided to compile them for posterity, leaving the logistics of how they would be distributed to be determined.

Virginia always broke new ground in each of her books. No two were alike. As I read the mound of speeches, it became clear that the same was true of this genre. Always original, Virginia never gave the same speech twice. Certain themes — her background, her thoughts about parallel cultures, her liberation literature — were a constant; many stories, particularly those about family, were lovingly retold. But given her extensive speaking commitments — on top of her writing and family obligations as well as health issues we now know about — I fully expected we'd find many duplications. There wasn't one. Even if the titles were the same, or similar themes were discussed, entirely new speeches, filled with fresh insights and details, were written. Virginia respected her audiences, but her own intellectual curiosity and integrity demanded more than simply repeating herself.

We've identified more than 150 complete or nearly complete speeches, essays, and interviews covering thirty years, 1971 to 2001. There are easily two or three dozen more that we have not been able to reconstruct yet because pages are either missing or not labeled. In addition to the typewritten manuscripts, we scoured every anthology, publication, and textbook in the house to be sure we had found as much as possible of her published speeches, essays, and conversations.

The majority of speeches were written on a typewriter or early word processor. For most of those written on a computer, a printout was all that remained. I would find myself holding the one and only copy of a Virginia Hamilton original. Still, except for major speeches — such as the Newbery and Hans Christian Andersen acceptances and the Arbuthnot Lecture — compiling the pieces in this book was not as simple as it may appear.

Virginia carefully placed some speeches in labeled folders or neatly paper clipped them together with an identifier, such as a location (e.g., Montana or Dallas) or organization (IRA, ALA), typed or written on the top of the pages. But as often as not, there was no identification or only one notation on the first page. If the pages were separated, reuniting them was difficult. Detective work was needed. Forensic evidence included paper color (the original color as well as how aging had affected it) and thickness, type fonts, or scrawled messages that were difficult for even Arnold to decipher.

Determining the year a speech was delivered was easier. In addition to penciled equations in the margins where Virginia calculated how long she'd been writing professionally, she always mentioned her most recently published work. Then, using her old calendars, letters, and—for more recent speeches—her website, we were able to pin down the specifics of the audience or occasion.

Arnold told me that we have Virginia's innate shyness and perfectionism to thank for this collection. I think that is a lovely way to look at it. "If she had not cared so much about getting it all exactly right, while just wanting to stay home and write," Arnold said, "she might have done more improvisational public speaking." And we would not have this significant record of the insights and reflections of one of the world's most brilliant and innovative thinkers and writers of children's literature.

As usual, Virginia said it best:

While it is still true that many children's books are created through the prism of popular culture, which tends to avoid the broad cultural foundation of this country, things are changing. I think that my books have been responsible for many of these changes, because I have broadened the field and created a canon at the same time. Yes, there was a cultural children's literature before me, but there wasn't the diversity of genre and subject matter I've created in the more than thirty books I've published over the years. Nor has there been another writer for young people, black or white, who has done the amount of speaking and writing I've done about writing and my particular parallel culture. You can follow the history of my books through my published speeches. When you trace my history, you see that my books have widened the cultural landscape and provided a bridge to the past and between the generations.

MY LOVE and gratitude go to my children, Leah, Jacob, and Ben, who, besides managing their own busy and productive lives, have helped me to maintain my Columbus/Yellow Springs balancing act. When I say they keep the home fires burning, I'm in no way referring to that one minor grease fire in the kitchen.

ARNOLD: LATE AT NIGHT IN GINNY'S OFFICE

WE BUILT THIS house in 1969 on the last few acres of the Hamilton family farm. By 1974 it was full of books and papers and our two children, of course. So we added this room on the cool and shaded west side of the house: sliding glass doors and long window lights. I built the bookcases out of the best heavy redwood. No sags.

Each working morning, after the kids had gone to school, and later on, after the kids had gone out into their own worlds, I would make the coffee, load the washing machine, and head upstairs to my office. Over those thirty-two years, we wrote and published more than seventy books.

I measured Ginny's progress on each project by her voice floating up to me on some late afternoon or as we met in the kitchen to refill our cups. There was always time to follow her into the office, sit in my chair by the sliding doors, and listen as she read to me. I loved that process of listening to chapters of a new novel, or her new telling of an old tale. Sometimes M.C. Higgins and Paul Robeson on some same afternoon.

We would have long conversations, discussions, and sometimes arguments. She would elicit my reactions, my thoughts, then play on those sounding boards until she was satisfied. Then she would go back to work. There was always the sharing of ideas and information and opinions. But always, her own vision was paramount.

We wrote and published and raised our children and traveled. We lived the kind of "life in art" we had dreamed about when we were young and starting out. And as the years and books and awards and honors built into her special and significant career, she began to write more speeches and present her own views around the world.

And the process in her office was the same for the making of speeches as it was for the discussions of character and tone and place in her novels. We were writers who lived within that duality of our literature and a world view of politics and race and generation. It was a most wonderful time of thought and talk and writing and speaking. It was a wonderful process of moving forward. No sags.

Now, seven years after her death, I sit in this office and marvel at the files stacked neatly on those shelves. Kacy Cook and I have counted and catalogued more than 150 speeches written over a thirty-two-year period. And after two years of our efforts, there are a few stacks of files yet untouched.

Ginny read me her drafts of each speech, each article. I was present at almost all of the occasions, as participant or part of the audience. And I still marvel at the number and variety of these nonfiction pieces created during the writing of more than forty books.

Building this collection was almost as complex as the making of one of these speeches. Despite my own skills as anthologist and editor, there is no way I could have worked alone and succeeded with any degree of accomplishment.

Kacy Cook brings keen intelligence and experience to this project. She has that great love of youth literature, especially Virginia's novels, combined with the energy and technical wizardry so necessary for this kind of project. Many of the choices were hers, as we discovered and read and ascribed priorities. This was a true collaborative effort.

And Kacy possesses that enthusiasm and optimism which, many times, pulled me forward into the realms of possibility when I became mired in those comfortable past times. As we worked on this book, she would always move me, gently but with loving firmness, into the work. Into the future. And always no sags.

GREAT THANKS and love to my friends and (very) adult children, Jaime Levi and Leigh Hamilton, accomplished artists in their own evolving lives. They are as strong and focused as their mother.

Thanks to Dick Robinson, CEO of Scholastic Inc., for suggesting this book project to Virginia, several years before her death. And for his continuing commitment to this collection these past years.

Thanks to Andrea Davis Pinkney and Suzanne Murphy and David Saylor and Jacky Harper and all our friends at the Scholastic helm.

Thanks to the publications where a few of these pieces first appeared.

All love to Rudine Sims Bishop and Leo and Diane Dillon for decades of friendship and their superb work and encouragement.

Finally, to my editor, Bonnie Verburg, thanks beyond thanks. I always recall staying up all night in our living room, many years ago, as I added wood to the fire, refilled the glasses, and observed the "magick" of process. I am proud of my own books she has edited in the past and the unique place she had in the making of many Virginia Hamilton creations. And her steadfast commitment to this collection.

Peace.

LEIGH: REMEMORY

THERE ARE SO many things I remember about my mother, but most of them have nothing to do with her speeches or her writing. She was not only a genius of an artist, creator of a new art form, and winner of every prize that children's literature had to offer, but she was also a truly amazing mother. Most of my memories are of this Virginia Hamilton. Simply my mother. Sadly, I didn't really get to see her speak much. By the time her career had exploded and she was out and about speaking regularly, I was already away from the house, pursuing my own life and career. I'm sorry I don't have more of that Virginia Hamilton to share with you, more of those memories, as opposed to just the "mom" ones. Although for me, these memories are the most sustaining; they nourish my spirit as I miss her, remember her, and celebrate her every day. The memories I have are sweet and clear and sun-filled yellow, and play over and over, and are a comfort and great happiness to me. I would like to share a few of them with you.

What I can tell you, or I should say, what I remember so vividly, is that when I wanted to run track *and* play in the orchestra, the school thought it was too much and I should pick just one. But I didn't pick just one, and Mom drove me to every meet and concert. She would bring my track spikes and concert gown and violin in our old Gran Torino station wagon, and I would change in the "way back" as she drove me to the next venue, so to speak. Never a complaint, never an "oh, that's just too much, I just don't have time." Simply doing it, because that's what you did when your Leigh-la wanted to do it all. And of course I never thought for a moment I couldn't do it all; she told the school that I *could* do it all, and so we did, she and I together. She driving me, and me running or playing. We did it all. And I won most of my races, and was concertmaster in the orchestra, and I know, because I remember, that it was really because of her.

I can tell you she was an amazing cook. I remember her cooking all the old family recipes that were handed down—from my great-grandmother to my granny, from Granny to my mother, and then of course from my mother to me. I would watch as she would put a pinch of this in here, and a shake of that in there, all the while talking about family stories as I sat with my back against the warm stove, always a bit in the way, listening, smelling, absorbing it all. I remember that very well. Still today, in my own kitchen, I can feel her presence as I make the old family favorites that were handed down to me—a pinch of this, a shake of that, sometimes feeling as if she is guiding my hand, sometimes. When I got a bit older, she would tell me of a new idea for a book, or if she was in the middle of one and not sure which way the characters were going to go, we would talk about it. I would give her suggestions, and she would laugh because they were mostly awful. But it was fun, as she cooked and I listened, tasted, watched, smelled. I remember it all so well, yellow sun and pure, as if it had just happened.

I can tell you my mother was the most disciplined person I've ever known. She loved her work; she loved the creative process; and she loved storytelling. I do remember her going into her office where her typewriter (later a computer) was, and hours later pages and pages of words would come out with her. I remember that it just seemed sort of normal: You went into a room and came out with art, with words that became alive and jumped across the page, magic somehow. I remember that, and I remember thinking how wonderful it was that my mom was a magician of sorts, creating lives and places and times that existed between the pages.

I remember knowing I was loved and cherished above everything, and that also meant her being brutally honest and direct with me. Ginny was tough. I remember doing my first voice recital, and afterward, after everyone else had congratulated me, she talked to me alone. She pulled me to the side and commented on the few notes that were out of tune. It was shockingly honest, but it was true. From that moment on I made sure to work in a way so that it wouldn't happen again. I have her to thank for that, for that honesty—that she cared enough to be tough, for showing me that nothing simply slipped by, and that being just good enough wasn't enough.

These few little remembrances of mine will hopefully give you a glimpse of the other Virginia Hamilton. You will have read her speeches, and they will tell you of her work, her writing style, and the astounding artist she was. I wanted you to know a little bit of who the private woman was, the mom, or Ginny, or Ginger-bell. This part is as important, and really makes up the artist Virginia Hamilton as a whole.

I hope you enjoyed my visit to another time and place. I thank you for allowing me to indulge myself in calling it all up, in putting it down on paper. Seeing the words that are my memories seems lovely somehow, as if I can see her face on the page.

JAIME: REMEMORY

MOST PEOPLE know my mother as an incredible writer of books for children, which of course she was. But if you never saw her "live," as they say in rock 'n' roll, then you really missed out on an important part of her genius. Her speeches were, in essence, a microcosm of her very being. In them, her soul, intellectual prowess, and insatiable curiosity were all on display at the highest level. To hear a Virginia Hamilton speech was at once an education, an entertainment, and a passport into a creative world that knew no bounds.

My mother was a consummate professional in everything she did, be it writing a novel, giving a speech, or cooking her famous baked-corn casserole. She expected nothing but perfection from herself and worked hard every day to achieve it.

I remember watching her prepare for a speech, painstakingly going over every word, every pause, every inflection. Reciting it over and over and over again, like a pianist practicing a concerto or an opera singer rehearsing an aria. Making music with her words, her knowledge. Guiding us through sometimes uncharted waters, rocky terrain — turning what we thought we knew on its head, teaching us that sometimes upside-down is better than right-side-up.

Some years ago, before my first book was published, I had the chance to give my very first speech. *In front of my mother.* It was the one and only occasion in which we appeared together professionally. I was excited, confident, and eager to show her what I could do if given the mic. I had done my homework, working long hours on the writing of the speech, doing multiple drafts and countless revisions. I had practiced and practiced and practiced some more. I was ready.

At the conclusion of my speech, I sat down next to my mother. A sense of profound accomplishment encompassed me. I knew I had done well and couldn't wait to hear what she thought of it. I quickly turned to her and asked, "So, what did you think?"

She replied without hesitation, "It was pretty good, but you need to look at the audience more, and don't say 'um' so much." Seeing that my face had dropped into my lap, she added, "Don't worry, it takes time, you'll get it." That was Mom. Always the truth. Always teaching. Always giving it to you straight. She was treating me like a professional, a fellow writer. Telling me what I *needed* to hear instead of what I *wanted* to hear. And to this day I am deeply appreciative of her loving honesty.

I hope you have enjoyed this tremendous collection of her speeches. And I hope you will take from it the love, understanding, and wisdom that were my mother's intent. In this collection, you see a rare glimpse into what is possible: each speech a magical moment in time, when style and substance came together to create a symphony for the ears, the mind, the heart, and the soul.

ARNOLD: INTO THE FUTURE

Virginia's novels and biographies and collections of folktales are vital and instructive and illuminating. Her work carries forward the thinking of Dr. Du Bois and Hegelian philosophy, Zora Neale Hurston, and William Faulkner.

She was a student of the visions of Freud and Gertrude Stein, Richard Wright and Ralph Ellison. Her novels are manuals of survival. She created a unique body of work out of the African American specifics of her own history and the universalities of the most diverse "human" experiences. She was one of those true American originals who gave voice and meaning to all young readers and their older allies.

After her death in 2002, as a family, we began to devote our energies and resources to bring this life and art into our evolving future. This collection of Virginia Hamilton's speeches, essays, and conversations is one of the more joyous fruits of our labor.

Here is a list of institutions and activities devoted to these continuing efforts:

At the Yellow Springs, Ohio, Community Foundation there is the Virginia Hamilton and Arnold Adoff Endowment to help fund youth activities at the Yellow Springs Library, with emphasis on creative diversity and cultural inclusion.

A corner of that library is devoted to young adults, where they enjoy the use of our commissioned reader's couch. The original portrait of Virginia, by Leo and Diane Dillon, which graces the jacket of this book, hangs on the wall. A unique story rug, visualizing many of her books and aspects of her life, is on display in the community meeting room named in her honor.

In 2009 we celebrated the twenty-fifth annual Virginia Hamilton Conference on Multicultural Literature for Youth at Kent State University in Ohio. We have also established an endowment with the Kent State University Foundation to fund outreach grants for teachers and librarians who use multicultural materials. There is a scholarship for a student to assist with our papers as they are being deposited into the Kent State Library Special Collections, where they will be available to all.

An endowment at the Ohioana Library Association fosters the use of multicultural books for young readers in Ohio classrooms and libraries.

We are providing major funding for an expansion of the Bolinga Center, a cultural facility and student resource at Wright State University in Dayton, Ohio, with a strong emphasis on African American students and their cultural and literary heritage. Upon completion of the renovation, we will deposit our own resource and research books and materials as a collection to be used by the Wright State students and faculty, and colleges throughout the area.

Virginia Hamilton's book manuscripts and supporting materials are deposited at the Library of Congress; a full listing is available on their website. Eventually, all of the manuscripts for her speeches and articles will be deposited there as well.

This year we will update the current Virginia Hamilton website (virginiahamilton.com) with additions of her speeches and other nonfiction. These dozens of pieces, not included in this book, will be available for reading and downloading.

In 2010, the American Library Association and the Coretta Scott King Committee will present the first Virginia Hamilton Award for Lifetime Achievement at its annual convention in Washington, D.C. The recipient will alternate yearly between an author or illustrator and a librarian.

ABOUT
VIRGINIA HAMILTON

BOOKS BY
VIRGINIA HAMILTON:
A CHRONOLOGICAL
LISTING

MAJOR AWARDS:
AN ALPHABETICAL
LISTING

CONTRIBUTORS

CELEBRATE
HER LIFE

ABOUT VIRGINIA HAMILTON

VIRGINIA ESTHER HAMILTON was born, as she said, "on the outer edge of the Great Depression," on March 12, 1934. The youngest of five children of Kenneth James and Etta Belle Perry Hamilton, Virginia grew up amid a large extended family in Yellow Springs, Ohio. The farmlands of southwestern Ohio had been home to her mother's family since the late 1850s, when Virginia's grandfather, Levi Perry, was brought into the state as an infant via the Underground Railroad.

Virginia graduated at the top of her high school class and received a full scholarship to Antioch College in Yellow Springs. In 1956, she transferred to The Ohio State University in Columbus and majored in literature and creative writing. She moved to New York City in 1958, working as a museum receptionist, cost accountant, and nightclub singer, while she pursued her dream of being a published writer. She studied fiction writing at the New School for Social Research under Hiram Haydn, one of the founders of Atheneum Press.

It was also in New York that Virginia met poet Arnold Adoff. They were married in 1960. Arnold worked as a teacher, and Virginia was able to devote her full attention to writing, at least until daughter Leigh was born in 1963 and son Jaime in 1967. In 1969, Virginia and Arnold built their "dream home" in Yellow Springs, on the last remaining acres of the old Hamilton-Perry family farm, and settled into a life of serious literary work and achievement.

In her lifetime, Virginia wrote and published forty-one books in multiple genres that spanned picture books and folktales, mysteries and science fiction, realistic novels and biography. Woven into her books is a deep concern with memory, tradition, and generational legacy, especially as they helped define the lives of African Americans. Virginia described her work as *liberation literature*. She won every major award in youth literature.

Following is a brief account of the highest of the highlights of her remarkable career. Listed dates note years of publication, rather than when a prize was awarded.

1967. Virginia's first book, *Zeely*, is published. It is named an ALA Notable Book and wins the Nancy Bloch Award.

1968. *The House of Dies Drear* wins the Edgar Allan Poe Award for Best Juvenile Mystery.

1971. *The Planet of Junior Brown* is named a Newbery Honor Book and wins the Lewis Carroll Shelf Award.

1974. *M.C. Higgins, the Great* wins the Newbery Medal, making Virginia the first African American author ever to receive this honor. In addition, the book wins the National Book Award, the Boston Globe–Horn Book Award, the Lewis Carroll Shelf Award, a *New York Times* Outstanding Children's Book of the Year citation, and is chosen as a Hans Christian Andersen Honor Book, among its long list of awards. This marks the first time a book has won the "grand slam" of Newbery Medal, National Book Award, and Boston Globe–Horn Book Award. This feat has rarely been repeated.

1979. Virginia is a delegate to the Second International Conference of Writers for Children and Youth in Moscow.

1982. *Sweet Whispers, Brother Rush* is chosen as a Newbery Honor Book and wins the Coretta Scott King Award, the Boston Globe–Horn Book Award, an IBBY Honor Book citation, and the American Book Award, among others.

1984. The Virginia Hamilton Lecture in Children's Literature is established at Kent State University in Kent, Ohio. The Virginia Hamilton Lecture grows into the Virginia Hamilton Conference on Multicultural Literature for Youth and is the longest running event in the United States to focus solely on multicultural literature for children and young adults (http://virginia-hamilton.slis.kent.edu/).

1985. *The People Could Fly: American Black Folktales* wins the Coretta Scott King Award, a *School Library Journal* Best Book of the Year citation, a *Booklist* Editor's Choice citation and is a *New York Times* Best Illustrated Book of the Year, among others.

1987. Virginia and Arnold are named distinguished visiting professors at Queens College in New York.

1988. *In the Beginning: Creation Stories from Around the World* is named Newbery Honor Book, an ALA Best Book for Young Adults, a National Science Teachers Outstanding Science Trade Book for Children, a *Parents* magazine Best Book of the Year, a *Time* magazine Best Book for Young Readers, and wins the Lewis Carroll Shelf Award, among others.

1989. Virginia is named distinguished writing professor, Graduate School of Education, The Ohio State University.

1990. Virginia receives the Catholic Literary Association's Regina Medal. The only criterion for this award is excellence. The Regina Medal is awarded annually to a "living exemplar of the words of the English poet Walter de la Mare 'only the rarest kind of best in anything can be good enough for the young,' for continued, distinguished contribution to children's literature without regard to the nature of the contribution."

1992. Virginia wins the Hans Christian Andersen Award, the highest international recognition bestowed on an author or illustrator of children's literature. She is only the fourth American to win the award, which has been presented every other year since 1956.

1993. Virginia delivers the May Hill Arbuthnot Honor Lecture in Richmond, Virginia.

1993. Virginia speaks at the Pacific Rim Conference in Kyoto, Japan.

1995. Virginia becomes the first children's book author ever to receive a MacArthur Fellowship, nicknamed the "genius award."

1995. Virginia is awarded the Laura Ingalls Wilder Award for her "substantial and lasting contribution to literature for children."

1996. Virginia is the recipient of an NAACP Image Award for *Her Stories: African American Folktales, Fairy Tales, and True Tales.*

2001. Virginia is awarded the De Grummond Award for lifetime achievement in children's literature. This is Virginia's last public address. It also marks the first and only time she appears professionally with her son, Jaime Adoff.

She continued to write, travel, and lecture, spending time with her son, Jaime, in New York City and daughter, Leigh, in Berlin, Germany.

Virginia Hamilton died of breast cancer on February 19, 2002. Three books have been published posthumously: *Time Pieces, Bruh Rabbit and the Tar Baby Girl*, and *Wee Winnie Witch's Skinny*.

Her first grandchild, Jaime's daughter, Anaya Grace Adoff, was born November 26, 2008.

BOOKS BY VIRGINIA HAMILTON:
A CHRONOLOGICAL
LISTING

1967. *Zeely.* Illustrated by Symeon Shimin. New York: Macmillan. In this female initiation story, Geeder Perry and her brother, Toeboy, go to their uncle's farm for the summer and encounter a six-and-a-half-foot-tall Watusi queen and a mysterious Night Traveller.

1968. *The House of Dies Drear.* Illustrated by Eros Keith. New York: Macmillan. Winner of the Edgar Allan Poe Award. Thomas Small and his family move to the great and forbidding House of Dies Drear, a home that was on the Underground Railroad, and trouble begins.

1969. *The Time-Ago Tales of Jahdu.* Illustrated by Nonny Hogrogian. New York: Macmillan. Four lighthearted tales celebrate the deeds of a "strong black boy," who is a world-class trickster.

1971. *The Planet of Junior Brown.* New York: Macmillan. A Newbery Honor Book. Junior Brown, a 300-pound musical prodigy, plays a piano with no sound while his homeless friend, Buddy Clark, draws on all his wit and New York City resources to protect Junior and save his disintegrating mind.

1972. *W. E. B. Du Bois: A Biography.* New York: Crowell. Here is a study of the great scholar's life, through which he strives to live up to his enormous potential and to liberate himself from all manner of governmental, political, and societal constraints.

1973. *Time-Ago Lost: More Tales of Jahdu.* Illustrated by Ray Prather. New York: Macmillan. More tales of the world-class trickster.

1974. *M.C. Higgins, the Great.* New York: Macmillan. Winner of the Newbery Medal, the National Book Award, and the Boston Globe–Horn Book Award. Mayo Cornelius Higgins, called M.C., sits atop a forty-foot pole on the side of Sarah's Mountain and dreams of escape. But poised above his home is a massive spoil heap from strip mining that could come crashing down.

1974. *Paul Robeson: The Life and Times of a Free Black Man.* New York: Harper & Row. The importance of the famous athlete, singer, movie star, and political activist becomes clear in this compelling biography.

1975. *The Writings of W. E. B. Du Bois.* New York: Crowell. A selection of essays, articles, speeches, and excerpts from writings by W. E. B. Du Bois records his views on a variety of social injustices. Edited by Virginia Hamilton.

1976. *Arilla Sun Down.* New York: Greenwillow. This novel of psychic realism follows the story of a biracial family in which the daughter, Arilla, is uncertain of her identity in light of her older brother's overwhelming Amerindian warrior presence.

1978. *Justice and Her Brothers.* New York: Greenwillow. The first book of the Justice Trilogy (also called the Justice Cycle). In these novels, the protagonist, Justice Douglass, her brothers, Thomas and Levi, and a friend, Dorian, mind-jump to a future Earth a million years from today, only to find a wasteland controlled by an entity known as Mal.

1980. *Dustland.* New York: Greenwillow. The second book of the Justice Trilogy.

1980. *Jahdu.* Illustrated by Jerry Pinkney. New York: Greenwillow. More tales of the grand trickster.

1981. *The Gathering.* New York: Greenwillow. The third book of the Justice Trilogy.

1982. *Sweet Whispers, Brother Rush.* New York: Philomel. A Newbery Honor Book, winner of the Boston Globe–Horn Book Award and the Coretta Scott King Award. This novel, which confronts issues of child abuse, single-parent families, and the death of a young person, turns on the appearances and disappearances of a ghost, Brother Rush.

1983. *The Magical Adventures of Pretty Pearl.* New York: Harper & Row. A fantasy—part myth, part legend and folklore. When Pretty Pearl comes down from the god home of Mount Kenya to live among real people, she discovers the diaspora of the slave trade and forgets all her brother god's warnings about being true to the goddess within her.

1983. *Willie Bea and the Time the Martians Landed.* New York: Greenwillow. This old-fashioned, humorous novel tells about the night in October of 1938 when Orson Welles broadcasted his famous radio

357

adaptation of H. G. Wells's tale of a Martian invasion of Earth and scared legions of Americans who believed it was really happening.

1984. *A Little Love.* New York: Philomel. Sheema Hadley searches for the father she never knew, who never wanted to know her, and ultimately finds new strength in herself.

1985. *Junius Over Far.* New York: Harper & Row. A cross-cultural adventure set in America and the Caribbean.

1985. *The People Could Fly: American Black Folktales.* Illustrated by Leo and Diane Dillon. New York: Knopf. Winner of the Coretta Scott King Award. These twenty-four selections present a significant body of black folklore and bring us closer to the hearts and minds of the people who first told them and passed them on to us.

1987. *The Mystery of Drear House.* New York: Greenwillow. The conclusion of the Dies Drear Chronicle.

1987. *A White Romance.* New York: Philomel. A contemporary coming-of-age novel, with sex, drugs, and rock and roll, and a none-too-subtle biracial theme.

1988. *Anthony Burns: The Defeat and Triumph of a Fugitive Slave.* New York: Knopf. Winner of the Boston Globe–Horn Book Award. A historical reconstruction of a poor man's life, with a backdrop of the Civil War, in which this common man is the center and point of his own struggle.

1988. *In the Beginning: Creation Stories from Around the World.* Illustrated by Barry Moser. San Diego: Harcourt Brace Jovanovich. A Newbery Honor Book. Twenty-five stories from cultures around the globe, explaining the creation of people and the universe.

1989. *The Bells of Christmas.* Illustrated by Lambert Davis. San Diego: Harcourt Brace Jovanovich. An ALA Notable Book. A traditional story about a prosperous African American family in Ohio and their 1890 celebration of Christmas.

1990. *Cousins.* New York: Philomel. Three cousins set out on an emotional journey over a summer in which there is rivalry, deep hostility, and a death.

1990. *The Dark Way: Stories from the Spirit World.* Illustrated by Lambert Davis. San Diego: Harcourt Brace Jovanovich. An illustrated collection of compelling multiethnic and multicultural scare tales from around the world.

1991. *The All Jahdu Storybook.* Illustrated by Barry Moser. San Diego:

Harcourt Brace Jovanovich. An illustrated revision of Hamilton's three Jahdu books, all rolled into one.

1992. *Drylongso.* Illustrated by Jerry Pinkney. San Diego: Harcourt Brace Jovanovich. A family struggling against forces of nature—weather, climate, and a huge dust storm—meets a stranger named Drylongso, who, with his divining rod, finds a life-giving underground spring.

1993. *Many Thousand Gone: African Americans from Slavery to Freedom.* Illustrated by Leo and Diane Dillon. New York: Knopf. This nonfiction story collection about the plantation era in America presents factual slave escape stories and portraits of real people in their historical context.

1993. *Plain City.* New York: Blue Sky Press. In the stillness of winter, Buhlaire Sims is ready to get some answers about her family in this coming-of-age novel about people of various colors and classes.

1995. *Her Stories: African American Folktales, Fairy Tales, and True Tales.* Illustrated by Leo and Diane Dillon. New York: Blue Sky Press. Winner of the Coretta Scott King Award. This all-female collection spans the generations, from girl child to elder woman, in stories ranging from Cinderella fantasy to long-ago folktales and true narratives of real women.

1995. *Jaguarundi.* Illustrated by Floyd Cooper. New York: Blue Sky Press. Endangered animals must make their way to freedom in this original picture-book story.

1996. *When Birds Could Talk & Bats Could Sing: The Adventures of Bruh Sparrow, Sis Wren, and Their Friends.* Illustrated by Barry Moser. New York: Blue Sky Press. Here is a wonderfully humorous collection of bird tales collected from plantation era slaves, retold in colloquial speech.

1997. *A Ring of Tricksters: Animal Tales from America, the West Indies, and Africa.* Illustrated by Barry Moser. New York: Blue Sky Press. Eleven of the best animal trickster tales ever, gathered from the storytelling ring of the slave trade during the American plantation era.

1998. *Second Cousins.* New York: Blue Sky Press. In this sequel to *Cousins,* a family reunion brings two sophisticated second cousins from New York City—setting Cammy's world off balance.

1999. *Bluish: A Novel.* New York: Blue Sky Press. A new girl arrives at school in a wheelchair, and some of the children call her "Bluish." Her leukemia makes her seem different, but Dreenie's overwhelming curiosity leads her and another student, Tuli, to reach beyond their fear.

2000. *The Girl Who Spun Gold.* Illustrated by Leo and Diane Dillon.

359

New York: Blue Sky Press. This stunning picture-book folktale runs parallel to the classic "Rumpelstiltskin," where a girl must spin gold for a king or die. In this West Indian–based telling, Quashiba must guess the name of her magical helper, Lit'mahn Bittyun.

2002. *Time Pieces: The Book of Times.* New York: Blue Sky Press. In this semi-autobiographical novel, Hamilton weaves together the present time and slave times. Published posthumously.

2003. *Bruh Rabbit and the Tar Baby Girl.* Illustrated by James Ransome. New York: Blue Sky Press. Hamilton adds her magic to a popular African American story and tells it in authentic colloquial speech. Published posthumously.

2004. *Wee Winnie Witch's Skinny: An Original African American Scare Tale.* Illustrated by Barry Moser. New York: Blue Sky Press. A wild night ride of bewitchment and fright based on an 1800s African American scare tale about a woman who outwits a witch and steals her skin. Published posthumously.

2004. *The People Could Fly: The Picture Book.* Illustrated by Leo and Diane Dillon. New York: Knopf. The title story of the powerful folktale collection of the same name is presented here with award-winning full-color illustrations. In 2007 the publisher issued an edition which included a CD reading of the story by Virginia Hamilton and James Earl Jones.

MAJOR AWARDS:
AN ALPHABETICAL LISTING

VIRGINIA HAMILTON was one of the most distinguished authors of twentieth century youth literature. She received nearly every award in the field during her thirty-five-year career, including:

Arbuthnot Honor Lecture (American Library Association), 1993

Blackboard Book of the Year Award (*Her Stories: African American Folktales, Fairy Tales, and True Tales*), 1996

Boston Globe–Horn Book Award for Fiction (*Sweet Whispers, Brother Rush; M.C. Higgins, the Great*) and for Nonfiction (*Anthony Burns: The Defeat and Triumph of a Fugitive Slave*)

Coretta Scott King Award (*The People Could Fly: American Black Folktales; Sweet Whispers, Brother Rush; Her Stories*) and Honor Book Award (*Anthony Burns; The Magical Adventures of Pretty Pearl; The Bells of Christmas; Junius Over Far; A Little Love; Justice and Her Brothers*)

De Grummond Award, University of Southern Mississippi, 2001

Edgar Allan Poe Award ("The Edgar") from Mystery Writers of America (*The House of Dies Drear*)

Hans Christian Andersen Award, for the body of her work, 1992

International Board on Books for Young People (IBBY) Honor Book (*Sweet Whispers, Brother Rush*)

International Hans Christian Andersen Award, U.S. Honor Book (*M.C. Higgins, the Great*)

Jane Addams Children's Book Award (*Anthony Burns*)

John Newbery Medal (*M.C. Higgins, the Great*) and Newbery Honor Books (*Sweet Whispers, Brother Rush; The Planet of Junior Brown; In the Beginning: Creation Stories from Around the World*)

Laura Ingalls Wilder Award, for the body of her work, 1995

Library of Congress Best Books for Children (*Sweet Whispers, Brother Rush*)

MacArthur Fellowship ("Genius Award"), 1995

NAACP Image Award for Outstanding Literary Work for Children (*Her Stories*)

National Book Award (*M.C. Higgins, the Great*)

New York Times Outstanding Children's Book of the Year (*M.C. Higgins, the Great*)

Ohio Governor's Award, 2000

Ohio Humanities Council, Bjornson Award for Distinguished Service in the Humanities, 1993

Ohio Women's Hall of Fame, 1993

Ohioana Award: The Body of Work by Virginia Hamilton (1984); Career Medal (1991)

Regina Medal of the Catholic Library Association, 1990

Time magazine, Best Books for Young Readers, 1988 (*In the Beginning*)

The Virginia Hamilton Conference on Multicultural Literature for Youth at Kent State University, an annual event begun in 1984 and named for the writer

Distinguished Visiting Professor (Graduate School, Department of Education, Queens College, New York, 1986–87 and 1987–88; Graduate School, Department of Educational Theory and Practice, The Ohio State University, Ohio, 1988–89)

Honorary Degrees, Doctor of Humane Letters:

Bank Street College of Education, New York, New York

Kent State University, Kent, Ohio

The Ohio State University, Columbus, Ohio

Wright State University, Dayton, Ohio

CONTRIBUTORS

RUDINE SIMS BISHOP is Professor Emerita of Education at The Ohio State University, where she specialized in children's literature. She is a world-renowned expert in the fields of multicultural and literacy education and the premier authority on African American Youth Literature. Her major works include *Shadow and Substance: Afro-American Experience in Contemporary Children's Fiction* and *Free Within Ourselves: The Development of African American Children's Literature.* She makes her home in Columbus, Ohio.

KACY COOK was born in Columbus, Ohio, the second of six children. Her father was a federal agent and her mother was a dress designer. Kacy now has three children of her own, daughter Leah, and sons Jacob and Ben. Since attending The Ohio State University, Kacy has worked in journalism and publishing. She has edited a variety of media — newspapers, magazines, textbooks and other nonfiction books, and websites. In addition, Kacy writes books for young people, including *Nuts* (2010), a novel for middle-grade readers. She also contributed a chapter to *Women on Fire: 20 Inspiring Women Share Their Life Secrets,* compiled by Debbie Phillips. Her website is kacycook.net.

ARNOLD ADOFF is an anthologist and poet who has published more than thirty books for young readers and their older allies. Among his award-winning collections are *I Am the Darker Brother, Slow Dance Heart Break Blues,* and *Love Letters.* In 1988 he received the NCTE Award for Excellence in Poetry for Children. His long-awaited new book of poems, *Roots and Blues,* will be published in 2010. Arnold was married to Virginia Hamilton for forty-two years, and they have two children, Leigh and Jaime, and one grandchild, Anaya Grace. He lives in Yellow Springs, Ohio. His website is arnoldadoff.com.

LEIGH ADOFF is a well-known opera singer in Europe. She has sung more than twenty-five operatic roles and numerous concert works at various American and international opera houses and theaters, including the Houston Grand Opera, the Opera Manhattan, the Teatro della Muse di Ancona in Ancon, Italy, the Wiener Kammeroper in Vienna, and the Munich Philharmonic Mariinsky Theatre. Leigh's recent engagements include singing in *Teñoritas*, as well as a guest appearance in Oscar-winner Pepe Danquart's *Human Voices*. She followed this with the world premiere of the prize-winning opera, *Moshammeroper*, at the Neuköllner Oper in Berlin. Leigh Adoff makes her home in Berlin, Germany, with her husband. Her website is leighadoff.com.

JAIME ADOFF is a poet and novelist and formerly the leader of his own rock band. He is the author of the critically acclaimed *The Song Shoots Out of My Mouth: A Celebration of Music*, a Lee Bennett Hopkins Poetry Award Honor Book; *Names Will Never Hurt Me*; *Jimi & Me*, winner of the 2006 Coretta Scott King/John Steptoe Award for New Talent; *The Death of Jayson Porter*, a "poetic prose" novel for young adults; and *Small Fry*, an illustrated collection of poems for young readers. He is a highly sought after speaker, presenting across the country on teen issues, diversity, young adult literature, and poetry. He lives in his hometown of Yellow Springs, Ohio, with his wife and children. His website is jaimeadoff.com.

CELEBRATE HER LIFE

*A memorial service for Virginia Hamilton was held at
the Scholastic headquarters in New York City in May of 2002.
Here are two tributes by long-time friends and colleagues
and a note from her editor at the Blue Sky Press.*

VIRGINIA AND I have been friends since 1953, when we were students at
Antioch College. We've both played important roles in each other's lives.

Virginia always claimed, with a sly little smile, that I have her to thank
for my marriage to Lester Schulman. Back at Antioch, Lester had just broken
up with his heartthrob and had vowed to ask the first girl he knew in the
cafeteria line for a date. Virginia and I were having dinner together that
evening, and Lester's eyes fell on the beautiful, willowy Virginia Hamilton.
But she already had a date, so he turned to me and popped the question. I
guess I didn't mind being second choice. We were all friends.

Some years later Lester and I were Arnold and Virginia's witnesses at
their marriage in City Hall here in New York.

As long as I've known Virginia she was a writer. In the mid-1960s our
lives crossed professionally. I was working at Macmillan, doing what would
now be called marketing, and I remembered a story she had written for a
creative writing course at Antioch. It had not been written as a children's
story, but I urged her to let me take it to Macmillan because I thought it
could be made into a wonderful children's book. The story was titled "The
West Field." It was published as *Zeely*.

Before I left Macmillan I had the privilege of promoting her first five
books — *Zeely*; *The House of Dies Drear*; *The Time-Ago Tales of Jahdu*; her
first Newbery Honor Book, *The Planet of Junior Brown*; and her Newbery,
M.C. Higgins, the Great. It was such fun for me, bringing her to the attention
of the world, and, in retrospect, I would have to say that promoting her

365

books was probably the most personally satisfying aspect of my forty-some years in children's publishing.

Later, when I was the editor in chief at Random House and Knopf, I would rank *The People Could Fly* as the book I am proudest to have published.

When I think of Virginia, I think of her sitting cross-legged on her bed in our dormitory at Antioch, strumming on her guitar and singing the blues. She was awfully good. And then, of course, I think of her standing at a microphone, in a regal African dress, giving one of her never-to-be-forgotten speeches, usually a speech in acceptance of yet one more major award. She was awfully good at that, too. But mostly I just think of her as my good friend. I miss you, Virginia.

— JANET SCHULMAN
Random House

VIRGINIA HAMILTON, simply put, set the gold standard in children's literature. With the publication of her first book, *Zeely*, in 1967, she helped to launch the modern era of African American children's literature, and from there, she went on to become one of America's premier writers of children's literature. Her books were illuminations of what she called the American hopescape and, in particular, the distinctiveness of African American experiences within that context. Virginia had a magical way with words and a superb sense of who she was and what she was about as a writer. I once wrote something about Zeely, the character, having sprung from Virginia's head, full-grown like Athena, armed with self-knowledge, shielded by pride, and robed in dignity. Virginia liked the paragraph and thanked me for it, a small act of generosity typical of the way she befriended me. I realized later that pride, self-knowledge, and dignity were as characteristic of Virginia as they were of her creation.

It was a privilege to know her as a writer, teacher, colleague, and friend. In that same piece, I declared myself the president of the Virginia Hamilton Admiration Society. It is an office from which I will never retire.

— RUDINE SIMS BISHOP
The Ohio State University

❧

VIRGINIA HAMILTON was one of the greatest gifts of my life, and working with her was an extraordinary privilege. I loved to watch her brilliant, creative mind attack a complex concept—with a kind of hungry, focused curiosity. Then, over time, she digested the full range of possibilities and made her carefully considered decisions. She did this in all phases of her writing, from taking on an idea for a story collection to making editorial revisions. Nothing was random; each sentence was crafted with intense deliberation.

The process of writing every project was different. *In the Beginning: Creation Stories from Around the World,* for example, began as an idea, and with the speed of a rattlesnake, Virginia struck it and made it wholly her own. This was followed by months of research. Then, over dinner she would tell me the most outlandish—and often highly controversial—creation tales she had uncovered. Both of us were completely absorbed, but our final editorial sessions on this book were so contentious and highly charged it is a wonder we survived them. In retrospect, perhaps we had to lock horns early on to truly, deeply test our ability to be completely honest with each other.

The novel *Plain City,* a very different book, was conceived by Virginia during an Ohio snowstorm while she was trapped on a highway in a "whiteout" of snow. The related scene in *Plain City* vividly appeared to her that day, and the entire novel—so extraordinary in its detail and multilayered relationships—came to me in batches of fully written, unconnected scenes that Virginia then mysteriously wove together as if they were always one piece in her mind.

I was most surprised by the almost mystical *Drylongso,* which swept across the landscape of Virginia's imagination with the single-minded inevitability of the dust storm in the book. It flowed out in a manuscript that I published, word for word, exactly as it was written, with no editing or revisions whatsoever.

Virginia was also a powerful mentor in my publishing career; when I met her in 1985 she had already worked with many of the great editors of her generation: Janet Schulman, Richard Jackson, Susan Hirschman, Ann Beneduce, Frances Foster, Stephanie Spinner, Robert Warren, and Patricia Gauch. Her insights about publishing were invaluable, but an even greater gift to me was her friendship and the familial warmth and ease of it. More than anything, I miss those hours of teasing, clowning, and laughing. Even at the most formal functions, Virginia knew how to keep a straight face while making me laugh so hard that Perrier would come out my nose as I struggled to appear serious and professional.

On my desk I have a small photo of the afternoon we bought matching blue dresses and played hooky at an IRA convention in Orlando. We slipped away to go see Shamu. We thought our frilly new outfits made us sleek and glamorous, but the SeaWorld photographer's picture shows two frumpy, disheveled women in lopsided clothes, frowning at the camera. We *were* frowning. When we saw the camera, we thought Virginia was being stalked by news paparazzi.

Over the years, Virginia's vision dramatically elevated children's literature to new heights, and she educated and enlightened readers throughout the world. My years with her were precious beyond measure, and every book I publish is enhanced by what Virginia so generously gave to me.

— BONNIE VERBURG
The Blue Sky Press, an Imprint of Scholastic Inc.